SHORINJI KEMPO PHILOSOPHY

SHORINJI KEMPO
PHILOSOPHY

Shorinji Kempo No Tetsugaku

少林寺拳法の哲学

Robert Villiers

BSKF PUBLICATIONS
London

Original photography and illustrations by BSKF
Stock photography by Pixta and Adobe Stock
Cover design by Ben Perkins and Guy Jarman
Front cover image: Nio guard at Chuo-ji, Sapporo (Pixta)
Back cover images: BSKF Chief Instructor Tameo Mizuno, 8th Dan Seihanshi (BSKF)

Distributed in the United Kingdom by BSKF Publications.

Published by BSKF Publications, 6 Tylers Court, Vicars Bridge Close, Wembley, Middlesex, HA0 1XT. Copyright © 2019 BSKF Publications. All rights reserved.
Printed in the United Kingdom.

ISBN 978-1-9161319-0-3
First edition, 2019

British Shorinji Kempo Federation (BSKF), teaching and promoting the art of Shorinji Kempo in the UK since 1974. BSKF and the BSKF logo are registered trademarks in the United Kingdom.

www.bskf.org
contact@bskf.org

Contents

Introduction

Gassho! Welcome to this book presenting a comprehensive review of Shorinji Kempo philosophy topics for students. It is designed to supplement the teaching you receive in your dojo, stimulate conversation with fellow students and promote wider reading.

What is Shorinji Kempo?

Shorinji Kempo is a modern Japanese martial art based on a combination of traditional body conditioning, self-defence techniques and Zen-inspired philosophy. It was created in 1947 by Doshin So (宗道臣, also known as Kaiso 開祖 or 'founder'), drawing on his experience with both Chinese and Japanese traditional martial arts, Zen Buddhist religious practice and philosophy, and his own unique life experiences before, during and after the Second World War.

About the BSKF

The British Shorinji Kempo Federation (BSKF) is an organisation of clubs from around the UK that teach Shorinji Kempo. It traces its origins back to 1974, when Tameo Mizuno was sent by Kaiso to London to establish Shorinji Kempo in the UK. We formed the British Shorinji Kempo Association (BSKA) in 1976 and became the British Shorinji Kempo Federation (BSKF) in 1989.

Acknowledgements

This book has been written and edited by Sensei Robert Villiers 6th Dan Daikenshi (City University Branch). We also acknowledge the input of a number of other senior BSKF instructors, to whom we are most grateful for giving their time and expertise to make this considerable undertaking a success. They are: Sensei Tony Leith 4th Dan (Glasgow University Branch), Sensei Sean Dixie 4th Dan (Imperial College Branch), Sensei Ben Perkins 4th Dan (East London Branch), Sensei Kavita Kapoor 3rd Dan (Camden Branch).

Many historical photographs and reproductions of historical artworks used throughout this book are considered to be in the public domain in accordance with the appropriate copyright laws.

Stock photography is used under licence from PIXTA and Adobe Stock.

Original photographic works are copyright of BSKF. We would like to thank Sensei Mike Sadler 5th Dan (Bristol City Branch) and many other dedicated senior BSKF members for providing them.

We are also ever grateful for the guidance and input of Sensei Tameo Mizuno 8th Dan Seihanshi, Founder and Chief Instructor of the BSKF.

Style note:

Japanese terms in *romaji* (Roman lettering) are *italicised* unless in common English usage (like 'dojo'). Japanese script *(kana* or *kanji)* is normally in brackets. English translations of terms appear in single quotation marks.

About the Author

Robert Villiers holds the rank of 6th Dan Daikenshi in Shorinji Kempo, and is the Chairman of the Council of Branchmasters of the British Shorinji Kempo Federation (BSKF). He has been studying the art since 1989, and is a direct student of BSKF Chief Instructor Tameo Mizuno, 8th Dan Seihanshi, himself a direct student of the founder Doshin So. Robert first started teaching in 1994 and is currently the branchmaster of the City University Branch in central London. He has also represented the UK in international competitions in both Japan and Europe, winning medals in World Shorinji Kempo Organization (WSKO) Taikais in both 1993 and 1997, and has participated in many other competitions and public demonstrations.

Purpose and Structure of the Book

This book is primarily intended as a resource for students of Shorinji Kempo, '*kenshi*', to both help in their general understanding of the broad sweep of Shorinji Kempo philosophy and to use when preparing for their regular grading examinations where particular topics will be set for discussion. However, despite varying amounts of occasionally technical content specific to the practice of Shorinji Kempo as a martial art, the lessons within can also be applied much more broadly and, as such, it is hoped that the material will be of interest and use to a wider audience of those not actively involved in regular Kempo training.

The book first introduces Shorinji Kempo and its founder, Doshin So (Part I), and then describes the distinctive ideas that form the core of the philosophy (Part II). Part III introduces ideas about how to make progress in both training and other areas of life, while Part IV includes a more thorough discussion of the technical aspects of Shorinji Kempo. A detailed examination of the scope and role of *ki* (energy) forms Part V, followed by a short account of the history of Shorinji Kempo and the BSKF in Part VI. Finally, Part VII deals with the fundamental ideas of *Kongo Zen* and Buddhism which underpin the philosophy as a whole. Appendices at the end cover the text of the *Dokun* in English and Japanese; a summary of useful lists; a table of the *kenkei* or technique families of Shorinji Kempo; a table of *bukai*, *hokai* and *sokai* rankings; the current BSKF philosophy syllabus by grade.

Part 1

What is Shorinji Kempo?

We begin the book with an introduction to Shorinji Kempo and its founder, Doshin So. The story of its creation takes us from his birth in early 20th century Japan to his experiences of war and its aftermath in China and at home. We then detail some of the most basic aspects of the discipline, describing both the fundamental purpose and structure of the training, and a selection of practical information and advice for new students.

Doshin So and the Founding of Shorinji Kempo

What is Shorinji Kempo?

Shorinji Kempo is a modern Japanese martial art, based on a combination of traditional body conditioning, self-defence techniques and Zen-inspired philosophy. It was created in 1947 by Doshin So (宗道臣, also known as Kaiso 開祖 or 'founder'), drawing on his experience with both Chinese and Japanese traditional martial arts, Zen Buddhist religious practice and philosophy, and his own unique life experiences before, during and after the Second World War.

Early life of Kaiso

Kaiso, born Nakano Michiomi (中野道臣) in 1911, was orphaned at the age of eight and sent to Manchuria, then occupied by the Japanese, to live with his grandfather, a well-connected figure of noble *samurai* background and an important member of an organisation known as the Black Dragon Society (*Kokuryukai* 黒竜会). This was an influential Pan-Asianist group and secret society active in what was then the Empire of Japan. It was under his grandfather's instruction that the young Nakano received his first experience of traditional Japanese martial arts such as *kendo* and *jujutsu*. Following the deaths of his mother, sisters and grandfather in quick succession, Kaiso returned to Japan in 1926. After a period living in Tokyo, in 1928 he enlisted in the army, at the age of 17, and joined the *Kokuryukai* in his turn. Though accurate independent accounts are impossible to come by, it appears that he undertook wide-ranging covert surveillance missions throughout China, making maps and conducting surveys, using as a cover his burgeoning study of both Buddhism and the martial arts. It was then that Kaiso met his first teacher of Chinese *quán fa* (Japanese: *kempo* 拳法): Chen Liang, a Taoist priest and master of the White Lotus style (Japanese: *Byakurenmon ken*, Chinese: *Báiliánmén quán* 白蓮門拳).

Returning to Japan once more in 1931 due to illness, he joined the Air Corps; however, he was almost immediately put out of action by a heart attack, and on his recovery was given only a short time to live by his doctors. This news caused him to redouble his commitment to his nationalist activities, and he returned to China to work with and study from Chen. Chen also successfully applied his traditional acupressure healing techniques to Kaiso, who would later codify these skills into the system of *seiho* (整法) as part of Shorinji Kempo.

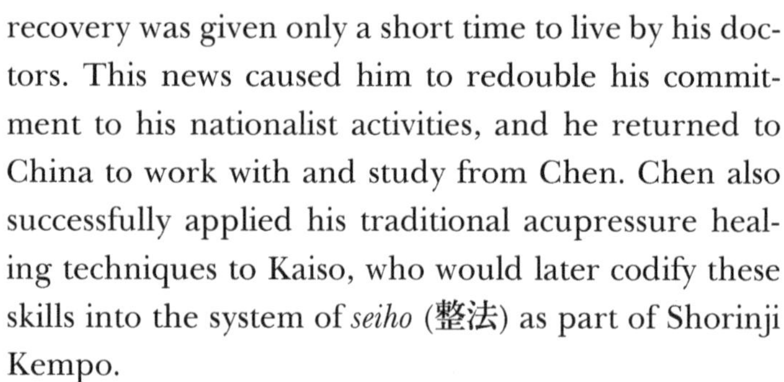

Figure 1 Michiomi Nakano in 1931

With Chen's introduction, Kaiso was subsequently able to study as a disciple under the grandmaster of the *Giwamon ken* school (Chinese: *Yihemén quán* 義和門拳), Wen Taizong. Wen introduced him in turn to Huang Longbai, under whom he had studied at the Songshan Shaolin temple in his youth. It is claimed that Wen formally granted Kaiso the title of 21st grandmaster of *Arahan no Ken* (阿羅漢の拳) at a ceremony at the then ruined temple in 1936.[1] *Arahan* is a rendering of the Sanskrit *arhat* (*arahant* in Pali[2]), which means 'enlightened one', or 'highly developed practitioner'.[3]

Figure 2 Japanese troops evacuating from Manchukuo in 1945

Kaiso was in Eastern Manchuria in 1945 when Russia invaded Manchuria and initiated hostilities against Japan. On 15th August 1945, Japan surrendered, and in the aftermath, Kaiso witnessed many atrocities and suffered many

1 See below under 'Bodhidharma, Zen and the Shaolin Temple' for further details and qualifications. *Giwa* means 'righteous harmony'.

2 Linguistic note: many terms relating to the Indian origins of Buddhism are better known in their Sanskrit form, rather than Pali, a closely related dialect in which the earliest scriptures and accounts were written.

3 The Chinese reading is *āluóhàn* or simply *luóhàn*, and in Japanese it is also sometimes *rakan*, as in the *rakan* ken family of advanced *juho* techniques.

hardships. According to some accounts, wounded Japanese soldiers were left behind to die while the army retreated, and many Japanese civilians committed mass suicide. Kaiso managed to escape to Japan with the help of friends in Chinese secret societies, finally being repatriated in 1946 after a year living in the now Soviet-occupied province. His first-hand experience of the total military defeat of a once oppressive occupying force made a lifelong impression on him. He saw a world with broken societal structures ruled by violence, and witnessed extreme suffering. It was during this time that he began to formulate his ideas for how the society he remembered and cherished could be rebuilt, and putting these thoughts into words, he stated:

'The person, the person, the person! Everything depends on the quality of the person!'

人,人,人,すべては人の質にある! *hito, hito, hito, subete wa hito no shitsu ni aru!*

Kaiso realised that the outcome of all the important events in life – from the most personal encounters to the grandest scales of national politics and global war – depends on the decisions of the actual people involved, rather than resulting solely from the workings of implacable impersonal forces like ideology or religion. Whilst those forces do indeed drive people to act in the ways they do and thus create such momentous outcomes as war or peace, terrorism or heroism, ultimately it is still the individuals concerned, acting in the moment, who determine the course of history. For this reason, the quality of those decisions, and therefore the quality of the people who make them, is of huge importance. Kaiso's conclusion was that the best way to construct and maintain a just and peaceful society is from the bottom up, not from the top down, by creating people who can think for themselves, consider the welfare of all others, and have the strength of will and body to act decisively in order to realize their ideals. Not everybody needs to become an *arhat* to help create such an ideal world; it is sufficient that there is a minimum critical mass of good people in a society to keep it on the right track and avoid the disastrous and tragic outcomes seen so often throughout history when peaceful nations have been led astray by small minorities of dangerous zealots.

Figure 3 Kaiso c1940s

Founding of Shorinji Kempo

In 1946 Kaiso travelled back to Japan and, following a spell in business in Osaka, he settled in the small industrial port town of Tadotsu, on the southern island of Shikoku. What he found there was not the Japan of his memories, but a country broken by defeat in war and foreign occupation. The people of Japan, to Kaiso's eyes, had lost faith in all that was good about their country and culture. Pride, dignity and morality had all been sacrificed in favour of mere survival during this hard time; black markets were the only means of obtaining food and staple items, and these were ruthlessly controlled by organised criminal gangs of *yakuza*[4] who ruled through violence. Kaiso was determined to do something to improve this state of affairs and decided to try to preach the philosophies and ideas he had collected from his studies in China and synthesised throughout his life to the young people of the town. His idea was to teach them mental and spiritual resilience so that they could resist despair and take action to change their situation for the better. However, his initial efforts at philosophizing seemed to make little impact on the people he most wanted to reach, and he realised that mere talk and abstract ideas were not sufficient to get their attention, beset as they were by such hardship and danger. Instead, what they wanted and needed was something more immediately useful in helping them face the perils of their daily lives.

Figure 4 Kaiso c1950

Therefore, he decided to set up a small dojo in his house and began teaching the fighting skills of *Arahan no Ken*. He intended to use these practical techniques as a 'hook' to tempt young people into his dojo; once they were there, he would then have the opportunity to teach them the philosophy behind the techniques, and show how they constituted a means for understanding the value of self-discipline and the benefits of working with others. Inspired by the famous murals in the

4 Japanese organized crime groups. The role of the Yakuza in Japanese society is somewhat ambiguous, and not as straightforwardly violent or negative as, for example, the Mafia in Italy or the US. However, it is fair to say that despite some evidence of their providing a form of local policing and even disaster relief (e.g. after the Tohoku earthquake and tsunami in 2011), they have a long history of criminal activity enforced by sometimes extreme levels of violence.

Shaolin Temple[5], which depict both Indian and Chinese monks practising their techniques together in pairs with each participant smiling (see '*Kumite Shutai*'), he decided to create an art that revolved around not only dynamic techniques, but also mutual cooperation, friendliness and Buddhist philosophy.

During this period, Kaiso was developing, systematizing and expanding the techniques of the arts he had studied throughout his life into a single holistic system that he would later name Shorinji Kempo. He worked with several key early students[6] to construct a comprehensive syllabus, and also began collecting and writing philosophical material under the banner of *Kongo Zen*.

Figure 5 Shorinji Kempo training in Tadotsu, c1950

However, as his reputation grew, he came to the attention of the various local gangs who at the time controlled many aspects of life in Tadotsu. They were not happy that a Buddhist monk had appeared in their town and was teaching people to stand up to their corrupt and exploitative rule. In frequent encounters, Kaiso and his earliest students confronted and faced down the gangs, even converting and recruiting some of their leading members. From there, Shorinji Kempo spread rapidly throughout Japan, taking an especially firm hold in the country's university system. Eventually, it was transmitted around the world, where it is now practised in more than 30 countries. It has been established in the UK since 1974, when Sensei Tameo Mizuno came to Britain with the encouragement of Kaiso, to start teaching and to create the organization that would later become the British Shorinji Kempo Federation, or BSKF.

---

5 The murals are in the *Avalokitesvara* or White Robe Palace hall (Chinese: *bai yi dian* 白衣殿) and date from the *Qing* dynasty period, around the 17th century CE.

6 In particular Nakano Sensei, the husband of his first daughter Tomiko, who adopted the family name.

Figure 6 The port of Tadotsu c1930

Figure 7 Headquarters of the World Shorinji Kempo Organisation in Tadotsu today

Kaiso's motivation and purpose – 'Give me Leaders, not Followers!'

Kaiso's vision is a radical alternative to the great ideological movements of the 19th and 20th centuries – the powerful and destructive '-isms' that caused so much havoc and conflict in the world, like fascism and communism – and also to the more ancient – but no less damaging – absolutisms of religious extremists. These belief systems seek to impose a view of the perfect society on humanity from above, demanding a single interpretation of what is good and how to achieve it, disregarding the consequences and collateral damage such impersonal and inflexible dogmas always wreak. In contrast, Kaiso's idea was to seed society – in all countries – with self-actualized individuals who had done the hard work of building their mental, physical and spiritual personalities by their own efforts, so that they could provide a bulwark against the kind of collective insanity that had for example led the Japanese Empire to engage the vastly more powerful United States in a highly risky and ultimately unwinnable war. And his message continues to be relevant today, in an era when the universalist secular ideologies of the 20th century have retreated in the face of religious extremism, growing intolerance and nationalism. The individuals he called for would not be spoon-fed a set of opinions or directives about what is right and wrong, but rather would be trained to use their own judgement, thinking for themselves and relying on intellectual and ethical resources built from the intense study and self-examination that is required by Shorinji Kempo training. That is to say, it is not by telling people what to think, but by showing them how to 'polish the mirror of their hearts'[7], and so find out the truth of good and evil actions for themselves, that lasting change and a true hope for peace can finally be obtained.

Figure 8 Tameo Mizuno with Doshin So (1977)

Kaiso's call – 'Give me Leaders, not Followers!' – was particularly aimed at his initial

7 This phrase, given in response to the question "What is *Chan* (Zen)?", is associated with the monk Nányuè Huáiràng (南嶽懷讓, Japanese: Nangaku Ejo) (677–744), who succeeded the 6th *Chan* Patriarch Huineng on the basis of his answer.

target audience: the dispirited young Japanese he found in his hometown on his return to Japan after the war. Society and culture in Japan, and east Asia more generally, have historically placed a high value on harmony and collective action, in preference to the individualism that is thought to be characteristic of Western cultures. In reality, all peoples display varying amounts of each attribute at different times and in different ways, but the fact is that, while both qualities are potentially useful – conferring the great power of people working together in unison, or the power of innovation and creativity respectively – both can also lead to negative outcomes when taken to extremes. Similarly, respect for one another and for authority is a vital ingredient for any society to function smoothly, but taken to excess it can mean that citizens fail to evaluate critically either their leaders' actions, or those which they, as citizens, are being asked or coerced to undertake on their behalf. The upshot of all this is that Kaiso wanted his students to deploy the optimum combination of independence and cooperation to ensure a well-functioning, prosperous and just society.

Note: on religion

It is important for *kenshi* to recognise that, despite the heritage of its basic ideas in Buddhism and specifically Zen, Shorinji Kempo is not a religion, and that its practice and principles are consistent with all mainstream faiths. It has nothing to say regarding supernatural matters or topics such as what happens after death – neither endorsing or rejecting such ideas – but merely chooses to focus instead on what is knowable, and the world as we find it. Shorinji Kempo does, in one sense, fit with the ancient meaning of the word 'religion', in that it involves a 'binding' (from the Latin *religo*, 'I tie') of oneself to a set of actions and principles that one believes are true, just, and above all helpful. However, *kenshi* should never take any idea or principle of this philosophy as an article of blind faith; rather, they are expected to question and challenge everything, and to think critically and independently.

The Unique Nature of Shorinji Kempo

Healthy Body, Healthy Mind, Self-Defence

Our goal in practising Shorinji Kempo is to strive to attain these three things – a Healthy Body, a Healthy Mind and practical Self-Defence skills – in order that we may develop to our greatest potential as individuals. Shorinji Kempo is a system for helping us to live our lives to the fullest and in the most positive way possible, and it does this by addressing our needs in both the physical and mental or spiritual realms (see '*Ken Zen Ichinyo*'). But what makes Shorinji Kempo unique as a practice and a way of life is that it utilises fighting techniques and training to achieve such progress in an integrated 'psychophysical' method. Hence, the three aspects when united together make up the Unique Nature of Shorinji Kempo: Healthy Body, Healthy Mind, and Self-Defence.

Healthy Body

To be as healthy and fit as we can be is a necessary condition for a good life. With a healthy body, we feel both physically and mentally ready to tackle the daily challenges we confront; not being in top condition can make all other aspects of our lives more difficult. Such an idea is hardly controversial; however, it can prove very difficult for many people to put it into practice in their everyday lives. One reason for this is that typical fitness regimes become boring very quickly, and rapid initial gains are not followed by consistent long-term progress. On the other hand, participation in many team-based or individual sports becomes increasingly difficult over time: as you get older, there is both a greater risk of injury and a relentless decline in ability and competitiveness. In contrast, Shorinji Kempo is particularly effective as a means of physical training, just because it is both challenging and rewarding, while having a very low rate of injuries due to the style and structure of practice. This means it can be continued over a lifetime at a sustainable and moderate level, and thus contribute much more effectively to long-term health than an activity that is tried and abandoned after an initial brief burst of effort.

Healthy Mind

The unique nature of Shorinji Kempo training helps us to develop psychological, emotional and intellectual skills and habits that enable us to manage stress, prioritise effectively, improve willpower, and master a host of other useful cognitive attributes. This benefit comes as a result of its integrated approach to both physical and mental self-improvement. The psychological challenges of training – whether facing a tough *randori* (free sparring) opponent, or your own frustration with mastering a difficult technique – provide an excellent way to build up mental toughness gradually, whilst encouraging a 'Growth Mindset' (see below). By learning to cooperate with a range of partners, we build confidence, trust and the ability to understand and interact with others, boosting our so-called 'emotional intelligence'. And finally, the requirement to study the philosophy syllabus topics – to understand them, debate them and ultimately to put them into practice in your everyday life – offers an intellectual and ethical quest that will enrich your experience of life and the relationships you have with those around you.

Self-Defence

One challenge that can rarely be met through intellect alone arises if you are physically attacked or are compelled to intervene in an attack on somebody else. *Kenshi* are absolutely forbidden to use Shorinji Kempo techniques to initiate unprovoked attacks and must use them only for self-defence or the defence of others (see 'Self-Defence and Violence' and '*Shushu Koju*'). When applied correctly, the techniques are very effective and are a formidable resource, but they are always a last resort, when all else has failed and no other course of action is possible. Please remember: any actions must be taken with a sense of good judgement, responsibility and awareness for the consequences to ourselves and our opponents, including, but not limited to, legal ramifications. We are all responsible for our own actions and will be judged on them. At the same time, however, we have a duty (not to mention a natural desire) to protect ourselves and those close to us, if at all possible, and failure to do so decisively can leave mental as well as physical scars, or worse. Such events are fortunately very rare in our current society in the UK, but they do still occur and can have disproportionate effects on our life for such brief moments; therefore, it is of more than passing importance to study ways to protect and defend ourselves and others. In all our practice of Shorinji Kempo, at all times, we need to keep this idea firmly in the front of mind: we are training to fight, both to *not lose* (see '*Fuhai Shoju*'), and ultimately, to survive and thrive. If we lose sight of the fundamental place that self-defence has at the heart of Shorinji Kempo, we are merely dabbling in sport or dancing.

How to Behave at the Dojo

Kyakka Shoko

The first step in your training begins when you enter the dojo (道場, now used to refer to a training hall for martial arts, but originally the place monks used for practising meditation at a Zen temple): start by examining yourself. This is *Kyakka Shoko* (脚下照顧), which means in Japanese, 'to shine a spotlight on your feet'. The process starts with putting your shoes and any bags you may have neatly on the floor as you enter the dojo; as is traditional in Japanese and other Asian households, shoes are not worn indoors and are placed neatly by the door, rather than thrown carelessly aside. This self-examination is not limited to just your kit; try to consider your own feelings, emotions and physical state before you dive into training, to give yourself a chance to focus your efforts on achieving your goals both for the class and for your wider practice. In this way, your practice can start even before you enter the dojo and continue long after you leave. During the class as well, you must pay meticulous attention to the details of your practice; for example, is your stance correct – the exact copy of your Sensei's? Have you taken on board the general points or specific corrections you have been given? The smallest changes can make big differences and have dramatic effects (like the 'butterfly effect' of Chaos Theory legend), so never be careless, and make sure the attitude of mental tidiness and rigour is maintained not just at the dojo, but in your everyday life in general.

Figure 9 Kyakka shoko: shoes arranged at the entrance of a room

Gassho Rei

When we enter the dojo, we place any bags we may have on the floor (see above) and perform *Gassho Rei* (合掌礼): literally, 'meeting palms respect' (*gassho* can also refer to a handshake). This is our way of showing respect to each other and to the dojo, a place we make special by our commitment to train seriously there, wherever it may be. It is also how we greet each other as *kenshi* (拳士: literally, 'fist samurai', but better rendered as 'ladies and gentlemen of Kempo'). In Shorinji Kempo, we do not bow as in many other Japanese martial arts. Following the teaching of Buddha, we treat each other as equals, and this is reflected within *gassho rei*, which is also a common friendly greeting throughout (Southern) Asia. The joining together of two open hands symbolizes the coming together of two individuals as people of equal human potential. As important as showing our respect as we enter the dojo, is performing *gassho rei* as we leave. These actions give us a chance to pause for thought, putting a formal close on the day's training, and serving as a reminder to take the lessons of that training back into our normal lives.

Figure 10 Gassho rei

Samu

Please make every effort to be on time – this actually means to arrive a little early, as most dojos will require some form of *samu* (作務), which refers to the chores assigned to the monks in a temple; for example, cleaning. *Samu* is when we prepare the dojo for the lesson to come. It involves making the dojo clean and safe by removing anything that might cause a danger; mopping the floor or putting down mats; and anything else that can make training a better, safer and more enjoyable experience. *Samu* is performed by everyone, regardless of rank and can be seen as another element of *kyakka shoko*.

Dress

Please come to the dojo appropriately attired. This means a clean and, if necessary, ironed *dogi* (道着, training suit, 'clothing of the Way'). Fingernails and toenails should be cut short and clean. All jewellery must be removed or, if removal is not possible, protected by a plaster or tape. Long hair should be tied back. And don't forget basic personal hygiene to avoid strong body odour or bad breath etc.! These things are not only important for safety and hygiene, but also show basic respect for your fellow *kenshi*, not to mention respect for yourself.

Spirit

Always try to have an enthusiastic and constructive attitude in your training and try to cultivate *Kisei* (気勢) and *Kihaku* (気迫): spirit and determination. Remember that, even if you are feeling a little low, the energy you bring to the dojo will be given back to you tenfold by a strong group all working hard together towards a common goal. So it is up to all of us individually to contribute our utmost efforts to help both ourselves and our fellow *kenshi*.

If you're late

If for any reason you're late for the class, simply sit down at the back of the dojo in *seiza* (静座, the formal kneeling position) and, with your eyes closed, mentally run through the lines of the *Dokun* while practising deep breathing (*chosoku* 調息). The reason for taking these few moments before joining the class is simply to remove any stresses you will be feeling due to being late and to mentally prepare yourself for the remainder of the class, and constitutes a particular form of *kyakka shoko*. Once finished, or if requested to join, start your own warm-up (*taiso* 体操) and join in with the remainder of the class without rushing.

Basic Elements for Beginners

Before new students can begin to practise basic movements (*kihon*) or techniques (*hokei waza* 法形技), they should be aware of these basic elements that inform all our physical training in Shorinji Kempo. *Kenshi* should try to keep these elements in mind as much as possible during their practice and, indeed, in normal daily life outside the dojo, not just when they are reminded to focus on a particular aspect. They should become routine, habitual, ultimately almost instinctive, and allow *kenshi* to feel, stand, see, breathe, move and think better, at the same time as performing any chosen activity.

Rei

As described above, *rei* refers to the act of paying respect. As well as on entering and leaving the dojo, *kenshi* as a group will perform *gassho rei* to the Sensei at the beginning and end of each section of the class, and to each other when starting and finishing pair-form practice together. However, please don't *rei* too often; we show our respect, but do not want to form the habit of a subservient, deferential or diffident mindset – far from it! As in all things, balance is key.

Kesshu

Kesshu Gamae (結手構) is our most basic stance and, just like our fighting stances, it has a purpose and a function: to send a message to others, and to create both a physical and mental change in ourselves. The hand position (the word itself means 'joined hands') superficially indicates peaceful intention, as the normally more dangerous right hand is held or covered by the left; this is analogous to the Western handshake, where a proffered right hand means that the other person can see clearly you are unarmed. The position has a deeper significance, however; it is a *mudra*, a hand position used in traditional Yoga practice (as is *gassho rei*) which is designed to create a stable but alert energy in the *kenshi*. This state of readiness is also reflected in an upright posture, steady breathing, and an open heart and mind, respectfully alert and ready to receive teaching and participate in the class. *Kesshu Gamae* is the default position for a *kenshi* any time they are not in some other stance or activity.

Figure 11 Kesshu gamae

Seiza and Anza – sitting

There are several points during a typical class where *kenshi* will sit on the floor: when receiving instruction, listening to the *howa* of the Sensei, or practising *zazen* meditation. There are two styles of sitting used for these occasions – *seiza* (正座) and *anza* (安座). *Seiza* ('proper' or 'upright sitting') is the traditional polite method of sitting used in Japan to indicate respect and a certain level of formality, and is thus used when receiving instruction, at least at first until the Sensei calls for *anza* – 'easy sitting'. *Anza* is also the position adopted most frequently for meditation as it is more comfortable (for most people) to maintain for an extended period of time.

Seiza is performed by drawing back the right foot, going down onto the right knee and then kneeling fully, with upright posture, good breathing and an alert attitude. To stand, simply reverse the order of actions. *Anza* starts in the same way as *seiza*, but once the right knee is touching the floor, tuck the right foot under the left thigh and sit down into a cross-legged position, bringing the left foot and ankle over the right, if possible[8], or under if not. While this position is more comfortable for most people, given the reduced pressure on the knees, it is in fact harder to maintain correct upper body posture in *anza* than in *seiza*; so concentrate on keeping the back straight and shoulders back, not hunching over or letting the neck come out of alignment with the spine by nodding forwards or tipping the head back. To stand, again reverse the order of actions: disengage the left foot and place it flat on the floor in front of the right foot; rock forwards and then up into a half-kneeling position with the right knee down; bring the right foot directly behind the right knee and then stand up, bringing the right foot forwards at the end to complete the movement to *kesshu gamae*. Try not to use the hands (either on the floor or the knees) when sitting or standing; rather, starting from *kesshu gamae,* place the arms by the sides with palms flat on the thighs while moving, and revert to *kesshu gamae* when finished.

Many Western students unused to sitting on the floor will find one or both of these positions uncomfortable, either straight away or after a short period. If there is no injury or other structural problem, try to maintain the positions for as long as possible before shifting to a new one (either from *seiza* to *anza,* or from *anza* to something less formal). That means not moving at the first sensation of discomfort, but testing yourself – moderately, as always – to endure the challenging feeling for a little longer each time. Both positions are also yoga *asanas* – poses designed to promote health and vitality – and the stretching of the legs and opening out of the hips that they encourage is an important part of gaining increased mobility and stability. But, as ever, pay attention to your own condition: if you have an injury that may be exacerbated by sitting in either way, find a modified way to sit which is manageable without causing pain; if you find the circulation becoming restricted, resulting in numbness or tingling, take care of the situation by changing position, stretching out if necessary. In either case, it is polite to ask the Sensei's permission before adopting a different position.

---

8 *Anza* is technically just the simple cross-legged position, whereas if one foot or ankle is placed on top of the other (normally, but not necessarily, the left on the right) the position is the same as the 'half lotus' position of yoga and is known as *hankafuza* (半跏趺坐) in Japanese. Both positions will be referred to as *anza* in this text.

Kamae – posture

Beyond *Kesshu Gamae* and the sitting methods described above, all techniques and movements in Shorinji Kempo are performed from one or other of the stances, or *kamae* (構), such as *chudan gamae* (中段構 'mid-level stance') or *ichiji gamae* (一字構 'stance of the character for 1'). And while the word 'stance' in English is derived from the word for 'stand', *kamae* instead refers to 'structure', and thus can be equally applied to a form in motion or to a stationary pose (compare with this the idea that in Yoga, *asana* or poses are not necessarily meant to be static, but can flow from one into the next). In practice, this means that *kenshi* should strive to maintain good posture at all times, both when still and in the course of performing basic movements or more complicated *waza* ('techniques'). Like *kesshu gamae*, the named stances each have a purpose, typically to have an effect both on the opponent and on the practitioner – sometimes to intimidate but sometimes to trick; sometimes to bolster our courage and sometimes to calm us down. By being conscious of *kamae*, their details and their purpose, and by maintaining good body structure always, not only will techniques become much more effective, but the mind and spirit will be reinforced too.

Happomoku

Happomoku (八方目) literally means 'eyes in 8 directions' – the 8 directions being those of the Chinese Zodiac – that is to say, 360⁰ vision! More realistically, we should strive to cultivate our peripheral vision and become sensitive to what is happening – especially to movement – at the borders of our awareness. When facing an opponent, we should look them straight in the face, but simultaneously be aware of everything else about them; naturally, this means the position and movement of their hands, feet and limbs, but it also includes more subtle information like the rate of their breathing and the set of their weight and balance. Furthermore, we must also be aware of as much of the surrounding environment as possible – any obstructions, the quality of the surface, what is behind us – as well as taking note of any other people or sources of danger or assistance in the vicinity. Thus, 'looking in all directions' has both literal and metaphorical significance, and is one more aspect of being fully open to our environment. This radical openness should be extended to all your senses – hearing, touch, smell, even taste – and should therefore not cease when you are not using your eyes; for example, when in *zazen* meditation or darkness. The key, as with vision, is not to grasp at the objects of perception, and thus close out other available information by focusing too narrowly on a small subset of the available inputs.

Chosoku

Chosoku (調息) means to regulate the breath. Control of the breathing is a vital element for improving physical performance as well as calming and settling the mind; for the breath is perhaps the most obvious bridge between the two aspects of body and spirit, *Ken* and *Zen* (see '*Ken Zen Ichinyo*'). *Kenshi* should strive to breathe deeply and evenly whenever possible, and to harmonise this with their movement and actions (see '*Kiai*'). When out of breath from strenuous exertion, make a conscious effort to bring down the rate of breathing (and thereby, the heart rate) as quickly as possible, and try to breathe through the nose with the mouth closed when recovering. When practising as a group, the Sensei may call for *shinkokyu* (深呼吸), 'deep respiration'; take this opportunity to get your breath back with maximum efficiency by using the movement of the arms and upper body to perform two very deep breaths, finally sealing the movement with the hands pushing away and the exhalation deliberately cut short at the end.

Figure 12 Shinkokyu

Kiai

An important special case of breathing control is *kiai* (気合) – the spirited shout that many martial artists use to bring focus and power to actions such as strikes, blocks, throws, and even breakfalls. We can also hear it in the enthusiastic grunts of top tennis players when they hit a mighty serve or powerful backhand. *Kiai* begins with a shout, but ultimately it is the focus of energy that is important. The word itself means 'unifying (the) *ki*', and it has both physical and psychological elements. From a physiological point of view, *kiai* causes tension in the core muscles of the torso, thus bringing greater control and transmission of power into complex whole-body movements such as punches, kicks and throws. Additionally, this tension creates a momentary protective effect, making the body less vulnerable and sensitive to impact. On the mental level, *kiai* allows us to focus all our will and attention on the result of an action – rather than becoming overwhelmed by the many important details of even the simplest techniques, we can bundle all we have learned into a single explosive expression of intent, unifying body, mind and spirit through the medium of breath. Do not be bashful or diffident in your *kiai*; as a beginner, look to make as much noise as possible to show your enthusiasm and fighting spirit, and to encourage others to join with you in giving 100% in your training efforts. *Kiai* is also an essential part of self-defence – a sharp shout or yell at the right moment can destabilise or discourage an attacker with great effect – but practice is essential, so do not hold back!

Tai sabaki and ashi sabaki

Shorinji Kempo is a very fluid art, and body movement is at the core of its effectiveness. Therefore, there is strong emphasis on the various different ways of moving the body, not just dodging for defence but also for offense, with or without stepping. Movement of the head and trunk in isolation is called *tai sabaki* (体捌), and footwork is *ashi sabaki* (足捌) or *umpo ho* (運歩法). While there are quite a few different body movements and steps to be mastered in the early stages, it is important to realise that the different elements are all part of the effort to move with maximum efficiency and speed, to enable both defence and attack with the minimum of wasted effort whilst maintaining balance and power generation. Just as with *kamae*, consciousness of accurate and nimble footwork, together with proper dodging and body movement, should become completely habitual and instinctive over time. However, this requires close attention from the beginner at the outset, together with continued self-monitoring (cf *kyakka shoko)* as you progress and develop. It is all too easy to miss these details and focus instead only on the most obvious aspects of a technique – the hand that blocks or releases, for example – when in fact the body and foot movements can be just as important, if not more so, in determining success or failure.

Chinkon

Chinkon-gyo (鎮魂行 'soul calming discipline') is the counterpart to *ekkin-gyo* (易筋行 'muscle easing discipline') and forms an important part of every Shorinji Kempo class[9]. It consists of a short period of seated meditation (*zazen* 座禅) surrounded by the spoken pledges of the *Dokun* (see next topic). Just like *ekkin-gyo*, our technical practice, *chinkon* is fundamentally a practice with multiple dimensions: mental, physical and spiritual. However, its methods and style are quite different from the moving, active challenges of *kihon* (basics) and *hokei* (set technique) practice; it provides another angle, a method shaped over millennia (meditation as a discipline was already common in India in the time of Buddha) to achieve the central aims of Shorinji Kempo, which are to develop the self and learn to live in harmony with others. Therefore, you must not ignore or downplay this aspect of training – it is as fundamental as *ekkin-gyo*, and all *kenshi* must work hard to get the most from these relatively brief opportunities to 'salve the soul'[10].

Figure 13 Dabo during chinkon gyo

9 *Chinkon* can be conducted at the beginning of a training session, in the middle – between basic and technical practice – or at the end.

10 The blend of physical training and meditation into a unified system of personal development was arguably the great innovation of the Shaolin temple method, and a key reason why Doshin So adopted the name of that famous institution. See 'The Shaolin Monastery: History, Religion, and the Chinese Martial Arts' (2009) by Meir Shahar.

Mind

Reciting the *Dokun*, as described in some detail below, allows us to imprint the basic ideas of the philosophy of Shorinji Kempo in our minds, at the same time as giving us a chance to reflect on their meaning or on our recent successes or failures in living up to their precepts. Then, when seated for *zazen* meditation, we strive to calm our minds and improve our mental functioning by deliberately trying to let go of the busy chatter of our thoughts, the seldom-quieted restlessness of our ever-wandering attention and the unending analysis of every thing we perceive or imagine[11]. Note that in both parts of *chinkon* – recitation and meditation – there is by design very limited space for conscious declarative thought, such as brooding over some failure or worrying how we will deal with a looming problem in our lives. It is this very absence of grasping with the mind that can heal and strengthen it, and prime it for enhanced performance, not only in our training, but in the rest of our activities too, be they work, study or leisure[12].

Body

Zazen is also a challenging physical practice – it is not supposed to be either easy or relaxing! However, the precise method of sitting and breathing is designed to maximise the recuperative effect and to rapidly induce a sense of mental calm and physical well-being. This is achieved first and foremost through the adoption of good posture, which is vital to ensure comfort and efficient circulation of both air to the lungs and blood throughout the body; then through an active process of inhalation and exhalation that acts to fill the body with energy, drawing strength from the air surrounding us. This physical effect produces an immediate impact on our mental state, which in turn influences our bodies via calmer, deeper breathing and a reduced heart rate. It is the deliberate actions of *chinkon* that accelerate and enhance this beneficial effect relative to just flopping down after exertion or relaxing at home in front of the TV; it is an active form of recovery and recharging that also brings with it mental and spiritual benefits.

---

11 This sort of perpetual mental activity of grabbing onto sensory input and internal ideas has been dubbed the 'monkey mind' by some Zen teachers (which may be an unfair slight on our simian cousins). Modern psychologists refer instead to the 'Default Mode Network'.

12 Many leading businesspeople and celebrities now practise, and attribute their success to, various forms of meditation.

Soul

The word *chinkon* can sometimes refer to a funerary rite or requiem mass, which gives an indication of its true meaning – 'tranquillity for the soul'. That is to say, the purpose of reciting the *Dokun* and performing *zazen* meditation is primarily to quieten the mind[13] and thus allow the spirit to flourish, unburdened by the stresses and turbulent emotions of everyday life. The consequences of this, from a spiritual perspective, are that we can learn from this practice how to see beyond the words and concepts of our 'grasping' analytical minds, and thus begin to get a sense for the nature of reality as it truly is. Such a sense is valuable, in that it can help us to avoid being deceived by our own or others' narratives – convenient stories about the world that may in important ways be misleading or false thus causing us to come to the wrong conclusions or take the wrong actions based on them. The endpoint of this process is called *satori* (悟) or enlightenment, but it is useful even for the novice who has just begun the practice, for this is not an all-or-nothing kind of event – it is an endless process of chipping away at the wall of illusion and ignorance that first created and then limits our human consciousness.

13 The underlying meaning of the Sanskrit word *nirvana* is 'extinguished', as in a raging fire, or the cooling down of a patient recovering from a fever.

How to Sit and Breathe During Zazen Meditation

Kamae – posture

Zazen meditation is most often performed in *hankafuza* or *anza*, but it can also be performed in *seiza*; for example, after arriving late to a class, or if *anza* is not possible owing to injury[14] (see above for details of the position and how to sit and stand correctly). In this position you can remain comfortable and grounded for long periods, focusing on the breath and posture. At the same time, you can become aware of the flow of *ki* energy through the body as you breathe in and out, and the flux of sensations, perceptions, thoughts and emotions which pass through your mind and body. However, it is not necessarily easy to establish this position, so careful attention must be paid to posture in both the lower and upper body, and the awareness and avoidance of tension throughout. It also takes effort and energy to maintain, though with practice the amount of conscious effort becomes progressively less.

Figure 14 Zazen meditation

---

14 When *seiza* is adopted for meditation, a different set of *kanji* can be used from normal (正座), but with the same sound – 静座, with the meaning 'quiet' or 'calm sitting'. The *tai gamae* (体構え 'body stance') is the same, but the *kokoro gamae* (心構え 'heart stance') is different.

From the stable triangular foundation formed by the crossed legs and the tailbone (coccyx), allow the spine to rise up as vertically as possible, with the head balanced on top, but tilted slightly forward – this is because the cervical spine does not enter the skull at the middle of its base, but closer to the rear (the occiput). Release tension from the hip flexors and shoulders as much as possible, allowing them to fall to the lowest position allowed by your current level of flexibility (which you can also improve with targeted but gentle stretching), and in so doing, allow the chest to expand and the heart to open. With this *kamae* ('structure' as well as 'stance') you are in position to breath most easily and deeply.

During *zazen*, the Sensei's designated assistant will check the posture of the seated *kenshi* in the group, one by one, using a long staff or *shakujo*. This is called *dabo* (打棒[15]) and is a valuable opportunity to check your own alignment and balance. It is easy to be unaware of incorrect posture, and the gentle corrections given at this point will help you to learn what in fact it feels like to sit up straight. In recognition of this help, *kenshi* must show gratitude with *gassho rei*, but it is important first to wait for the adjustment to be complete, and secondly not to disrupt the corrected posture by making a large or jerky movement with the hands.

Chosoku – breathing

There are several possible breathing techniques that meditators can utilise, and indeed, traditional yoga practice has a whole field of study devoted to the subject (*pranayama*). Here is the characteristic Shorinji Kempo method used by *kenshi* during *zazen* meditation. Note that precise timings and levels can be adapted to your own initial state – particularly as this will change from class to class depending on your physical condition and what you have been doing immediately beforehand – but also during the *zazen* session itself, as you become more deeply relaxed (or perhaps sometimes less comfortable).

1. Breathe in slowly and deeply through the nose, with mouth closed.
    a. For example, count for 5 - 7 seconds, trying not to rush.
    b. Start the breath from the bottom of the lungs by contracting (and so pulling down) the diaphragm – this, in fact, feels more like pushing the belly out – which draws air into the lungs.

15 Literally, 'hitting stick'; this may refer to the tradition in Zen temples of striking students with wooden practice swords (*bokken*) if they were caught napping during the long *zazen* sessions required of initiates.

   c. For extra capacity, use the muscles between your ribs (intercostals) to expand the upper chest cavity and draw in more air.

2. Pause when the lungs are full.

   a. Either simply stop breathing in, or compress the air in the lungs slightly by holding the breath consciously, stopping the flow of air through the airway (trachea) and slightly tensing the muscles of the torso. Avoid any action that introduces tension to the neck or shoulders or causes a visible movement of the upper body.
   b. Count for 3 - 4 seconds; feel the energy *(ki)* brought by the new oxygen suffusing throughout the body from the chest outwards.

3. Exhale slowly and deeply through the nose, with mouth closed.

   a. Allow the intercostal muscles to relax first, then the diaphragm.
   b. Count for 7 - 10 seconds.
   c. A stronger exhalation can be achieved by tensing the lower abdominal muscles at the end of the outbreath. Again, take care not to let any tension spread to surrounding areas.

4. Pause before the lungs are completely empty, with 20%-30% of the air remaining.

   a. Count for 3 - 4 seconds.
   b. Start to inhale again when you feel ready; do not rush.

The whole cycle of one breath in and out should be as long as you are comfortable with, and can range from 10 to 30 seconds, depending on the oxygen demands of your system at the time (e.g. after strenuous *randori* practice, you will need to breathe more rapidly, at least at first, than if you had been inactive).

When the *zazen* session comes to an end, the assistant with the *shakujo* (*dabo*) will strike it on the floor to make a sudden, sharp noise, together with a loud *kiai*, thus rousing the group from its quiet and peaceful state. At this moment, as soon as you hear the crack of the *bo* and the shout of the *kiai*, make you own *kiai* to match it with as little delay as possible. This discipline is designed to give you practice in immediately reacting to a change in situation, and requires that you are both relaxed and prepared at the same time. This is also why you should never completely empty the lungs, as then you would have no breath with which to make your *kiai*.

The Dokun

The *Dokun*[16] (道訓 'teaching of the way') is the set of pledges we recite either side of *zazen* (seated meditation) during training, and can be seen as a kind of mission statement for all *kenshi*. Some of the sentiments expressed are obvious; some less so, and some may even be controversial. However, it is important to both understand and to mean the words as spoken out loud during every class, for in this way the true meaning of the commitments expressed can take root and become part of our lives, rather than remaining mere empty slogans. Take this time as an opportunity to reflect on how far you have lived up to these ideas in your daily life, and to renew your commitment to doing so in the future.

Seiku 聖句 'verse of scripture'

1. 'Rely on yourself and not on others; no one is as reliable as your own well-disciplined self.'
2. 'By committing evil, you defile yourself; by avoiding evil, you attain purity.'

This text is taken directly from two verses (v.160 and v.165) of the *Dhammapada* – a collection of sayings of the Buddha which is one of the most widely read and best-known Buddhist scriptures. The two verses deal with the requirement to develop yourself (*Jiko Kakuritsu* – see 'Establish Yourself, Live in Harmony with Others') and take responsibility for your own conduct, by trying to see clearly that good actions are fundamentally beneficial to a person, and vice versa (mirroring the concept of *karma* or *innen* 因縁; see Part VII).

16 See Appendix below for the full text of the English translation and the Japanese original with romaji transliteration.

Here is an alternative translation from the 19th-century scholar, Max Müller (1881):

'One is one's own refuge, what other refuge can there be?

With self well subdued, a man finds a refuge such as few can find.'

'By oneself the evil is done, by oneself one suffers; by oneself evil is left undone, by oneself one is purified. Purity and impurity belong to oneself, no one can purify another.'

There is much that can be written about these few short lines, but the most obvious point to make is that it is about individual human flourishing (what Aristotle called *'eudaimonia')*. In a nutshell, you (and you alone) are responsible for your own happiness and you cannot rely on anyone else to provide it for you; the best way to ensure it for yourself is to improve yourself and avoid doing 'evil' – what might more commonly be called 'the wrong thing'[17]. Startlingly, there is no other positive commandment (such as avoiding certain foods or committing to certain rituals or practices): work to improve yourself, avoid the negative stuff, and everything else will follow naturally. But what is not said is how you determine what is positive and what is negative, and the attempt to do just that forms the central part of the work of people striving for enlightenment – how to see things for what they really are.[18]

One other important point to note is that when we say 'rely on yourself and not on others', we are not denying the importance of the networks we make and form part of in our lives, where of course we rely on and are relied upon by family, friends and even strangers. It is this symphony of mutual cooperation and support that enables us to achieve so much as individuals and as a society. Rather, we are saying that within such a network, we should try to be the strongest node in our local group – one that strengthens and feeds energy to its surrounding connections, rather than one that drains energy and is parasitic; taking and not giving back.

---

17 Also cf. Mark 7:15 (KJV) 'There is nothing from without a man, that entering into him can defile him: but the things which come out of him, those are they that defile the man.'

18 In traditional Buddhist thought, the three 'defilements' (*kleshas*) are ignorance, craving, and clinging. It is really these that we should strive to avoid, and in so doing attain true clarity of vision, or purity.

Seigan 誓願 'pledge'

1. 'In acquiring this art, we pledge to honour our founder and not betray our masters, to respect our elders and not slight the young; as comrades, we pledge to help each other and to cooperate for the accomplishment of these teachings.'
2. 'We pledge to leave our past aside and to devote ourselves to mastering the art as plainly and naively as infants.'
3. 'We pledge never to perform our art for selfish reasons, but for the benefit of all mankind.'

While *Seiku* focuses exclusively on the individual, *Seigan* expands the view to include the environment of the dojo, your teachers and training partners and the wider community of *Shorinji Kenshi* throughout the world. We consider our place within that structure, our attitude to training and the wise exercise of the skills that we (will) have learned.

We first affirm our commitment to maintaining the original intention of the founder, Doshin So (in a nutshell, 'to create an ideal world' and to foster world peace), and to keeping a proper sense of perspective about the hierarchy of experience within the organization. Doshin So created Shorinji Kempo by assembling the disparate elements of his broad studies in martial arts, philosophy and spirituality, together with a good deal of his original design; we should recognise that great achievement, and respect it as a coherent vision and comprehensive system that has brought, and continues to bring, huge benefits to very many *kenshi* and the communities of which they are part. At the same time, that system is transmitted, maintained and (occasionally) adapted by the whole group of those who teach and practise it now as a living art, with those who have gone before (note that the word *'sensei'* literally means 'born before') and have devoted more time and effort to practice having a naturally greater authority than those who are newer. This is the basis for the respect that we accord to masters, teachers and our seniors, and it is not derived from a slavish subservience to unearned authority.

Following on from that, we also commit to giving as well as to receiving help, and to acting cooperatively to bring the dream of the founder closer to reality. This part underlines the importance of acting together to achieve this goal – together, we are much stronger than we could be separately.

The next point talks about coming to training with an open heart and mind, and being as receptive as an infant to new information. There is a famous story of a

Zen master[19] who pours a cup of tea for a know-it-all visitor, but does not stop as it overflows:

> *'Nan-In filled his visitor's cup … and kept pouring. The professor watched the overflow, until he could restrain himself no longer: "Stop! The cup is overfull, no more will go in." Nan-In said: "Like this cup you are full of your own opinions and speculations. How can I show you Zen, unless you first empty your cup?'*

The moral of this tale is that we need to have an 'empty cup' to be able to receive new information or insight, or we will not be able to recognise, understand or process it; and this applies equally to master and student. Discarding our 'baggage' – preconceptions, unhelpful habits of mind and body, and inaccurate estimates of our own worth (whether too high or too low) – is a crucial precondition for learning and growth.

Finally, the third point reminds us of our responsibility as the beneficiaries of skills and capabilities we did not have before and would not have otherwise. We must be modest and not use these purely to raise our status, or to exploit others for money without offering them something of value in return. However, and this is very important, this point does not forbid us from ever earning money from the art, or otherwise being compensated appropriately for our contributions. Despite the fact that many teachers and administrators gladly give their time without charge, it is quite acceptable to be paid for those things[20], and *kenshi* should at all times be prepared to pay an appropriate amount for their education. Indeed, not charging students for the privilege of learning the art is a sure way to cause them to judge it accordingly, as having no value.

Shinjo 信条 'creed'

1. 'We are grateful that we are endowed with our souls from *Dharma* and our bodies from our parents; we determine to make every effort to return their blessings.'
2. 'We love our country and determine to better the welfare of our people.'
3. 'We love justice, respect humanity, observe courtesy, keep the peace and determine to be true and brave.'

---

19 In this version the *Meiji*-era master Nan-in. Quote from Osho News.

20 Many early branch masters in Japan benefited from Doshin So's *tokkin* (特金) system of fee sharing.

4. 'We strive to master the art and discipline our bodies and souls; we love our comrades and help each other; we cooperate and endeavour to establish an ideal world.'

Shinjo takes the broader focus of *Seigan* and expands it progressively to our families, communities, nations and, ultimately, the whole world. It also includes multiple references to gratitude and love. This is very important, and a feature not lost on all major world religions – by acknowledging blessings and expressing thanks, we create a more positive and balanced mental attitude that can protect us from the corrosive effects of chronic stress and worry with which we are afflicted in our modern existences. This may be because, as a matter of simple survival, humans have evolved to be much more sensitive to threats, risks and negative outcomes than to positive ones. Indeed, it has been estimated by neuroscientists that a positive event requires as much as five times more reinforcement than a similarly negative one to have the same force in a person's memory and future motivations[21]. But in a modern life where most existential threats have been banished by lawful and organized societies, technology and healthcare, this evolved bias causes long-term harm. Restoring the balance of positive reinforcement through mindful repetition of these words can help us to be both happier and more connected to our world.

The first point mentions *dharma*. This is one of the most fundamental concepts of Buddhism (and several other Indic religions and philosophies such as Hinduism and Jainism). We go into a more thorough discussion of this topic later (see Part VII, *passim*) but in this context it is easiest to think of it as representing the force of nature, or the law of the universe, in the same sense that we might talk of the laws of physics. However, note that there is much more that can be said on this topic, and the preceding ideas are merely a good place to start, not a final definition. In any case, the thrust of this point is that we should recognise and be grateful for the source of our physical being; that is to say, the chain of life of which we are a part and, more specifically, our parents. They not only created us biologically, but (sadly, not for everyone) helped to create our mental and spiritual selves by bringing us up with love and discipline. We – out of the millions of possible genetic variants jostling for the chance of life – have been given the awe-strikingly rare gift of conscious life and we must do everything we can to show our gratitude by making the most of that opportunity. Ask any parent what they want from their children in return for the massive investment of time, money and energy that is parenthood, and they will tell

21 Dr Rick Hanson *Hardwiring Happiness: The New Brain Science of Contentment, Calm, and Confidence.*

you that it is for their children to prosper, thrive, be happy and achieve their full potential (which is not to say that a little gratitude does not go amiss either); we should always bear that in mind, and strive to do the same for the broader force that has granted us life: *dharma*.

The second point then broadens this awareness to the wider community and nation where we live. Some may recoil from any sentiment that could be perceived as nationalist, in the sense of a narrow-minded, inward-looking and xenophobic perspective. But this is very much not the intention here; if anything, it can be seen as the best sense of patriotism, and there is a crucial distinction: patriotism celebrates one's own nation's strengths and distinctive culture, at the same time as being open to exchange and discourse as equals with other nations. It is the direct corollary of the pride, loyalty and love we should feel for our families.

As humans, we have evolved from collections of individuals living in tight-knit family, clan and tribal groups, to larger communities that have coalesced into discrete nation states. It is conceivable – even likely[22] – that this progression might arrive one day at the kind of globally undifferentiated society we sometimes see in futuristic films or TV shows, where national distinctions seem to have vanished. But that is clearly not the case today; nor is it likely any time soon, and it is deeply important to recognise this, especially for people with limited experience of the world who might not be sufficiently aware of the significant differences that will continue to divide national groups for the foreseeable future, in cultural and linguistic terms, and even in their ways of thinking and seeing the world.

The third point is more straightforward, though the injunctions it contains are by no means easy to uphold. Scoring well on these items requires courage, intelligence, compassion and energy; however, just as in physical training, the way to develop these strengths is by exercising those capacities on a regular basis.

The final point is essentially a summary of everything that has gone before: train your whole self, interact constructively with your network, and when enough people are thinking the same way, we have the chance to create 'an ideal world'.

Further study – the Kyoten

Note that, while we refer to this group of statements overall as the *Dokun*, in Japanese dojos there is traditionally another section between *Seigan* and *Shinjo* called

22 See *Sapiens* by Yuval Noah Hariri, chapter 9ff (Harper, 2011) for a discussion on the progressive assimilation of all prior cultures into one.

Dokun that goes into more detail about the behaviour expected of adherents of *Kongo Zen*. Another section called *Raihaishi* (礼拝詞 'words of worship'), spoken only in private dojos (*doin* 道院), talks about *dharma* and *innen* (see Part VII for a further discussion). The full set of statements is referred to as the *Kyoten* (教典), which means 'teachings' or 'religious code'. They were left out of the original translations into English of the basic Japanese textbook (*fukudokuhon*) as being too overtly religious in nature; however, they are included in the appendix for reference.

What Is Budo and Why Do We Practise It?

Traditional budo and bujutsu

Shorinji Kempo is – among other things – a martial art; that is to say, a system of techniques and exercises designed to increase skill in combat. The Japanese word for martial art (or, more precisely, 'martial way') is *budo*, and this term has become well known in the West. This can be attributed to the prominence of Japanese arts – particularly Karate – in the explosion of interest in martial arts by Western viewers and practitioners that occurred from the 1960s onwards. This cultural invasion was spearheaded by the films of Bruce Lee[23] and supported by Hong Kong's prolific kung fu movie industry, but was underpinned by other factors, such as the exposure of American GIs to oriental fighting systems when stationed in Japan, Korea and the Philippines. *Budo* as a socially recognised activity has been present in Japan for longer, although its origins are not, in fact, ancient: before the advent of Kano Jigoro's *Kodokan* Judo, in the Meiji period of 19th-century Japan, traditional martial skills were often the jealously guarded secrets of noble *samurai* families; these activities were known as *bujustsu* (武術): 'martial craft'.

To stop two spears

By the time of the founding of Shorinji Kempo in 1947, the meaning of the word *budo* had reverted to equivalence with *bujutsu* – that is, a purely practical collection

23 Ironically, Bruce Lee – as a proud denizen of Hong Kong and an inheritor of the distinctively Chinese *wing chun* style of Ip Man – was occasionally prone in his films to jingoistic portrayals of Japanese martial arts and artists as boorish, unsophisticated and ultimately less effective than his Chinese ancient and modern hybrid style. Given the (at the time) recent history of the two peoples, this partisanship is understandable.

of fighting techniques – and had lost the associations of the 'way' (derived from Confucian and Taoist traditions) that Kano had intended. Indeed, it had become associated with the use of arcane fighting skills for mere show, to oppress the weak and vulnerable, or to settle disputes with brutal and excessive force[24]. Kaiso wished to reset the meaning of *budo* for his followers, and drew inspiration from the structure of the *kanji* (ideogram) for *bu* (武, see below) which contains three simpler elements – 'two' (二), 'spear' (弋) and 'stop' (止) – reinterpreting it as 'to stop two spears'.

By this, he meant that *budo* (and by extension *bujutsu*) is more than a set of fighting techniques; rather, it is a general method for promoting a better society, by creating peacemakers who can settle disputes not just physically, but in all areas of conflict. This interpretation is almost the opposite of the popular conception of the vengeful martial artist, but is, in fact, very close to Kano's original lost vision.

Why practise budo?

A useful question we can ask ourselves is why we are practising a martial art at all. For most of us, violence plays little or no part in our lives. Spending thousands of hours over many years mastering an unarmed combat system might seem of little practical use in today's world, where violence is relatively rare. This compels us to look further and more deeply into the true meaning of the martial way. *Budo* is a means of overcoming ourselves and of training our minds and bodies in ways that will have manifold uses, whether or not we ever actually encounter physical violence of the sort that our techniques are designed to counter.

Budo offers us a concrete way of realising the two central pillars of Shorinji Kempo and the two vital ingredients of a good life, which are to develop ourselves through our own efforts (*jiko kakuritsu*) and to learn to live and prosper in harmony with others (*jita kyoraku* – see 'Establish Yourself, Live in Harmony with Others'). The first of these is achieved through the effort and hard work required by the

24 Note that this is still a common conception of *budo* in the West, too.

training; the second through learning the skills of conflict resolution that are at the heart of 'stopping two spears'[25]. Kaiso stated that everything in our lives depends ultimately on the quality of specific people – on ourselves and on those in a position to help or harm us. *Budo* develops our qualities by giving us the skills to resolve conflicts in many different arenas. This, in turn, gives us the confidence to stand up for what we believe is right, and the wisdom to cooperate with others, both to inform those judgements and to help make them a reality.

---

25 These two aspects are also known as *bu no tai* (武の体) 'the body of *bu*' and *bu no yo* (武の用), 'the application of *bu*'.

Part 2

The Fundamental Ideas of Shorinji Kempo

The topics in this section explore the fundamental ideas of Shorinji Kempo philosophy, based on the teachings and writings of the founder, Doshin So, reflecting his unique personality and experience. The characteristic mixture of traditional Zen Buddhism with insights drawn from the world of *budo* which he brought to his message was expressed in a typically direct and iconoclastic way. The result is a collection of simple precepts that encapsulate his thought, and which can serve as an invaluable touchstone for *kenshi* (and other readers) seeking to take practical steps to improve their lives and make the world a better place.

Gyo – The Discipline of Shorinji Kempo

As should already be clear, Shorinji Kempo is not merely a fighting art or simple method of self-defence. Kaiso created Shorinji Kempo as a *gyo* (行, 'discipline') – a tool we can use to develop ourselves to our greatest potential and to help us learn to live in harmony within our societies, promoting peace and happiness. To understand more of what this means, it is instructive to look at the word *gyo* to see how it is used and to uncover its deeper underlying meanings.

The meaning of gyo

A *gyo* is a discipline or practice that can be thought of as any activity capable of being conducted with a spiritual ulterior[26] motive. This activity can be practically useful in its own right (self-defence or cleaning, for example) or not (meditation or chanting). It is a concept used often in Buddhist teaching, particularly Zen, but it is also common to many other traditions of religious devotion, or even in the secular pursuit of excellence in arts or crafts. Some examples from the Japanese Zen tradition are flower arranging (華道 *kado*), the tea ceremony (茶道 *chado*) and, of course, many of the traditional martial arts; for example, archery (弓道 *kyudo*). The fact that these examples all end with the suffix *do* (or 'way') is no coincidence, for the idea of a way of life – an ongoing process, a spiritual journey – is key to the whole concept.

Figure 15 Chado: the tea ceremony

26 'Ulterior' here means 'lying beyond' and does not necessarily indicate ill intent.

In fact, from the point of view of Zen, any activity can be endowed with this significance if it is conducted with due mindfulness and reverence, with total involvement and concentration on excellence, even if it is the lowliest and most menial task[27]. Extending this idea, you can view the whole of your life as a kind of large-scale *gyo* – a practice optimised to enhance your understanding and bring you closer to enlightenment.

It is also worth mentioning that, in Japanese, *gyo* (or *shugyo*) can refer more narrowly to a type of unforgiving asceticism, verging on self-mortification. This became popular in some schools of Japanese Buddhism[28], despite Buddha's own disdain for such a path (see 'The Middle Way'). It should be obvious that the *gyo* of Shorinji Kempo is more in tune with Buddha's direct advice to avoid extremes and to seek meaning in balance and moderation in both physical and spiritual practices.

The origin of gyo

The character for *gyo* (行) is most simply read as the verb 'to go'; and here, the connection with the word for 'way' (道 *do*) is obvious: it refers to an iterative process (n.b. '*iter*' is the Latin for 'journey') that takes you somewhere you want to go. It is something you keep on doing; for the wise, it can be seen to have value in its own right apart from the goal of getting to the destination. Indeed, the character has been interpreted to represent a left and right footprint, as well as a crossroads; this view, then, adds the idea of constantly beginning anew with each step, seeing every moment as a new opportunity (see '*Ichigo Ichie*').

Kaiso introduced a further interpretation. For him, the character reveals two strong figures facing each other, each carrying on their back someone weaker or in need of

27 It is said that the most sought-after chore (作務 *samu*) among the devout in Zen temples was the job of cleaning the latrines.

28 For example, *taki no gyo* 'waterfall austerities' involves standing under a waterfall, and the nine-day fast of the *doiri* of Nichiren Buddhism often resulted in the ascetic's death. See the *Encyclopedia of Monasticism* by William M. Johnston for further examples.

help. This illustrates his vision of creating strong and just individuals who can help the needy and co-exist peacefully with others in a mutually cooperative society[29].

Types of gyo

Within Shorinji Kempo there are two main types of *gyo* – *ekkin-gyo* (易筋行) and *chinkon-gyo* (鎮魂行) – broadly delineating the physical and mental spheres of the discipline. It goes without saying that both areas are vitally important in cultivating the qualities sought in a *kenshi*, although, having said that, the relative time spent on *ekkin-* versus *chinkon- gyo* in a typical class points arguably towards Kaiso's own views on the right balance between the two. And these are ultimately just broad reminders that the whole of our practice – *kihon, embu, randori, zazen, seiho*, *tetsugaku*, charitable activities – should be seen in this light and conducted in this way: as a discipline, a never-ending journey of self-discovery and self-improvement.

29 See http://www.zendoctor.com/ShugyoMeaning.html for an interesting discussion of the meaning of *shugyo*.

Half for Your Own Happiness, Half for Others'

半ばは自己の幸せを、半ばは他人の幸せを
Nakaba wa jiko no shiawase wo, nakaba wa hito no shiawase wo

Kaiso used these memorable words to describe the balance between self-interest and altruism that *kenshi* should strive for. They are quite self-explanatory, but note (as is often the case) that the order of the words is significant: look after your own needs first as your primary responsibility, to avoid being a burden on others; then look to help those around you. A good and fulfilling life must involve service to others, but you must develop yourself sufficiently first to be of any use. This encapsulates all we are trying to do with our training and, ultimately, our lives. To achieve happiness – or *eudaimonia,* to use Aristotle's term[30] – is our ultimate goal, but while this appears simple in some ways, it is no easy task. Doshin So's prescription is just this: work hard to improve yourself (*Jiko Kakuritsu*, see below); then enjoy your life, but fill it with service to others (*Jita Kyoraku*, again below). This precept has a central place in Kaiso's teaching and is very similar to a verse of the *Dhammapada* (v.166) that comes immediately after the two verses which make up the *Seiku* section of the *Dokun* (verses 160 and 165). It states:

> *Let one not neglect one's own welfare for the sake of another, however great. Clearly understanding one's own welfare, let one be intent on the good.*

---

30 From the *Nicomachean Ethics*. He stressed the cultivation of *arete* – 'virtue' or 'excellence' (αρετή) – which as a concept has much in common with the goals of personal improvement and good relationships with others that Kaiso emphasised. As a result, many modern commentators prefer 'human flourishing' over 'happiness' as a translation for *eudaimonia*.

It is also important to reflect on the distinction between your own happiness and that of others, and between self-interest and altruism. From the Buddhist perspective, where one of the fundamental tenets is that the difference between self and non-self is an illusion, the above distinction in fact melts away: contributing to the happiness of others directly improves your own wellbeing, as it is the same thing. You could even say that helping others is, in some sense, fundamentally selfish, as is everything else you choose to do, and that is how it should be. With this perspective, then, the difference between self and others is not one of kind, but of proximity: you are connected indivisibly to everyone and everything, but you are still you, and your first duty and your first opportunity to make the world a better place starts with yourself. Therefore, it is important to have balance, and to devote enough of your energy to promoting your own happiness – which you are uniquely placed to do – in order to provide the necessary condition for promoting the happiness of others.

Establish Yourself, Live in Harmony with Others

Jiko Kakuritsu 自己確立 – Establish Yourself

The idea that true happiness arises as the result of a self built up to be physically robust and mentally sharp, well-educated and self-disciplined, is an ancient one[31]. The three ideals of Shorinji Kempo ('Healthy Body, Healthy Mind, and Self Defence') fit squarely in this tradition, though with a distinctive and characteristic emphasis on *budo* as a uniquely effective method of education. Therefore, this building of character alongside physical development is the first goal of our practice and is referred to by the phrase *jiko kakuritsu* (literally 'self-establishment'). Achieving it is that part of the 'ulterior motive' referred to above in '*Gyo* – The Discipline of Shorinji Kempo'.

This project of self-construction – finding out who we are, who we want to be and taking committed action to realise those goals – is at the very core of the discipline of Shorinji Kempo and pervades and informs everything we do and how we go about it. Through constant, iterative practice, we can improve our strength, which is of course vital to having a healthy body, and thus helps our state of mind too (see '*Ken Zen Ichinyo*'); but we also develop self-confidence and the ability to make decisive and courageous decisions in our lives. By understanding ourselves at a deep level – what we believe in and what we stand for – we can insulate ourselves from the forces of social pressures, empty hedonism or seductive but misguided ideologies that can cause so much harm and lead those less firmly established astray. And this development will not just affect us: as everything is ultimately connected (see 'Fate and Free Will'), a well-established individual will act as an example of stability and

31 The early (pre-Socratic) Greek philosopher Thales of Miletus put it thus: τίς εὐδαίμων, ὁ τὸ μὲν σῶμα ὑγιής, τὴν δὲ ψυχὴν εὔπορος, τὴν δὲ φύσιν εὐπαίδευτος ('What man is happy? He who has a healthy body, a resourceful mind and a well-educated nature').

quiet strength to those around them. This is exactly what Kaiso's vision for the creation of an 'ideal world' calls for (see 'Doshin So and the Founding of Shorinji Kempo' and 'The *Dokun, Shinjo*') – a critical mass of self-actualized individuals within society to act as beacons of true strength, good judgement and compassionate action.

Jita Kyoraku 自他共楽 – Live in Harmony with Others

The expansion of our outlook from our own selves – where everything must begin, of necessity, as the only thing over which we have direct, deliberate control – to our surroundings, our families, friends, communities, societies and eventually the whole world, is the subject of *jita kyoraku* (literally, 'self and others mutual enjoyment'[32]). This idea resonates with Kaiso's interpretation of the character for *gyo* (行): while the first, more conventional reading shows the idea of a journey and a process of self-improvement (and so corresponds with *jiko kakuritsu*) Kaiso's take shows strong people helping the weak and cooperating with others in a mutually beneficial way. This is the essence of the meaning of *jita kyoraku*.

The idea that we are enmeshed in a web of social and kin relationships – that we are dependant in a myriad of ways on those around us at varying degrees of separation – and that we should therefore behave as if the concerns of our neighbours are our own, is an old and universal one, and is often called 'the Golden Rule'[33]. Kaiso's philosophy recognises this interdependence whilst simultaneously stressing the importance of self-reliance – a seeming contradiction that is, in fact, resolved on looking more deeply at the substance. For it is only by establishing ourselves as strong and independent in both mind and body that we can truly co-exist with others as equals in mutual harmony and respect. And this once again brings Kaiso's famous saying to mind: 'Half for your own happiness, half for others''.

32 Kaiso's phrase bears the clear imprint of the philosophy of Kano Jigoro, the founder of modern Judo, who promulgated the almost identical phrase *jita kyoei* (自他共栄), 'mutual welfare and benefit'.

33 Variations on the theme can be seen in the teachings of (among many others) the ancient Chinese sages (Confucius and Lao Tzu), of Buddha, the ancient Greeks (Thales) and Romans (Seneca), and the Abrahamic traditions.

The Key Teachings of Shorinji Kempo

少林寺拳法の特徴
Shorinji Kempo no Tokucho

The following six topics – *ken zen ichinyo, riki ai funi, shushu koju, fusatsu katsujin, go ju ittai, kumite shutai* – form the core of Kaiso's original teachings[34] about the key characteristics of Shorinji Kempo. They can be further subdivided into three groups of two: ideas for how to develop ourselves and how to live our lives (*ken zen ichinyo, riki ai funi*[35]); ideas for the proper way to use our skills (*shushu koju, fusatsu katsujin*); and ideas for how to train those skills most effectively (*go ju ittai, kumite shutai*). These six canonical topics are joined by a seventh, encapsulating Kaiso's injunction: 'Don't Lose!' (*fuhai shoju*).

34 The topic names are all composed of four characters put together (四字熟語 *yoji jukugo*); this is a classic format for expressing Zen teachings in a concise way.
35 This first pair can in many ways be seen as directly parallel to the ideas of *jiko kakuritsu* and *jita kyoraku* discussed earlier, in that they offer the means to achieve the ends expressed in them.

Ken Zen Ichinyo

拳禅一如
The Unity of Body and Mind

Ken Zen Ichinyo can be considered the most fundamental of the Six Characteristics of Shorinji Kempo. As a concept, it encapsulates the essence of both Shorinji Kempo in particular and of martial arts practice in general, and beyond that, of the whole nature of reality itself, as perceived by our embodied minds. It teaches first that martial arts and mindfulness are two aspects of one unified discipline, and that both *ken* (martial arts) and *zen* (mindfulness) must be practised together in order to develop effective and responsible individuals. Finally, it asks us to look behind and beyond the false dualism of words and things and so come to attain a deeper understanding of reality and our place within it.

'Oneness of Fist and Zen'

Ken (拳) means 'fist', and in the context of *ken zen ichinyo,* it stands for the physical practice of martial arts, and ultimately by extension, everything related to the physical body.

Zen (禅) means 'meditation'. However, given the broader significance of the religion and philosophy that bears this name, the word is hard to translate directly into English. In this context it can be understood as meaning the practice and mindset of meditation, or what we in the West would call 'mindfulness'[36].

---

36 The word *zen* is the Japanese reading of the Chinese *chan*, itself a version of the original Sanskrit word *dhyana*. In its original form, before the establishment of the Chan (Zen) school of Buddhism in China in the 5th century (see 'Bodhidharma, Zen and the Shaolin Temple'), it simply meant the practice of seated meditation that was already common in Indian spiritual practice even before the time of Buddha.

Ichinyo (一如) is translated as 'oneness' or 'unity', and it refers to having the quality of being a unified whole. It is often used to convey the idea that where we may conceptually consider two things to be separate, they may actually be aspects of one and the same thing, like two sides of a coin, or descriptions of some one thing from two different angles. It can also – and not without tension with the first sense – indicate 'unification'; in other words, that disparate elements have been combined into a newly united whole.

Thus, ken zen ichinyo can be read literally to mean that the practice of martial arts (*Kempo*) and of mindfulness (*Zen*) cannot be separated – that they are, in fact, aspects of the same underlying truth – and that the apparently different spheres of physical and mental training should therefore be brought together in theory and practice. Not only is mental and spiritual education a requirement for the proper direction of the physical skills learned in martial arts training, but the very activity itself is uniquely suited to promoting both types of development – body and mind – simultaneously.

Beyond 'Fist' and 'Zen'

Ken can also be understood as representing the whole body, and *Zen* as the trained mind and spirit. Additionally, *Ken* is both the physical training method by which one comes to understand more truly the indivisibility of body and mind, and also that physical nature in its entirety. Likewise, *Zen* is both the mental training method through which one learns to control (and eventually let go of) the mind in order to direct the body effectively, and also the expanded consciousness itself. The mind directs the body, and the body carries out the will of the mind. The two cannot act independently; thus, *Ken Zen Ichinyo* can also be interpreted to mean that 'body and mind are one'[37]. This wider formulation can be seen both as a description of the way things actually are (though it may not always be obvious), and as a call to action – to unify the two seemingly disparate spheres of body and mind in our training and in everyday life.

Unity of Body and Mind

The interconnected nature of our minds and bodies can be seen in how mental and physical health affect each other in any individual. Long-term illness or physical

37 This more general formulation in Japanese is commonly expressed as *shin shin ichinyo* (心身一如).

strain will inevitably have an impact on mental well-being, and there is considerable evidence, likewise, that adverse life events which impact mental health can directly affect physical health; for example, by affecting the body's capacity to resist infection and illness through the immune system. Positive effects also flow in both directions from healthy bodies to healthy minds and vice versa. Indeed, the very existence of the 'placebo effect' (and its opposite sibling the 'nocebo effect') should be evidence enough for the proposition. Modern neuroscience has also demonstrated that the practice of disciplines like Shorinji Kempo over time changes the physical structure of the brain, as new neural connections are made and reinforced through the process of learning[38]. In a sense, the physical act of training over a sustained period can change the physical basis of our consciousness – the 'hardware' on which the 'software' of our minds runs – in a positive way. As the Roman poet Juvenal famously observed[39], *mens sana in corpore sano* ('a healthy mind in a healthy body') is truly the greatest of treasures.

Unify the Body and Mind!

Another aspect of *ken zen ichinyo* we become aware of through practice is that physical disciplines like *chosoku* (調息, breathing control) can help us to control our psychological and emotional state. Our reaction to crisis situations – the so-called 'fight, flight or freeze' response – is physiological and largely involuntary, and results in changes in breathing patterns, heart rate, and the release of large amounts of adrenaline. These can help to ensure our survival, but can also be associated with emotional responses (fear and alarm) which may be incapacitating. Being able to do something as basic as exercising voluntary control over one's breathing (which is an intrinsic part of Shorinji Kempo training) can help to control these physiological responses, and thus help maintain control of our psychological and emotional state.

The goal of physical training in Kempo is conditioning the body to respond appropriately and instinctively in a situation of physical conflict. First, you must strengthen the body and copy the outward forms of techniques to learn them. Next,

38 See, for example, *The Effects of Martial Arts Training on Attentional Networks in Typical Adults* (A. Johnstone & P. Marí-Beffa) in *Frontiers in Psychology*, February 2018.

39 In *Satire* 10, line 356. The subsequent list of virtues echoes closely the ideas of *jiko kakuritsu* and *jita kyoraku* and concludes with this assertion: '*semita certe tranquillae per virtutem patet unica vitae*' ('for sure, the only road to a peaceful life is through virtue'). See also the note on *eudaimonia* and *arete* (virtue) in the section on 'Half for your own happiness, half for others'.

you must condition your responses through repeated practice in many different scenarios to develop instinctive reactions. In a real fight, if you have to consciously decide to perform each new movement, it will be too late. When your body can instinctively react to the opponent's attack, and when you can immediately draw on conditioned responses, the mind can be freed for tactics and strategy: close observation of the opponent, broader situational awareness, and the ability to be 'one step ahead'.

Once a student has attained enough awareness and muscle control to practise the techniques without intense concentration, they will then be able to shift their awareness from their immediate body to reflecting on the overall practice and being 'present in the moment'. By engaging this level of awareness, you can begin to train the mind to read the dynamic between you and your training partner, and learn to strategize in response to the developing situation.

The final stage of this practice is what is sometimes called 'flow', or 'being in the zone'. It is letting go of active reflection to completely immerse oneself in the activity, allowing oneself to act and respond intuitively to one's partner. It is not the same as not paying attention. The mind is focused and clear but does not dwell or reflect on any one point or moment. This level can only be achieved after having internalised the required movements and gaining a good degree of proficiency in the techniques through long practice.

Figure 16 Bodhidharma (detail from painting at Himeji castle, Hyogo Prefecture)

Seeking balance

These two sides of training – mental and physical – are deeply interlinked, and it is important not to focus too much on one and neglect the other. Kaiso told the story of how Bodhidharma, on his travels through China, arrived at the Shaolin temple[40]. The monks there practised ascetic meditation and spent all their days sitting in contemplation. As a result, their physical condition was very poor, leaving

40 See 'Bodhidharma, Zen and the Shaolin Temple'.

them weak, both unable to fully apply themselves to their meditation and easy targets for bandits and robbers. Moved by this, so the legend goes, Bodhidharma taught the monks a series of physical exercises to reinvigorate them. This physical training fortified and strengthened their bodies, not only allowing them to apply themselves more effectively to their meditation, but also to improve their condition and better defend themselves. Over time their condition vastly improved, and the monks of the Shaolin temple became formidable and famous warriors.

Kaiso likely told this story to emphasise the importance of the balance between physical and mental training in martial arts, as well as life in general. If you focus exclusively on meditation you may become enlightened, but what use is that if you are weak and unhealthy, unable to defend yourself from ailments or others from violence? Equally, if you focus exclusively on physical or fighting practice, then of what benefit are you to society?

Riki Ai Funi

力愛不二
Strength and Compassion are not separate

This four-character phrase literally means 'strength and love are not two' and is the second of the two most important and profound teachings of Kaiso; together, these two topics form the first pair of the Six Characteristics of Shorinji Kempo, which deal with ideas for how to develop ourselves and how to live our lives. But for all its depth, it can also be understood simply and applied readily both in the dojo and in everyday life. First of all, 'strength' must be understood as both physical and mental strength; that is, the strength of willpower, determination, decisiveness and of rational, declarative intellect. 'Love', on the other hand, means something closer to 'compassion' or 'charity' in the Christian tradition, rather than romantic love, and also includes empathy, altruism and physical gentleness.

Funi 不二 – Not two

Furthermore, as with many of the compact Zen sayings that pervade the teachings of Doshin So, it appears to contain an opposition, a *koan*, even (a Zen contradiction in terms that is designed to allow students to break free of confining thought patterns). Thus, it can be understood both as a claim that the two opposites are not in fact different, but are actually the same, or merely superficially different aspects of a single underlying reality (see first bullet point below), and also as a clear instruction to merge the two apparently opposed attributes into a whole which is more representative of the truth that lies beneath (second bullet). This re-integrated quality of strength and compassion is what Kaiso called 'True Strength'.

Funi thus calls for two responses on our part:

- First, a recognition of what is really the true nature of the thing: real strength is in fact the same thing as effective compassion. Power without a foundation in compassion is ultimately flawed and weak (as well as dangerous), while superficial compassion without the physical, intellectual or moral strength to back it up is both ineffective and false.
- Secondly, a commitment to make ourselves into an example of that truth: we should train ourselves both physically and spiritually to unite these two seemingly opposed qualities. This will help us 'establish an ideal world'[41], as far as we are able, both for ourselves and that part of the world we can directly influence.

The writer Rolf Dobelli makes the point acerbically:

> *'Let me state this even stronger: Caring without action is inhumane. It gives us the illusion of making the world a better place. Truth is, we do it for us. We revel in the marinade of caring. What does it change? It makes us feel good (humane if you like) but doesn't help a thing. I don't care about people who care. Empathy – if it remains empathy – is useless. I deeply care about people who help.'*

Riki Ai 力愛 – Justice and Mercy

In a case where you witness injustice, your sense of right and wrong will tell you that something needs to be done. This is *ai*: your innate and learned inclinations towards compassion and love. However, only with *riki* (strength and courage) will you be able to go about making any difference to the situation. Unfortunately, injustice is all around us. As Kaiso taught that everything depends on the person, it is up to us as *kenshi* to foster a strong sense of justice (which is a mixture of unwavering principles and the empathy to put oneself in another's place) and to build our courage to take positive action when necessary, facing down wrongdoing. This obligation does not only apply in situations where we (or others) face a direct physical threat, but in all our relations with other beings.

Kaiso also taught that the exercise of compassion towards aggressors is only meaningful from a position of superior strength and is strictly conditional on their ability and willingness to change for the better. We must be ready to forgive if they can truly demonstrate that they have learned the lesson – that bad actions cause bad

41 *Dokun, Shinjo* no.4.

results for them sooner or later[42] – but clearly, a lesson can only be learned if it has first been communicated effectively. Otherwise, your forgiveness will have no impact on, or meaning to, a person who must have already discarded morality and fellow feeling in order to carry out their aggression. Therefore, a necessary but not sufficient condition for someone to be changed as a result of suffering an unexpected defeat at the hands of their intended victim is that they must fail, and you must be in control both of the situation and of the person (whether physically or psychologically). Justice must come before mercy.

Be the good guy

With that said, it is very important to stress that the lesson that should be taught is not that 'might makes right', but rather that you can be strong, just and merciful all at the same time. If you subdue an attacker and seek to impose your view of morality on them by force, you are thereby validating every idea they have ever had about the strong dominating the weak. There is no way that hurting them beyond what is necessary to defend yourself will make them suddenly revise that worldview. What you must do, always, is to be 'the good guy': never act out of hate, spite, revenge or superiority. It is only by offering a tangible example of a better way – the way of the *Arhat* – that some people might (just) be shocked into reconsidering their life choices and change their future behaviour.

Other connections

Riki Ai Funi can also be seen to be related to many other topics within the philosophy of Shorinji Kempo; indeed, as an idea, it can function as a kind of bridge between them[43]. For example, the concept of duality and unity in *Ken Zen Ichinyo* corresponds neatly to *Riki Ai Funi*, with the physical realm of martial arts and the body (*Ken*) being equivalent to *Riki*, and the contemplative and reflective realm of *Zen* being equivalent to *Ai*. Another close correspondence is with *Go Ju Ittai*, as the hardness of strength – here, both physical and mental – contrasts with the softness of compassion and caring. More broadly, we can see the toughness of *Riki* as what we

42 This is *Innen* or karma, and such rare occasions as envisaged here can give an unusually direct lesson in its workings, that for all their rarity may be the only way that some lessons can be taught or learned.

43 This is not to suggest that the topics are identical or express only the same ideas.

require to achieve *Jiko Kakuritsu:* hard work, discipline and inflexible determination. On the other hand, the openness and sensitivity to the feelings and experiences of other people *(Ai)* is what makes *Jita Kyoraku* possible. Accept and love yourself as you are *(Ai)*, but never be satisfied and keep on striving *(Riki)*. And so on.

Finally, while these connections are suggestive, they are ultimately limiting too, for it is in the very nature of these ideas that they seek to go beyond the simple equivalences of a=b to reveal, as stated so often here, the deeper truth beneath.

Shushu Koju

守主攻従
Defence before Attack

We now turn to the two topics that deal with the proper way to use the skills we learn. The first of these, *Shushu Koju*, literally means 'defending comes first, attacking is secondary'.

Moral considerations

Shorinji Kempo is a martial art that has at its core the idea of self-defence, rather than fighting for ego, winning competitions or exploiting others. Therefore, the techniques are structured around the primacy of defence before counter-attack. This concept is founded on a deep commitment to ethical behaviour not only when it is convenient, but also in the most serious encounters we are likely to face. Simply put, the philosophy of *Kongo Zen* prohibits us from being the ones to initiate violence, and further requires that if we cannot avoid the use of violence due to the actions of others, we must respond judiciously, proportionately, and ethically to put into practice the lessons of *budo*: to 'stop two spears'[44].

Legal considerations

Importantly, we live in a society governed by laws, and we can be called to account for our actions by the authorities, who will rely not just on our word, but on that of

---

44 Note that, in addition to the prohibition on initiating violence, the very nature of Shorinji Kempo techniques is designed to cause minimum lasting damage to the aggressor, with maximum effectiveness. See also 'The Five Elements of *Atemi*'.

witnesses and even of the perpetrator themselves. This means that we must be very careful to be able to justify any actions we take; for example, by showing that we had good reason to believe that we faced a genuine and imminent threat, and that our response was both proportionate and necessary (see more discussion of these ideas in 'On Self-Defence'). It is much harder to do this, if all a witness can recall seeing is you strike the first blow in a confrontation that leaves the opponent injured or worse; whereas a clear demonstration that you do not want to fight can make a powerful impression on witnesses who may be able to sway a jury after the fact with their (perhaps flawed) memory of the event.

Therefore, the principle of *Shushu Koju* also exists to protect us from the consequences of impulsive actions, where we may risk losing far more by 'winning' an unnecessary fight than by avoiding it. UK criminal law[45] allows an individual to use 'reasonable force' in their own defence. However, this force must be both proportionate to the threat involved, and also necessary to allow that person to escape the threat (so, using such force when reasonable alternatives existed, or for revenge, for example, would not be permitted).

Technical considerations

As well as moral and legal advantages, the tactic of not attacking first need not impose practical disadvantages; indeed, it is a key reason for the effectiveness of the techniques. To understand this, it is important to consider the effect of surprise on the course of both attack and defence. A saying attributed to Sun Tzu from the *Art of War* teaches: 'The first move, if not a surprise attack, can be easily withstood or evaded.' Thus, in any violent confrontation where there has been reasonable warning that something is about to, or could potentially happen, the principle of *Shushu Koju* has obvious application. This is because we gain a great tactical advantage from being prepared[46] to respond to an attack from a strong defensive position. By waiting to see what attack does come, we can evade, frustrate or block it, and then launch a well-timed, well-aimed and decisive counter-attack at an enemy who has exposed themselves with a committed attack that missed its mark. It is by tempting the assailant to overextend and open up their weak points that we are given an

45 See the Crown Prosecution Service website:
http://www.cps.gov.uk/legal/s_to_u/self_defence/

46 The ability to calmly assess the situation and wait for the appropriate moment to act is one of the most important and difficult aspects of *budo* to master. See '*Heijoshin*'.

opportunity for an easy but effective counter. Their attack will be *jitsu*[47], but foiled by a strong or fluid defence (also *jitsu*), and this will create *kyo* – an opening (*suki* 隙) that can be capitalised on without hesitation.

Figure 17 Hasso gamae (left), taiki gamae (right)

So in this case, the surprise is not the initial attack, but the determined and immediate response of the defender. To magnify this effect, in Shorinji Kempo we learn ways to conceal our strength and level of preparedness, and this is expressed most obviously in several of our *kamae*: principally, the calm-looking *taiki gamae* (待気構), its yet more modest cousin *tate muso gamae* (立無想構), and the conciliatory posture of *hasso gamae* (八相構). The names of the stances here give us a further clue to their purpose: *taiki* means 'waiting spirit', and *muso* means 'without intention'[48]. Thus, these stances predispose us to *Shushu Koju*, while at the same time

47 See 'The Five Elements of Atemi' and 'Ma'ai' for a discussion of *kyo* (empty) and *jitsu* (full).
48 *Hasso* means '[hands] in the shape of the character for '8' (八)', so refers to the shape, not the purpose.

tempting a less calculating attacker into displaying typical 'alpha male' behaviour and launching an unconsidered assault.

Further considerations

It is worth pointing out that the quote from Sun Tzu above also implies quite clearly that surprise attacks are, in fact, very effective. For just this reason, people who are experienced in the successful use of violence to get what they want – these are the people who are overwhelmingly likely to attack you unexpectedly – will tend to use this tactic as much as possible. In these cases, by default, your move will not be the first one, and thus *Shushu Koju* does not apply[49].

On the other hand, some altercations seem to arise as a surprise to no one but the 'victim', due to their own heedless and provocative behaviour, perhaps violating the norms of an unfamiliar social group into whose midst they may have unwittingly stumbled. In this case, the attacker may actually perceive that they are the one who has been attacked first – if not physically, perhaps more seriously with regard to their honour or status, by the words or deeds of the intruder. You do not have to agree that this kind of behaviour is right to see that it is widespread and dangerous, and that someone who is sensitive to their surroundings and to the reactions of others should be in a better position to avoid or defuse this kind of situation than someone who is not. In this context, *Shushu Koju* means avoiding provocative or offensive behaviour; that is, not 'attacking' (even if unknowingly) first.

Some situations, on the other hand, are actually much less serious and require more nuanced responses. Because Shorinji Kempo techniques are inherently based on *Shushu Koju*, they always provide the opportunity to protect ourselves and choose the level of force to be applied in response. Whilst it is generally a given that if we offer no response, unless the incursion was an accident, then we must simply expect the infringements to continue, we do not always need to offer crushing counter-measures in response to milder attacks; for example, against very intoxicated assailants. As ever, judgement is key.

Finally, the situation is absolutely changed if a weapon is evident or is about to be brought into play. In such cases, much more drastic defensive actions are warranted – that is, both permitted and required – if no available avenues for escape are present. Given the gravity of the situation, such actions will include pre-emptive attacks and

49 What is highly relevant however is the principle of *ryaku*, or strategy, that can help to ensure that you are not in the wrong the place at the wrong time and selected as a weak target by such people.

the use of any suitable objects that may be to hand for improvised defence and counter-attack. This more extreme response is still consistent with *Shushu Koju*, however, as the introduction of an asymmetric threat like a weapon (and the clear intent, means and opportunity to use it) has effectively initiated an attack already.

Fusatsu Katsujin

不殺活人
Do not kill, but help others to live

Fusatsu Katsujin is the second of the pair of topics from the Six Characteristics of Shorinji Kempo that deal with the proper way to use the skills we learn, and is translated literally as 'not to kill, people to live'.

The simplest way of understanding this injunction is at face value: the techniques and capabilities acquired from training in Shorinji Kempo should never be used to take life, but rather should be directed towards improving the lives of others, through the judicious exercise of force in the service of protecting self and others and upholding justice wherever possible. The juxtaposition is clear: we are tasked with fostering life, not damaging or eliminating it.

Fusatsu 不殺 – Do no harm

Why is such a commandment[50] necessary? In a society like ours today which is highly regulated and very safe by historical standards, *fusatsu* may seem like an unnecessary instruction. However, it is worth remembering that martial arts have a history, both ancient and modern, of being misused for either personal gain or reputation; or worse – to exploit, harm, or even kill others. They have a long association, in China particularly, with organized criminal groups such as the Triads, who evolved from and with the many underground secret 'boxer' societies[51]. These groups made

50 This phrase has on occasion been rendered into English in the words of the biblical commandment 'Thou shalt not kill'.

51 Key groups were the 'Fists of Righteous Harmony' *Yihequan* (義和拳, *Giwaken*), the 'White Lotus Sect' *Báiliánjiào* (白莲教 cf. *Byakurenken*) and the 'Heaven and Earth Society' *Tiāndìhuì*

use of not just the techniques of martial arts, but also the military-style training, discipline and bonding that they fostered, to further their nefarious goals, and occasionally to participate in open revolt against the government of the day.

For most of us today, such activities are an unlikely occupation. However, there are some types of martial arts training that encourage indiscriminately violent counter-measures which could, in effect, be training their adherents to go to jail. In contrast to the more established mainstream competitive martial sports – such as Judo, Taekwondo (both Olympic sports), and more recent arrivals like Muay Thai and even MMA hybrids, which are, of necessity, governed by rules to assure safety, at some level, for the competitors – new styles of 'street fighting' or 'urban' self-defence (Krav Maga, for example) have become popular that recommend dangerous techniques which would result in permanent injury, blindness or death if applied as intended. Such training is very far from the ideals of *budo* that Shorinji Kempo holds as sacred, and is dangerous both to participants and to society at large.

In any case, we have a responsibility not just to refrain from criminal activity, but also to make sure that any application of our skills achieves its justified and reasonable ends with minimal infliction of damage. Such a responsibility is moral as well as legal (see '*Shushu Koju*' and 'On Self-Defence'), but there is also a deeper reason to avoid harm: in causing damage to others, we also harm ourselves through the workings of *Innen* (karma), by means of *Engi* (cause and effect). Even in purely superficial terms, you will have to live with your conscience if you cause lasting injury or death through your actions, and that sort of psychic or spiritual self-inflicted harm is best avoided.

The techniques are designed to be safe but effective

Fortunately for *kenshi*, the very structure of the techniques and the nature of the training are designed from first principles to achieve the maximum effectiveness in stopping a violent adversary with the minimum of damage. This means that while judgement and control are always important, the instinctive reactions that have been trained by countless repetitions will result in actions that are inherently safe and effective.

First, the way we strike (as detailed in 'The Five Elements of *Atemi*') is geared towards exploiting the body's natural network of weak points (*keimyaku hiko*

(天地會 cf. *Tenchiken*). The word 'triad' itself comes from the 'Three Harmonies Society' *Sanhehuì* (三合會 cf. *Sangoken*).

経脈秘孔[52]), and not towards breaking bones, damaging organs, or otherwise causing dangerous and permanent harm to the opponent. The point is that a particular kind of pain or bodily reflex action (such as being winded) – which is the primary (short-term) effect of the use of such weak points – can be more effective in subduing an adversary and taking away their desire to fight than actual damage, which they may not notice or react to in time to stop them from pursuing their attack.

We rely not just on weak points, but also on other mechanical, physiological and psychological principles (see 'Technical Principles'). These allow less force to be applied than would otherwise be necessary, and thus also contribute to the safe but effective nature of the system. Further, as described above in '*Shushu Koju*', our techniques are also constructed with a primary defensive premise that allows us the chance to exercise restraint wherever possible. Having said all this, it is important to be clear that defending oneself or others from genuine danger, especially if there are any weapons involved, will entail a high level of risk to both the defender and the attacker. The primary injunction in *Fusatsu Katsujin* is 'do not kill', not 'do not damage'; so while we strive to minimize harm to an attacker, taking measures to train ourselves in fundamentally ethical methods, we cannot rule it out entirely.

Katsujin 活人 – Develop human potential

The second part of the phrase *Fusatsu Katsujin* is perhaps easier for us to relate to, for it calls on us to 'make people live', or, to expand on that a little, to foster human potential. This potential is both your own – as in *Jiko Kakuritsu* – and that of others – as in *Jita Kyoraku*. And these others are not just your family, friends, and those to whom you generally feel a sense of mutual obligation, but even the people who try to cheat, rob or hurt you. This is where *Fusatsu Katsujin* suddenly becomes difficult, even controversial; but this is also at the heart of the *Gyo* of Shorinji Kempo – what makes it a spiritual discipline rather than simply a fighting method. *Kongo Zen* holds that all human beings, aggressors included, have the potential to learn and to change both themselves and the world for the better. Crippling injuries diminish that potential, and death negates it entirely; inflicting either is not the goal of Shorinji Kempo training. Some martial arts have promulgated sayings like *ikken hissatsu* (一拳必殺), 'one punch, certain death'. Shorinji Kempo instead chooses a different saying: *ikken tasho* (一拳多生), 'one punch helps many'.

52 Literally 'secret holes of the acupuncture meridians'.

Go Ju Ittai

The third and final pair of topics in the Six Characteristics of Shorinji Kempo, *Go Ju Ittai* and *Kumite Shutai*, deals with ideas for how to practise and train most effectively.

剛柔一体
Hard and Soft form one whole

Shorinji Kempo divides its fighting techniques into the two systems of *goho* and *juho*, 'hard' and 'soft'[53]. On the surface, this is an obvious distinction, as the two styles of technique are clearly different. However, Shorinji Kempo not only teaches that a fully rounded and comprehensive system of self-defence must include both, but also that they exist on a continuum, and that there is ultimately no clear dividing line between the two systems. This has consequences for the way we both practise and apply our skills.

Goho 剛法

Goho is the hard system of strikes, kicks, blocks and deflections, characterised by instantaneous contact with an aggressor. It responds to hard, striking attacks with strong blocks and counter-strikes, aiming to make an opponent give up or to incapacitate them through the use of *atemi*. It is generally fast and powerful, and typically utilises simpler, larger and more obvious body and limb movements – 'gross motor skills'. For this reason, it requires less training than *juho* to be effective, and is practically more available in a high-stress situation where freezing or clumsiness

53 The third 'system' (*ho* 法) of the physical division (*tai* 体) of Shorinji Kempo is *seiho*, healing.

caused by an 'adrenaline dump' (see 'The Eight Stages of Self Defence') can limit dexterity and make sophisticated or elaborate moves unrealistic and impractical.

Juho 柔法

Juho is the soft system of defensive locks, releases, throws, restraints and pins, characterised by more continuous contact with an opponent at very close quarters. It responds to grabs to arms, clothing, the body, or even hair that may be used for three broad types of attack: to immobilise, control, or drag the victim away; to facilitate a strike such as a punch, knee or headbutt; or to throw them down to the ground or into an obstacle. This difference in situation from *goho* puts a defender at a greater potential disadvantage, but also offers greater opportunities for manipulating the attacker, provided by the very contact they have given. With skilful application of *juho* techniques, an attacker can be evaded, subdued, thrown or restrained, and a more nuanced application of force is possible, rather than the comparatively crude methods of *goho*. But this sophistication comes at a cost: *juho* techniques are typically more difficult to learn and require highly coordinated movements of the body, arms and hands – 'fine motor skills' – that may not be realistically available in a crisis situation.

Why is softness required to achieve these results? Because too much speed or power can risk breaking the connection with the opponent that enables the manipulation to happen. Juho calls for sensitivity in order to feel the vectors of force being applied and to use them against the attacker, often tricking them into putting themselves into a disadvantageous position or even into throwing themselves (rather than being physically thrown by the defender).

Go Ju Ittai 剛柔一体

Given these different types of attack and different circumstances, a comprehensive method of self-defence must include them all in order to give students both the best chance of protecting themselves against varied and unpredictable assaults, and to offer a broader set of defensive options for situations where extreme force is not warranted or justifiable. Shorinji Kempo integrates the two systems in regular practice into one coherent whole – *ittai* actually translates as 'one body' – particularly in the design and performance of *kumi embu*[54], in order to stress their interwoven

54 *Kumi embu* is a form of practice unique to Shorinji Kempo, where partners design and practise a flowing sequence of both hard and soft techniques, combining to form a dynamic display. See 'Types of Training'.

nature and powerful interaction. Whilst initially they seem separate and are practised mostly separately, future practice increasingly combines and merges them; indeed, from the grade of 4th Dan onwards, the syllabus is no longer organised into discrete *goho* and *juho* elements.

But the descriptions above are, necessarily, just generalisations. For example, it is possible to respond to grabbing attacks with *goho* alone (indeed, our most basic *juho waza* all begin with *goho* elements, such as dodges of incoming strikes and *atemi* like *meuchi* 目打), and striking attacks can be met not only with counter strikes, but with *go ju waza* – takedowns and throws in response to punches and kicks, such as *oshi uke nage* (押受投) or *tora daoshi* (虎倒). And looking more closely, we can see that all techniques, in fact, have elements of both hard and soft: the sharp and powerful *nukite* movement of *kote nuki* (小手抜) has much in common with *gyaku zuki* (not to mention the *atemi* that start and finish the technique), while the soft, entangling *hangetsu uke* (lit 'half-moon block' 半月受) of *kaishin zuki* (開身突) creates *kuzushi* (崩し) just like a well-executed *kagite shuho* (鈎手守法). Thus, the separation of the two systems is more apparent than real. Basic patterns of body movement continually reinforced in *kihon* training apply equally to both *goho* and *juho waza*, and in different ways, each employs the same fundamental understanding of how to best exploit the impetus supplied by an attacker and how to avoid pitting strength directly against strength.

Beyond Hard and Soft

We can also expand the idea of hard and soft beyond the sphere of techniques: we can think of our mental attitudes in this way too, displaying iron determination or flexible sensitivity, as the situation demands; the courage to stick by our core values even in the face of doubts, and the wisdom to re-evaluate our unquestioned assumptions when necessary.

This illustrates a deeper point: like the other 'union of opposite principles'[55] that we encounter so often in Kempo philosophy, the true meaning of *Go Ju Ittai* is that, behind the apparent differences between the two concepts, there exists an underlying reality that is at once both of them and neither of them, for these words are just labels we use to help us approach and categorise that reality. If we do not understand that deeper level, we risk mistaking the words for the real thing, which can result in nasty surprises when reality fails to conform to our neat preconceptions.

---

55 See, for example, *Ken Zen Ichinyo, Riki Ai Funi* etc. etc.

Kumite Shutai

組手主体
Pair-form training is at the heart of Shorinji Kempo

Martial arts have been developed, practised and passed down through the generations for thousands of years. During that time, many methods have been tried for communicating and practising the hard-won discoveries and insights of previous masters, but the most enduring and fundamental ones are single-form and pair-form training (practice with and without a partner[56]). Shorinji Kempo naturally employs both methods, but chooses to put more importance on pair-form training for practical and philosophical reasons.

This is primarily because single-form training is, by necessity, only preliminary[57] in the study of a martial art that aims to teach students how to deal with real attacks. Once a sufficiently robust base has been put in place through solo practice, then the next level of study can begin, which is to understand how to apply those basics in real time with a moving and intentional opponent. This change in level of practice reflects the difference described elsewhere (see 'The Three Levels of Mastering an Art') between *gi* and *jutsu*, technique and application.

There are many practical lessons to be learned from pair-form practice – some obvious and some less so. We learn the essentials of accuracy, distance, power and timing. By training with different partners, we learn how to adjust techniques according to their size, weight, speed and flexibility. Learning how to break balance and adapt to the many different variations of possible position that we may encounter when executing techniques cannot be done on your own. Finally, practising on a live

56 Another method of great antiquity is the written instruction manual (or scroll), now joined by the proliferation of modern media products such as DVDs and online videos.
57 By preliminary we also mean fundamental. See on *kihon* in 'Guidelines for Effective Training' and 'Types of Training'.

opponent is the only way we can learn to control and direct the power of our take-downs, throws and pins – enough to be effective, but not so much as to cause unnecessary or disproportionate harm.

Single-form training

Tan'en (単演) or single-form training ranges from the simple – *junbi taiso* (準備体操, warm-up and conditioning exercises) – to the more sophisticated, such as *kata* (型, set forms). Some other styles of martial art (particularly Karate) place great emphasis on *kata*, and rely on that method to encode and transmit many of their arts' most fundamental teachings. While Shorinji Kempo also uses single-form *kata*[58], it focuses on various types of pair-form interaction that can more effectively teach both practical and spiritual lessons. These comprise *hokei* (法形), *randori* and *embu*. The importance of *Kumite Shutai* can be immediately seen from the fact that you cannot learn much from sparring alone, and a single-form *embu* is much less impressive than one with two partners.

Cooperation and mutual development

The famous murals on the walls of the *Baiyidian* hall in the Shaolin Temple (see 'Doshin So and the founding of Shorinji Kempo') show Chinese and Indian monks training together in pairs, not individually, cooperating and learning together, and, importantly, enjoying themselves. This illustrates perfectly the mental and spiritual aspect of the principle of *Kumite Shutai*. We learn that without cooperative training it is impossible to make real progress. A partner who also improves alongside you will enable you to continue your own improvement indefinitely. But on the other hand, if your gain comes only at the expense of your partner, they will soon stop training with you, which is why we must always reciprocate roles and ensure that they are getting as much benefit as we are. It is only by helping each other that we can really reap the full benefits of Shorinji Kempo and explore it to its fullest extent.

Figure 18 Detail from mural painting at the Shaolin temple, Henan Province (early 19th C)

58 But prefers to refer to them as *tan'en hokei* (単演法形, 'single-form set techniques').

Fuhai Shoju

不敗勝従
You must not lose; winning is secondary

Our true goal as martial artists in combat or in life should be to not lose, rather than seeking to win. Losing means being defeated either physically or mentally, and could involve injury, subjugation, or even death. At the most fundamental level it means giving up; therefore, in some (albeit limited) sense, if you never admit defeat and never give up, no matter how bad your situation, you have not lost. But on a more practical level, it means keeping safe in the face of danger.

Fuhai 不敗 – Don't lose, be invincible

In the context of self-defence, this can be seen as practical advice that both steers you away from unnecessary conflict – if victory rather than survival seems important, then maybe the fight is just posturing for status (social violence) and thus avoidable – and clarifies the goals you should have when faced with genuinely unavoidable danger. Thus, your priority is to defend yourself (and any others you feel you must) from harm, rather than scoring points or teaching a lesson to someone you believe is in need of such schooling.

Shoju 勝従 – Winning is secondary

We contrast that with winning, which involves defeating an opponent and claiming victory over them. Winning a competition is a perfectly laudable goal as far as it goes, but a limited one. It should not come to dominate our approach to practice[59]. Winning in life first means not losing – for example, by giving up on efforts to grow as individuals and improve ourselves and our surrounding environment – but it also means not seeking to dominate others or prevail only at their expense. Treating life as comprised solely of a series of zero-sum interactions – these are occasions when one person's gain is matched by a corresponding loss for someone else – leads to a constant state of antagonism and a chronic lack of cooperation, which may profit you to the detriment of someone else in the short term, but does nothing to increase the overall stock of happiness or resources, and is thus ultimately impoverishing for everyone. A purely competitive and confrontational approach is strongly inefficient, since it discourages members of society from working together to increase the welfare of all.

There are obviously many positive aspects to the notion of winning, such as defeating your fears or conquering a bad habit or even an addiction, quite apart from more prosaic situations like winning a race or getting good grades in an exam. The important thing to bear in mind is that these positive points are all related to the benefits of victory to the individual, whereas the negative aspects mentioned above typically relate to the effects of seeking to dominate others.

Beyond winning and losing

If others seek to dominate you – physically, or in some other way – to promote their interests at your expense, then you must resist as effectively as you are able. In combat, as in other confrontations, this always means more than just defending in the hope that they will eventually grow weary and leave you alone (this is a form of denial only slightly less dangerous than the classic 'head in the sand' syndrome). In addition to avoiding harm, sooner or later you must counter-attack to ensure that the aggressor is forced to stop, rather than merely continuing their assault until they are eventually successful. You must be decisive and uncompromising in your actions, but your motive is important for both tactical and spiritual reasons: too keen an eye on victory may lead you to overextend yourself, putting yourself at unneces-

59 This is why sporting competitions are not over-emphasized within Shorinji Kempo. They have an important place, but must not be allowed to dominate, or the art risks becoming like those that have, for example, attained the status of Olympic sports (Judo, Taekwondo etc.); the incentives on offer – fame, money – are too powerful to be balanced by any more abstract benefits of traditional practice, and have distorted those arts beyond the recognition of their founders.

sary risk – either of desperate counter-attack, or even subsequent official sanction for having gone too far – while a 'dominance mindset' puts you, in some small measure at least, in the same position as that of the original attacker.

> *'To secure ourselves against defeat lies in our own hands, but the opportunity of defeating the enemy is provided by the enemy himself.'* *Sun Tzu*

Part 3
Study Skills and Life Skills

This section of the book is concerned with useful training and study skills that can help you in all areas of life and learning. These ideas can ensure you get the most out of Shorinji Kempo practice, but they also apply to everyday life, whether you are studying at school or university, developing professional skills and qualifications during a career, or simply dedicating yourself to lifelong self-improvement for the love of learning itself[60].

60 Scientific studies are increasingly showing that keeping mentally active through new learning throughout life not only significantly improves the chances of avoiding serious neurological conditions in later life (such as dementia), but also improves outcomes in other diseases as well, such as heart and lung disease.

Guidelines for Effective Training

修行の心得
Shugyo no Kokoroe

The following is a list of important items to keep in mind when you think about your Shorinji Kempo training as a whole. Keeping focused on these can greatly improve the quality and speed of your learning and development and, given that for all of us time is limited (see '*Ars longa, Vita brevis*'), getting the most out of the time we do spend in training is a very wise investment.[61]

1. Purpose – understand why you are training and clearly establish your future goals

Why did you first start practising Shorinji Kempo? For each of us, the reason will be different. For some it might have been a friend's suggestion; others may have been looking for self-defence skills or have been interested in Eastern philosophy. Try to remember what your reasons were, and then take another moment to check if they have changed or evolved since you started. Given what you know now and the experiences you have had, have your goals also shifted or expanded with your knowledge? The reason this is important is that if you have a clear understanding of what you are trying to achieve, you are much more likely to achieve it in a reasonable time. Focusing your efforts towards a defined outcome, you can easily see if you are making progress in the right direction; if not, you can change course and modify your efforts, as necessary. Even on the timescale of one lesson, it can be very helpful to set a specific goal for the class, while at the same time being mindful of the deeper motivations that underpin your practice. Revisit these longer-term goals from time

61 See '*Gyo* – The Discipline of Shorinji Kempo' for more details on *shugyo*.

to time – every year at the closing ceremony[62] is an excellent moment to do this – for, as you climb higher up the mountain of your own potential, your horizons will expand commensurately.

2. Order – follow the syllabus

The Shorinji Kempo syllabus has been carefully structured to allow us to progress in the art in an orderly and incremental way. The very first techniques you will learn – for example, *gyaku gote* – are the foundation of many techniques that will come later in the syllabus. In addition, basic movements and principles are introduced in a carefully thought-out progression using simple techniques as the foundation for more complex ones later. This process is important, and takes a little time at each stage, so it is important to respect the wisdom embodied in the structure of the teaching as it has been handed down to us through generations of teachers and students. Don't be tempted to run before you can walk: trying to jump ahead or make over-rapid progress through the grades will set you up for failure later, when your grasp of the fundamentals proves to be inadequate for higher levels of attainment. On the other hand, a steady rate of progress through the grades, conducted with mindful effort and lots of energy, will allow you to make significant strides in a surprisingly short period of time.

3. Basics – always return to your foundation

Kihon (基本) is the word for the basics and literally means 'foundation'[63]. These basics form the building blocks of all movements and should be practised constantly, initially to simply learn them and then to ingrain them in your 'muscle memory'. Properly speaking, of course, muscles do not have 'memory' and this term refers to reinforced neural pathways in the brain, created and maintained by constant repetition which makes them available for use with a minimum of conscious intervention. At first, some of these movements may seem awkward, but with time and effort they become more like reflexes, enabling almost effortless execution of techniques with apparently automatic ease.

---

62 The Closing Ceremony (*heikai shiki* 閉会式) is a traditional event held at the close of each year, where all students come together to formally finish the year's training and reflect both on what they have achieved since the last such ceremony, and what they plan to achieve in the following year.

63 The second character *hon* (本) derives its meaning ('main') from the image of the trunk of a tree, something that supports and nourishes the outer branches.

Figure 19 Kihon practice (BSKF 2014)

All students, from the Sensei down to the newest beginner, will do *kihon* practice together, for this is work that is never completed: it is not as if you can practise for a few years and then declare victory. In a real way, it is like the work we do to purify ourselves through 'polishing the mirror of our hearts'; all of us must work to get them polished, and then we must work to keep them polished. But note that one of the reasons for constant practice is to give us the opportunity to correct small errors and engage in a process of continuous improvement and refinement (*haizen* 改善). Thus, be mindful and do not just practise blindly – watch your teachers closely, and watch yourself even more closely, to see if you are getting everything right.

4. Principles – understand what makes techniques work

Shorinji Kempo techniques are based on a number of key underlying principles that make them effective, and will always incorporate several at the same time rather than just one. Some are purely mechanical in nature, such as *hazumi no ri* 弾みの理 ('principle of the bounce / rebound') or *kuzushi no ri* 崩しの理 ('principle of breaking balance'); some physiological, like *keimyaku no ri* 経脉の理 ('principle of weak points'); and some psychological or tactical like *renhanko no ri* 連反攻の理 ('principle of continuous counter-attack'). The important thing to realise is that by understanding the principles at work in any given technique you can greatly accelerate your ability to master it. At first, simply copying your Sensei is essential for learning the initial outlines (*shu*, from '*Shu, Ha, Ri*'), but as your familiarity increases, so must your understanding – to truly get the best results, you must look for, and then fully exploit, all the underlying principles of each technique. Watch the technique; ask yourself: "What are the principles? How and why does it work?" When you have gained some understanding, put that to use in adapting the way you perform the technique in ways that will increase its effectiveness.

As an example, *goho waza* defending against the attack *jodan furi zuki* will often utilise *soto oshi uke* – a powerful striking block to the inside of the opponent's wrist. If this block is performed correctly, it will both strike a weak point on the wrist – *sunmyaku* (寸脈) – causing the attacker distracting pain, and contribute to disrupting their balance, making follow-on attacks much less easy for them. Knowledge of these two principles (*keimyaku* and *kuzushi*) enables you to guide your practice in ways that will make the overall technique more effective.

5. Repetition – practice makes perfect

For both the comparatively simple movements of *kihon*, and the more complex combinations of *hokei* techniques, repetition is essential to engrave the movements in your mind and body so that they become natural and instinctive. As mentioned already, such practice must be mindful and dedicated – you must always be on the lookout for errors (small or large) that may have crept into your form, and this constructive self-criticism must be relentless and indefinitely sustained. But with those conditions met, the key ingredients are simply time and repetition.

It is sometimes said nowadays that true mastery of a complex skill (such as a classical musical instrument, or a sport such as tennis) requires 10,000 hours of 'deliberate' (that is to say, not mindless or misguided) practice. While this is a great oversimplification of the underlying research, the kernel of truth in this idea is that 'natural ability requires a huge investment of time in order to be made manifest.'[64] That is also why one can continue to improve in Shorinji Kempo throughout decades of practice, and be more skilful and effective (despite inevitable age-related decreases in speed and strength) at a later age than when younger. This is because the benefits of more practice outweigh any deficits from ageing, especially as such deficits are held in check precisely by this kind of training! It may be daunting to take the notion of 10,000 hours literally, as that would mean almost 50 years of uninterrupted 'normal' practice (i.e. two two-hour classes per week); on the other hand, it is good to know that more practice and more work will certainly result in greater accomplishment, whatever your innate ability or starting point may be.

6. Balance – train all aspects of yourself

Shorinji Kempo is a broad and deep art (see 'The Structure of Shorinji Kempo') and there are many nooks and crannies within it that can be explored with almost limitless potential for study and growth. But even in its most fundamental areas of basics (*kihon*), syllabus techniques (*hokei*), sparring (*randori*) and philosophy (*tetsugaku*), it is important to maintain a healthy balance across all dimensions; both within each

64 Malcolm Gladwell, in an interview about his book *Outliers* (2008). The book was based on research into performance by K. Anders Ericsson.

activity and between the different ones. Some obvious examples here are the balance between the right and left sides, between hard and soft techniques, and between physical and mental training. Many elements important to a good overall balance of training will not be in your direct control, but will, rather, result from the decisions of your teachers about what to focus on in classes; for example, whether to use protective equipment sometimes, constantly or never ('sometimes' being the right answer), or how often to include *seiho* practice[65]. But whenever you do have a choice – and that can involve how much effort to put into repetitions on one side rather than the other, or whether to stay after regular class time to get in some extra *randori* practice – try to focus on the areas that are not as strong as your strongest ones, and bring them up to that highest level too. Examine your blind spots: are you avoiding anything, consciously or not? By seeking out and eradicating your own weaknesses, you are on course to becoming truly powerful.

7. Level – practise according to your physical condition

Shorinji Kempo training should always be conducted with regard to your own current levels of physical condition – stamina, strength and flexibility. Of course, the very process of training helps us to improve those exact qualities (though it is often a good idea to supplement your Kempo training with some other complementary activities; for example, resistance training in the gym, yoga or swimming, among many other possibilities). But the point to bear in mind here is that, to maintain a healthy regular schedule of training, it is not helpful to push too far, thereby causing exhaustion or injury which will disrupt your normal rhythm and not contribute towards your long-term health goals. Some aspects of our individual conditions may be more permanent, such as a particular physical limitation or medical issue; others may be temporary, such as a passing infection or a minor injury. In all cases, we must first recognise clearly what our strong and weak points are, and then take care to respect them when exerting ourselves in practice – this is a key element of taking responsibility for our own well-being. Training should be above all fun and interesting – something we look forward to each time – and not some punishing regime of hardship and suffering. Moreover, it should be something anyone can engage in, no matter what their starting point of fitness, male or female, young or old.

---

65 Note that, if you believe that important areas are getting less attention than they deserve, you should feel free to communicate those opinions in a respectful and constructive way, as all good *sensei* appreciate feedback and recognise that they too are learning and can improve the way they teach.

8. Never Give Up – don't quit!

If you really want to improve yourself and master the art of Shorinji Kempo, then – to state the obvious – Never Give Up! Especially in the early stages, try to maintain a regular rhythm of training. By persevering, eventually even the deepest and least obvious lessons of this subtle and layered art will become available to you, not to mention to the immediate and ongoing benefits to your health, happiness and personal safety. Have faith in yourself and your own abilities. Techniques that frustrate you now will 'click' and become natural with time. Absolutely the most important distinguishing characteristic of the great masters and teachers of modern and past times is simply that they did not give up, and this lesson is vital for all to take to heart: you too can achieve greatness if you persevere.

It is also worth mentioning that life will sometimes throw obstacles in our path, frustrating our desire to keep training regularly through issues with family, job or health. These constraints should be respected but not yielded to entirely: if you can maintain even a reduced attendance, perhaps with wide gaps, then the thread of your training history will remain unbroken and while you may not be making any great progress, you will be ready to resume your journey again once conditions change to allow more frequent practice. And of course, many *kenshi* who have quit for any of a variety of reasons do eventually find their way back to the dojo. However, they are generally the exceptions, since such a return demands great willpower and courage after an extended absence; so if possible, it is far preferable to preserve even the slenderest of connections to your practice and your dojo.

Finally, this lesson of perseverance is perhaps one of the most important that Shorinji Kempo has to teach us, and it is relevant for all aspects of our lives, not just martial arts training. Combined with the various other mindful approaches to our practice and our personal development listed above, this indomitable attitude can be like armour against the vicissitudes of existence.

Lifelong learning

These 8 points are clearly applicable to your Shorinji Kempo training, but they also apply – sometimes with a little imagination – to any kind of activity that we undertake to develop ourselves further, be it at school or university, at work, or just for fun. The same process of establishing your base (asking yourself why you are learning this thing, and what you hope to get out of it; focusing on the fundamentals), approaching study in a systematic and disciplined way (following the correct sequence; understanding the underlying principles; practising regularly and repeatedly; keeping a balance by not ignoring your weak points), and sticking to the task by respecting your own condition at the same time as simply refusing to give up – all these habits will serve you well in any new endeavour and are far from limited in application to just Shorinji Kempo.

The Growth Mindset

The *growth* mindset refers to the idea that if people believe they can change certain aspects of themselves – a belief in growth – they will not only try hard when presented with challenges, but persist in that effort when they encounter difficulties or failure. This is because they see such occasions as learning experiences that will actually make them stronger and more capable in the future, so they do not shy away from them. The opposite of this attitude is called the *fixed* mindset, and those who are prey to it are led to avoid difficult challenges for fear of being exposed as inadequate when measured on the scale of some quantity (such as intelligence) that they believe is fixed and not subject to improvement.

Suffice it to say that if you can steer yourself towards a growth mindset, then your life will be set on a doggedly persistent trajectory of never-ending self-improvement, whereas if you languish in a fixed mindset, you are doomed to mediocrity and stagnation. And what is the best way for *kenshi* to cultivate this quality? Simply by coming to training and experiencing the change you can make in your capabilities through even a small effort. If you can improve a little, you can improve a lot.

Carol Dweck on Mindset

The modern formulation of this idea is attributed to Stanford University Professor of Psychology, Carol Dweck. Dweck has spent her career studying learning, motivation and, in essence, what habits make people happy and successful in their chosen fields[66]. She argues that the growth mindset will allow a person to live a less stressful and more successful life; this way of thinking about learning is also integral to the very fabric of Shorinji Kempo and its mission to help people fulfil their highest potential. In a 2012 interview, she said:

66 For example, see her TED talk: 'The power of believing you can improve'.

> *'In a fixed mindset, students believe their basic abilities, their intelligence, their talents, are just fixed traits. They have a certain amount and that's that, and then their goal becomes to look smart all the time and never look dumb. In a growth mindset, students understand that their talents and abilities can be developed through effort, good teaching and persistence. They don't necessarily think everyone's the same or anyone can be Einstein, but they believe everyone can get smarter if they work at it.'*

Individuals' theories of intelligence or other acquired skills and capabilities – that is to say, their mindset – can be affected by feedback and other environmental cues. For example, students given praise such as 'You're very talented' are much more likely to develop a fixed mindset, whereas compliments like 'Good job, you worked very hard', are more likely to promote a growth mindset.

Mindset and learning Shorinji Kempo

Professor Dweck's research focus has been mostly on school-age children, how they learn and how they can be steered towards a better mindset by their teachers and overall school experience. However, it should be obvious that good attitudes towards learning by *kenshi*, and good habits in teaching by instructors, can make a big difference to the speed and quality of the progress that students make in their study of Shorinji Kempo. Indeed, they can even make the difference between sticking with it and giving it up. An ability to persevere in the face of difficulties that derives from seeing learning as an exciting challenge, rather than some kind of verdict on your ultimate worth as a person, can bring all sorts of benefits; for example, lower stress, increased engagement and, most importantly, greater success at gaining whatever skill is being studied. This kind of attitude is clearly helpful for Kempo, but also for learning any subject or skill throughout life. Nowadays, more than ever, this is of crucial importance as changes in technology and society upend old industries and professions at an ever-accelerating rate. Our time for learning should not end when we leave formal education – something all adult *kenshi* implicitly acknowledge by coming to training in the first place – not just for our moral edification, but also for practical reasons of staying competitive in a changing world.

Anyone can achieve greatness

One difference in the case of *kenshi* as opposed to schoolchildren is that Shorinji Kempo is a voluntary activity, unlike the mandatory primary and secondary education that is the rule in almost all countries now – you have already taken a big step towards believing you can change by turning up to training in the first place. Nonetheless, it is still common for some beginners to be very unsure of their own capacities, often seeing themselves as impossibly far removed in ability and potential from their seniors or Sensei. But this is not the case! Every beginner who walks into a Shorinji Kempo class for the first time has the potential to become a Sensei – the only thing they need is the belief that it is possible and the energy and determination to make it happen – and every Sensei was once one of those unsure beginners.

Keep learning and growing, and never give up!

How, then, can we put these ideas into action in our daily lives? Simply by going to meet the challenges of regular training; of learning new and difficult skills; of becoming fitter, stronger and more agile; of expanding our minds and hearts to encompass a broader horizon than before, and of never giving up. Shorinji Kempo training gives us manifold opportunities to overcome small difficulties and, in so doing, realise that we have the capability to overcome much bigger ones. There are also less frequent occasions when much more significant challenges appear – a big competition or demonstration, your first foray into teaching, or, most seriously, an encounter with real violence outside the dojo. You may not be able to choose the timing of these, in order to be mentally ready or properly physically prepared; nonetheless, they must be faced with just the personal resources you have accumulated by that point in your life through your own efforts. Having a Growth Mindset is an essential component of getting ready to face such challenges.

The illusion of the unchanging self

Finally, from the perspective of Zen, the idea that one is in any way 'fixed' is a huge and dangerous illusion. For, according to one of its most important principles – that of impermanence (*shogyo mujo* 諸行無常) – all things are constantly in flux and influence each other, including people and their environment, and nothing stays the same, whether you realise and accept that or not. Therefore, given that we do have the power of free will – the power to influence some of those changes for good or ill – it is up to us to be responsible for shaping them in a positive way (see 'Fate and Free Will'). This principle means 'not only believing that you can change yourself, but knowing that it is impossible to remain the same.'

Ars Longa, Vita Brevis

Don't waste time

This famous phrase is from the ancient Greek physician Hippocrates[67], translated from Greek into Latin; in English, it reads as 'Mastering the Art takes a long time, but Life is short!'. This underlying sentiment is common in the sayings and writings of Kaiso; perhaps most obviously in the 'Guidelines for Effective Training', where no. 5 instructs us to practise continually, and no. 8 exhorts us to 'Never give up!' The point can simply be expressed by the idea that Shorinji Kempo is a deep and broad art, and that to master this art takes a lot of practice and a long time. 'Art' here is also used in the slightly old-fashioned sense of 'craft' or 'technique' (or, indeed, 'martial art') and refers to both the physical and mental aspects of the system. A good parallel would be with studying a Western classical performance art like piano playing, which takes years of dedicated practice – both at the keyboard and studying theory – to achieve a technique and mastery that can seem truly magical, although it is based on simple building blocks and a constantly reinforced foundation.

Vita brevis

To achieve such 'magic' (bear in mind that actual magicians or conjurors are also using physical skill and psychological mastery to 'prevail' over others) you need to put in the hours. One reason for this is that you never know how much time you actually have. This is not to point out your inevitable mortality – though this is always worth keeping in mind, to preserve some healthy perspective on what is important in life – but the more mundane notion that life often gets in the way of

67 As in the Hippocratic Oath. From the *Aphorisms*: 'Ὁ βίος βραχύς, ἡ δὲ τέχνη μακρή'

regular, focused practice. Exams, a change of job, moving away to a new area, or a longer-lasting injury can all prevent us from keeping the practice going, so it is especially important to *carpe(re) diem* ('seize the day') and make as much progress as you can, while you can. So life is both short overall, and short in terms of how much can be used for important constructive activities like Kempo.

Ars longa

And the Art is long! There are *'Santei, Sampo, Nijugokei'*: 3 Vessels, 3 Systems and 25 Groups (see 'The Structure of Shorinji Kempo'). This is a good thing, since you are unlikely to get bored when there is always something new to learn, or some specialised topic that will repay further and deeper study. While it is crucially important to preserve a balance in training and not ignore less favoured areas (Guideline no. 6), there is also scope (once the basics have been put on a sound foundation) to explore more thoroughly some of the more specialised areas of the art such as *hoki* (法器 defensive weapons), *seiho* (整法 healing techniques), or *tetsugaku* (哲学 philosophy study).

In the context of a regular student at a regular dojo, the important takeaway is that you should try to train regularly: twice a week is a minimum to avoid unnecessary regression between classes. If you are lucky enough to be within range of several dojos, you can train more often if you like; visiting other classes can also help to maintain regular practice if you are not able to attend one of your 'home' dojo's classes for any reason.

Pass it on

As a final note – and slightly at a tangent to the main idea here – Hippocrates' aphorism has also sometimes been interpreted to mean that 'Life is short, Art eternal', or that artists come and go, but their art lives on forever. For practitioners of Shorinji Kempo, our art is not some work in a museum, but a living tradition crafted by generations of masters and their students, refining it and evolving with the times, and passing on to the next generation the sum total of their knowledge and experience. Thus, it is up to all of us to work as diligently as possible to both preserve the tradition we have been given and strive to develop it further in our turn.

The Three Levels of Mastering an Art

技・術・略
Gi, Jutsu, Ryaku

There are three levels to mastering any art, and in Shorinji Kempo these are called *gi* (techniques), *jutsu* (craft) and *ryaku* (essence). But it is first important to understand what is meant by 'mastering': this is not just learning the art thoroughly or studying deeply, it is fundamentally connected to the ability to use the art in real life for its intended purpose. To illustrate the concept, we can make an analogy between the art of not losing a fight – Kempo – and the art of winning an argument or debate.

The basic movements of *kihon* can be compared to the words in a sentence: these, collectively, are *gi*. The art or craft of applying the right *waza* (techniques) at the right moment, like using judicious phrases and sentences, is *jutsu*; and the tactics and strategy needed to manage a full encounter – whether a real confrontation, a choreographed embu, or a heated debate – is *ryaku*. To continue the analogy, as you move from the level of words to that of sentences, and on to that of a more extensive dialogue, you change your perspective and different things become possible. Rather than pointing out just simple objects or concepts, you can start to formulate more complex ideas and, ultimately, you become able to create and express something as powerful as a poem, a philosophy or a scientific theory. At the same time, the levels below become part of the background, or, to put it another way, your foundation – the ground you walk on to reach new possibilities. So to master the art of winning an argument, just as with winning a fight, you need to have such a natural grasp of the underlying fundamentals (words, phrases and sentences, or body movement, techniques and application) that you are free to operate on the higher plane of strategy: how to approach the whole problem; perhaps even how to avoid the confrontation entirely. In a word, you have grasped the essence – *ryaku* – of the art.

Operating at a higher level

This analogy shows the power of the nested hierarchy of levels, and it is something we can see around us everywhere in the natural and cultural worlds we inhabit, from the organisation of an ant colony to language, and even to the way computers work[68]. One word to describe the almost magical results of such a process of building new levels of organisation is 'emergent': new things become possible, emerging as if by magic from nothing.

So how does this help with our practice of Shorinji Kempo? Kempo is a complex system – an art – that is built upon a basic physical, mental and spiritual foundation, whose exercise can then be used to great effect for the benefit (or, conceivably, for the harm) of society. By keeping in mind this sense of the levels at which we are operating – both in learning and making use of the art – we can come to truly master the art in the broadest sense.

Gi 技

Gi is the actual body of techniques and movements that we learn through *kihon* and *hokei* training. Strikes, blocks, footwork, throws and other body movements are all included. *Gi* represents the building blocks for more complex aggregations and sequences of movement required to respond to whatever an attacker might throw at us. It also refers to our named individual techniques, called *waza*, which is another reading of the same character (技).

Jutsu 術

Jutsu is the refined and correct application of the techniques that you have learned; it is impossible to operate at this level without first mastering *gi*. *Jutsu* is more normally translated as 'art' and is familiar from the name of the martial art *jujutsu* (literally, 'the soft art')[69]. Therefore, we can think of it as the skilful application of indi-

---

68 Some other examples: the emergence of chemistry and then biology from the comparatively simple behaviour of quarks, electrons and other subatomic particles; or the emergence of consciousness from the physical organisation of neurons in the brain. In both cases there are multiple intervening layers.

69 Note that the Japanese for 'fine arts' such as painting and sculpture is *bijutsu* (美術), lit. 'beauty craft', which references the skill of the craftsman as much as the inspiration of the *auteur*.

vidual techniques in the right place and at the right time in order to deal with the particular problems presented by one or more attackers.

Ryaku 略

Ryaku is hard to translate directly but means something like 'synthesis' – the ability to move beyond the details of the actions required in the moment to something with a broader perspective. Hence, we use the term 'essence', though the word is often translated as 'strategy'.

Needless to say, your individual technique will fail if the underlying building blocks are not firmly in place, such as the skill to move correctly to avoid an attack, and being properly positioned to deliver a strong counter-attack or a powerful throw. But even a well-executed technique is useless if there is another assailant behind you who will not wait for you to deal with their accomplice before attacking[70]. So more than just technical skill is required; namely, strategy. This includes the wisdom to not be in that dangerous situation in the first place, or the capacity to use entirely different methods of dealing with it, such as escape or negotiation. But nothing works if the basic actions are not reliable, as the higher levels of operation rely on each of the successively more fundamental levels beneath.

Learn from the base, apply from the top

When you learn Shorinji Kempo, of necessity you start with *gi*, proceed to *jutsu* and perhaps only rarely think of, or practise, *ryaku* – tactical and strategic thinking. But when called on to use the art, the order is reversed. Strategy comes first: in self-defence, our goal is to Not Lose, and beyond that, to Stop Violence. To achieve that, we may have several options, which will depend upon the circumstances, how early we become aware of the threat and how decisively we can bring ourselves to act. That strategic plan will then suggest certain tactics, which themselves require particular actions. With this degree of mastery it is possible, at the highest levels, to transcend the technique on which that mastery is built and to operate in a way which is almost removed from the action – looking down at it from above, like the conductor of an orchestra or a general directing armies from afar.

---

70 This staple of action films is called 'mook chivalry'. Do not be under any illusion that attackers in the real world will observe its rules of engagement.

The Three Stages of Learning a Skill

守・破・離
Shu, Ha, Ri

Shu, Ha, Ri describes the process of learning an art, craft or skill, from initial simple mimicry, to a level of proficiency where a student comes to 'own' the techniques, and beyond this, to the point where an innovator leaves the original style behind by creating something entirely new and original. Conventionally translated as 'follow, adapt, master', it describes the three characteristic stages of learning a complex skill or set of techniques, and applies not just to Shorinji Kempo and other martial arts, but also to learning to play a musical instrument, to painting or drawing, or simply to speaking and writing a language.

Beyond being a description of the normal way this process happens – which can be useful in itself to offer some perspective to students on where they may be in the long and arduous journey towards mastery – it can also help us to focus our attention on the right kind of practice and effort we should be making in relation to any particular skill or technique we are currently trying to attain or master. However, the conventional translation of 'follow, adapt, master' in fact conceals the true meaning and relevance of the phrase for *kenshi*, and we should instead hold on to the more literal and relevant version: 'protect! shatter! be free!', as explained below.

Shu 守 – Protect

Shu literally means 'protect' or 'guard'[71], but is usually rendered as 'copy' or 'follow' in English. This is an interesting change of perspective and level (see *Gi, Jutsu,*

71 The character / word also appears in ***Shu**shu Koju* and *kagite* ***shu**ho* for example, meaning 'defence'.

Ryaku) which goes beyond being a simple instruction to the beginner to just faithfully copy the *kaku* (格 – 'style' or 'status') of the master, since it is an injunction to literally 'keep it safe'. This implies that it is a gift of great value, and the way to protect it is to study the teacher's form by paying minute attention to all the details, memorising them and embodying them in your own actions[72].

There is a strong connection between the idea of *shu* and that of *kihon* ('basics'). Even though *shu, ha, ri* describes three consecutive stages of learning, it is also important to remember that the *shu* stage is never really finished (nor, indeed, are the other two, but it is often easier to see that the later stages of *ha* and *ri* are works in progress). It is vital to constantly revisit the initial training method of faithful mimicry – this simply means to keep on working hard on *kihon* – as doing so will continue to reveal areas for improvement and new insights into the deeper levels and meaning of each technique. This is also why it is so important to keep intact the *kaku* of the master (or really of the style itself), since it is an invaluable resource that will yield ongoing benefits for those who dedicate themselves to its study. Moreover, we have a responsibility to preserve it not just for our own development, but for that of the students who will come after us.

Ha 破 – Shatter

Ha is normally translated as 'adapt' or 'adjust', but in fact the word refers to something much more violent and traumatic, like 'rip', 'shatter' or 'violate'[73]. Again, the normal translation hides some of the true meaning of the original expression; namely, that this second stage of learning is, in fact, a great struggle which cannot be achieved without breaking something. If *shu* was a place of safety – both for the student (since they did not have to worry or think, but merely slavishly copy the form they were shown) and for the *kaku* itself (since it was protected by this blind devotion) – then *ha* is a place of struggle and danger. This is the stage when, in the conventional account, the student has sufficiently mastered the basic form to be able to adapt it to their own situation – size, strength, personality – and thus begins to make the techniques more effective by being more efficient and more tailored to the individual practitioner.

---

72 The traditional term for a beginner or apprentice in Japanese is *minarai* (見習), literally 'see-learner'.

73 The *kun yomi* ('native reading') of *ha* is *yaburi*, which is used, among other things, to denote the now frowned-upon practice of 'breaking' a rival dojo: visiting it to challenge the sensei to a public contest, with the loser's students being claimed by the victor (*dojo yaburi*).

But a much more common experience is the discovery that the basic version of a technique which has been learnt does not, in fact, work very well (or even at all) under more realistic conditions, when confronted with less co-operative or more serious opposition[74]. It is this painful situation that requires *ha:* breaking from the thoughtless copying of *shu,* and making a real effort to work out what is not working and what needs to be changed. Only by going through this difficult process (for every technique) can a *kenshi* come to 'own' the techniques – to truly be able to call them their own.

Thus, *ha* is nothing less than another version of the relentless (but always constructive) self-criticism that is required for *jiko kakuritsu* – the establishment of the individual. Like that more general idea, it requires creativity and experimentation, reflection and brutal realism. There is no room for complacency or self-delusion, since to be wrong about the fundamental skills of Shorinji Kempo could result not merely in embarrassment or dishonour, but in serious harm at the hands of a true aggressor. As already noted, this is not a comfortable state, and mid-level *kenshi* often develop profound (but unwarranted and unhelpful) doubts about their own abilities and achievements due, paradoxically, to their constantly expanding awareness and understanding. Because most students will spend the longest part of their training careers in this state, relatively speaking, an appreciation of the lessons of *shu, ha, ri* is vitally important to give perspective and to reassure those on the lifelong path towards mastery that they are, indeed, on the right track and should not give up.

Ri 離 – Be Free

Ri means 'separation' – not so much in space as leaving a relationship. Indeed, the Japanese word for 'divorce' is *rikon* (離婚). Therefore, as much as it indicates a new freedom from attachment, it also has connotations of sadness and even loneliness. Again, the conventional translation of '[to] master' obscures the depth of the underlying idea, which is that eventually, once the struggle of the *ha* stage has been endured, a new stage can emerge that is almost like a re-birth – the creation of a new style – but also the leaving behind of the 'parent' teaching and the solitary path of a

74 This often happens when new *kenshi* try to demonstrate some technique on a non-martial-arts-trained friend or acquaintance – the technique fails because the opponent does not know what they are 'supposed' to do.

new master[75]. We often think of true *ri* as a vanishingly rare achievement, which may be correct in the strictest sense. However, it would be more accurate to say that many people attempt to 'separate', but few manage to do it convincingly; that is, to create a distinctively new style that is instantly recognisable and widely acknowledged to be a significant addition to the cultural or technical stock of humanity.

In less expansive terms, *ri* can also refer to the 'small enlightenment' of creating a new technique or a new way of doing a particular technique, or the intermediate phase of achieving distinctive mastery in a whole area of Shorinji Kempo[76], without having to depart fully from the system created by Doshin So (who himself achieved the full version of *ri* in transcending the many different arts he studied before creating it). The important feature of *ri* in this sense is the freedom from constraint earned through the long and arduous process of apprenticeship and strict adherence to the art: there is no longer the need to be bound by someone else's *kaku,* as the new master has created their own *kaku* – a new expression of the same fundamental underlying principles and purpose that informed the original one.

Superficial difference vs. deep similarity

One of the practical consequences of the fact that every practitioner of Shorinji Kempo – from the freshest beginner to the most wizened master – is positioned at some point along the journey from *shu,* via *ha,* to *ri*, is that *kenshi* will often be exposed to different ways (sometimes glaringly so) of doing the same technique when studying under an unfamiliar instructor; for example, at an international study session (*gasshuku*). This arises naturally from the efforts of those teachers to customize and better understand the things they have learned for themselves – the process of making them their own – and can result in outwardly divergent-looking methods that can be confusing, especially for less experienced students who are still seeking the reassuring certainty of *shu* themselves. This is why a skilful teacher should tailor the style of teaching to the level of the student, and ensure that, before trying to impart a more sophisticated understanding, the basic level of *kaku* that is shared by

---

75 This separation is reminiscent of the story of Siddhartha Gautama – the future Buddha – leaving his young wife and child behind as he set out on the ascetic quest that would eventually lead to his enlightenment. The loneliness of this new life was eventually compensated for by the creation of the *sangha* – the community of his followers.

76 Famous examples of great masters who have reached this level are Bando Kunio Sensei in *appo;* Mori Doki Sensei in *juho;* and Ueda Kiyoshi Sensei in *shakujo*.

everyone is solidly in place. They must also understand where and how their own *ha* (or even *ri*) versions of techniques differ from what *kenshi* may have been practising, and be able to clearly explain such differences and their purpose.

Exposure to these different perspectives can be one of the most powerful tools for *kenshi* to help kick-start the process of questioning and testing what is required to enable them to 'own' the techniques. Any discomfort they may feel at being given advice which is sometimes diametrically opposed to what they have previously heard is another manifestation of the struggle involved in the process of *ha*. One helpful way to think about such experiences is that what we are really trying to grasp in learning is the underlying essence of each technique, not merely the superficial manifestation of that essence as instantiated by one teacher or another, even though that is where we must start in our efforts to grasp this hidden reality. We can imagine this essence as a sculpture in a darkened room; each sensei's teaching will cast light on this object from a particular angle, but it may take several such beams of illumination to begin to fully grasp the whole nature of it, even though from different angles the same object may appear outwardly very different[77].

77 One other way to learn its nature would be by feel alone; this is reminiscent of the teaching style of Kaiso who, according to the accounts of his earliest students, would refuse almost all verbal explanation of even complex techniques and simply perform them on his suffering disciples until they either grasped the method or pretended to in order to save themselves further pain.

Ichigo Ichie

一期一会
Seize the moment

Ichigo Ichie (一期一会) is a Japanese phrase that describes a Zen concept linked with the famed Tea Ceremony (*chado* 茶道) master Sen no Rikyu. It is often brushed onto scrolls which are hung in the tea room. The term can be translated as 'for this time only', 'never again', or 'one chance in a lifetime'. For *kenshi,* it means that, being conscious that each moment is unique and will never be repeated, we should do our best to make the most of any opportunities that present themselves and not be hesitant or lazy, mistakenly thinking that we will have the exact same chance some other time. It is related to (though not the same as) the notion of being 'present in the moment', which shares the idea of being fully committed to doing your best in whatever activity you are engaged in, whether it is work, study, or even rest and play. In a different context, when confronted by danger and risk, we may well not have the luxury of hesitating or opting out – doing so could have negative or even disastrous consequences. However, a mind and spirit trained to act decisively – to take whatever opportunities present themselves immediately and without dithering – can be our greatest asset.

Figure 20 Portrait of Sen no Rikyu by Tōhaku Hasegawa (16th C)

Make your own luck

Of course, while it is a shame to miss opportunities through lack of awareness, courage or energy, we should not dwell on such failures, but rather try to be alert to the next ones that come along. Life presents such chances to us all the time, and learning to spot them and being ready to seize them is a great life skill that underlies the supposed 'luck' and 'good fortune' of many successful people. Indeed, blaming 'fate' and 'bad luck' for a lack of success in life is a sure sign of someone who does not have the imagination or energy to seize the many chances we are presented with during our lives. That is not to say that it is easy to do so, and often we are prisoners of our own narrow-minded perspectives, excessive risk-aversion and even outright fear of the new, of failure, or of looking stupid (see 'The Growth Mindset'). This is where the whole body of mental, spiritual and physical training that is Shorinji Kempo can show its true worth in our lives, by enabling us to see the world more clearly (that is, to get closer to *satori*) and giving us the energy and courage to put that insight to constructive use.

There is some logical tension between these two interpretations of *ichigo ichie*: that each opportunity is unique and should not be squandered, and that life (or *dharma*) is constantly offering us chances that we may not even notice. The point is not that we must seize every single opportunity, nor that we should be complacent in letting them forever slip by in the expectation that more are on the way. As ever, the approach of the Middle Way is the best – in this case, that means being open and alert to the chances that life brings without needing to grasp at everything that comes your way.

Part 4

Technical Features of Shorinji Kempo

This section of the book details the technical features of the system of Shorinji Kempo training, describing its various components as well as several key concepts that can contribute towards mastery of the techniques and their application.

The Six Types of Training

修行の六種
Shugyo no Rokushu

Shorinji Kempo practice is divided into six broad categories of study, and it is important that sufficient emphasis is given to each area in order to ensure both consistent progress across the categories and the balanced all-round development of an individual. These categories are as follows:

Kihon – basic movements
Hokei – practising specific techniques with a partner
Randori – free sparring
Embu – developing and perfecting a set demonstration
Seiho – healing methods
Tetsugaku – philosophy study

Kihon

As discussed earlier (in 'Guidelines for Effective Training'), *kihon* training is where we focus on the basics. It includes all types of *kobo yoki* (攻防用器 strikes and blocks), *kamae* (構え stances), *ashi* and *tai sabaki* (足と体さばき foot and body movements), as well as *ukemi* (受身 rolls and breakfalls). *Kihon* practice forms a part of every training session, and all participate equally, as the work of solidifying and improving these basic movements is never finally complete. Also, as noted in '*Shu, Ha, Ri*', the constant revisiting of the underlying elements of all movements can offer up insights even to the most experienced practitioner, consisting of hints or suggestions as to how to improve the efficacy, practicality or realism of more sophisticated techniques.

Hokei

Hokei (法形) is a term unique to Shorinji Kempo that designates the corpus of *wazu* – set techniques practised in pairs, and the relatively few set forms practised solo. It can be translated literally as 'the patterns of the system'. Therefore, it refers to the whole body of teaching about fighting methods included in the system (法 *ho*) of Shorinji Kempo. Other martial arts have different ways of encoding this knowledge for transmission to new generations of students, and one of the best known is the use of *kata*, as seen particularly in most types of Karate and traditional forms of Chinese *kung fu*.

Kata 型

The *kei* (形) of *hokei* is similar in both symbol and meaning to *kata* (型), since both mean 'shape' or 'pattern'. However, the two ideas are subtly different in an important way. *Kata* originally referred to a mould into which liquid metal such as bronze was poured to make a cast. This gives us the interpretation of *kata* as having a fixed, unchanging form – a template that produces the same results every time a faithful copy is made. *Kei* (which can, confusingly, also be read as '*kata*'), on the other hand, denotes something less rigid which is built up in a continuous process and can still be changed. Shorinji Kempo *hokei* are patterns that have been refined over many generations of masters in order to teach us, as martial artists, the fundamental elements of the system. Starting with simple, single-movement attacks and counters, and developing into more complex attacking methods with more elaborate and sophisticated responses, *hokei* builds within *kenshi* the essential principles required to master the fluid and dynamic self-defence techniques. Developing an understanding of these principles and how they are adaptable to every different situation is one purpose of *hokei* training.

Kumite Shutai 組手主体

This distinction illustrates a key feature of Shorinji Kempo training: *Kumite Shutai*, or the emphasis on training with a partner (and not predominantly on single-form training). *Hokei* are patterns that are necessarily flexible because they involve (at least) two people who will always be different, both in terms of the practitioners themselves and the circumstances in which they meet. There are countless variables in such practice; thus, a fixed set form cannot – indeed, should not – be used to capture the teaching of how to respond to a certain situation. *Kata* makes sense as a teaching method for elements where variation is not normally an issue, such as the basic movements of *kihon*, but it makes less sense as a useful means of preparing students for actual encounters with real opponents. This is why, in practice, there is such a focus on free sparring in most styles of Karate, which they call *kumite*, not coincidentally. What Kaiso did in designing Shorinji Kempo and its reliance on *hokei* training is to explicitly acknowledge that *kumite* – pair-form training – is indeed *shutai*, the main subject[78].

One important point to note here is that, while *hokei* practice typically involves set drills, where both attacker and defender execute known patterns that have been set in advance, this is not fundamental to the concept it represents; indeed, one of the main purposes of *randori* – free sparring – is embedding the lessons learned in fixed *hokei* practice by handling surprise and randomness whilst still trying to perform the appropriate *hokei waza* for any given situation. Indeed, ultimately, true understanding of *hokei* can only be obtained in this way by learning how to apply the principles instinctively and under realistic conditions of surprise, fear and stress.

Hokei embodies the teachings of all past masters

Hokei (and *kata*, for that matter) allows us to transmit knowledge which has been gained within the lifespan of one individual to the next generation, so it is not lost with the inevitable passing of that individual; indeed, such transmission is the very basis of all human culture. These dynamic[79] patterns capture the experience of

78 Observant *kenshi* will note that Shorinji Kempo does in fact have several single-form set *kata*, properly called *tan'en kihon hokei*. Their relatively small number, and unambiguous correspondence to the pair-form *hokei* techniques, reinforces the point made above that simple universal actions can efficiently be taught in this way, but, again, the majority of learning is to be done with a partner.

79 In the sense of flexible, un-rigid.

generations of master practitioners and refinements gained over many times more iterations of practice than would be possible in the lifetime of even the most dedicated single person. Kaiso was very clear in stating that he had not simply invented Shorinji Kempo from scratch, but rather had systematised his knowledge of Japanese and Chinese martial arts, as well as incorporating what he saw as the most relevant lessons from Western systems like boxing. *Hokei* can therefore be seen as an aspect of the *Dharma*, ('the Law of the Universe') in that it represents a kind of solidified learning that persists and evolves over time. As individual practitioners come and go, they contribute to the intangible, ever-changing, but still robust pattern of knowledge which resembles in some way the ephemeral but eternal progress of life handed down from one generation to the next.

Hokei as Gyo

Ultimately, the most valuable lesson of this kind of training is how it can teach us to co-exist with other people, based on the twin principles of *jiko kakuritsu* – self-establishment – and *jita kyoraku* – living together in harmony with others. The training is the primary means by which we accomplish the building of our bodies and souls, our physical and social skills, our courage and compassion. This, then, is the true significance of *hokei*.

Randori

Randori (乱捕 free-sparring practice) is an integral part of Shorinji Kempo. It is important to understand the role *randori* plays in the overall programme of *budo* practice – what it is and what it is not. It is also worth stating that, as an activity, it can be conducted in a great variety of different ways, with varying methods and goals; therefore, while some fundamental principles (such as safety) apply to all types, it is also good not to have too fixed or rigid an idea about the purpose or conduct of *randori*.

What it is; what it is for

Randori is a very effective tool for improving *hokei*; the set techniques that make up the body of the syllabus. The importance and significance of *hokei* is discussed above, but, in a nutshell, they form the core training in self-defence techniques against a variety of realistic and committed attacks. *Randori* can help to improve *hokei* by introducing the element of randomness[80] and surprise, which forces the student to adapt to a fluid and unpredictable situation with natural and instinctive responses if they want to survive and prevail. Therefore, when practising *randori*, it is very important to keep this purpose uppermost in mind: you are not primarily trying to win a bout, or even just block or avoid an opponent's attacks endlessly; rather, you must use the opportunity given by your partner's unpredictable moves to try to apply the right *hokei* technique at the right time. Success in this effort will naturally lead to the scoring of points or the winning of bouts; but that is not the main purpose of the activity, and failure to protect yourself or to execute

80 Helpfully, the *ran* (乱) of *randori* means 'chaos' or 'disorder', as in the title of the epic film by Kurosawa.

any valid counter-moves can be a valuable lesson, provided you are alert to the reasons for that failure.

Beyond this primary goal, *randori* is by its nature inherently competitive, and this can be a very positive means for *kenshi* to push themselves to achieve more, thereby accelerating their own personal and physical development (*jiko kakuritsu*). However, to gain this benefit, *kenshi* must have a fundamentally constructive (and therefore cooperative) attitude towards sparring: you must try not to lose; you must also try to win; but you must also recognise that your failures can be a powerful source of learning for you, just as your successes can be equivalently useful for your partners. This attitude – of trying to win in order to improve both yourself and your partner – is at the heart of the respect for yourself and others that enables *jita kyoraku*. Furthermore, the struggle to prevail not just against an opponent but against your own fear, confusion or fatigue is an excellent way to promote *heijoshin*. This is the state of mind that is represented by the *kongo* (金剛) of *Kongo Zen* – pure, calm and utterly indomitable (see 'Mental & Spiritual Power'). Such a state will also allow the more experienced practitioner the space to exercise their creativity as well as their muscles, and to design and implement tactics based on the fluid situation they are presented with; thus, *randori* can be intellectually rewarding as well as physically challenging.

Lastly, *randori* is an unparalleled method of improving your physical fitness, as it calls on all the main elements of stamina, suppleness and strength, and is inherently 'high-intensity interval training', or HIIT – a modality that is now widely recognised by sports scientists as producing the most efficient gains in cardiac capacity, VO2 Max and metabolic benefits[81].

Safety and its consequences

Safety is fundamental to the conduct of *randori*, as it is for all our activities in Shorinji Kempo, and this has certain significant consequences for how we practise it. First, it means that you must exercise great control over your actions – control that is proportional to the risks and mitigating factors involved. Such factors will vary according to experience, the relative size, strength and speed of the participants, the type of *randori* being practised, and the use and nature of protective equipment. Secondly, you must abide by any restrictions explicitly imposed by the Sensei, and those

81 See e.g. Laursen PB, Jenkins DG (2002). *The Scientific Basis for High-Intensity Interval Training*. Sports Medicine (Review). 32 (1): 53–73.

you may choose to agree with your partner, to foreclose any unusual or dangerous actions you are not ready to deal with. The most obvious, and generally unspoken, example of this is the restriction on grabbing and throwing (i.e. *juho*) in *goho randori*; however, it could equally apply to other attacks – kicks to the knee area, strikes to the back of the head, or hair pulling, for example. However, it is vitally important to realise that such attacks are not restricted because they could never happen in real life, or that it is somehow not necessary to consider them and practise responses to them; rather, this is because free-form sparring practice is generally not a suitable method for addressing such issues, whereas more carefully supervised practice, between more experienced *kenshi*, with appropriate protective equipment (for both attacker and defender) may be required to safely pursue such relatively advanced and difficult subjects.

In summary, safety considerations mean that we must pay close attention to instructions and respect both our own condition and that of our partner; we must conduct our practice in a constructive and civilized manner (*kumite shutai*), recognising that we are striving to improve ourselves whilst helping our partner improve at the same time (*fusatsu katsujin*); while not completely discounting the use of unorthodox or potentially dangerous attacks, we must exercise strict control over our speed, power and targeting.

What it is not; what it is not for

Randori is not self-defence; it is very different from real-world violence in almost every important respect, and *kenshi* should be absolutely clear about this when practising. To be more specific, while your opponent's exact choice of attack is not predetermined, the general context is well defined and both participants know what to expect: a single well-matched adversary (in terms of size or experience), with a (normally) limited menu of options; a set of explicit or mutually understood rules; a safe and clear environment; a clear understanding that a bout is about to begin or has ended; and, most importantly, the lack of real intent to do harm, or to get something from the other person by violence. In a real self-defence situation, none of these conditions is likely (or can be assumed) to obtain, and this difference is much more important than the superficial similarity of a contest of strikes or grappling. Having said all that, *randori* is an important component of Shorinji Kempo training and, as such, can be a significant aid in our preparation for real-world confrontations, but not necessarily in the way many martial artists might assume.

One final point: do not apologise reflexively if you manage to strike your opponent successfully – you should not feel bad for doing what you have been asked to do. You must, of course, exercise restraint and control, and if there is ever an occasion when you did not, an apology is certainly warranted; but it is counter-productive to reinforce an apologetic and diffident mindset by repetitively and unthinkingly saying sorry every time you actually succeed in what you are trying to do. When suitably effective contact has been made – as judged either by the *shimpan* or by mutual agreement in non-competition *randori* – partners must do *gassho rei* to each other, not to apologise, but to acknowledge the success of the 'winner', and to show gratitude for the learning opportunity provided to both partners by the successful move.

Types of Randori practice

Randori should be a part of your regular dojo training, in which case it is normally not competitive in the sense of a sport with rules, referees and scoring, leading to a winner and a loser. When done in this less formal way, *randori* is, as stated above, totally focused on promoting these key goals of Shorinji Kempo as discussed above: proficiency in *hokei* self-defence techniques, *heijoshin* (a calm and unflappable mind), the ability to work and enjoy training with others (*jita kyoraku*), and overall fitness training for strength, flexibility and stamina (*ekkin-gyo*).

To introduce variety and to focus differently on some of these aspects more intensively, your Sensei may specify some variations or limitations on the sparring, and this is known as *gentei randori* (限定乱捕)[82]. Such variations could include, for example, specifying one person as the attacker and one as the defender only for each period; restricting *kenshi* to the use of two or three particular attacks or *hokei* defences; the use of a training weapon, such as a foam *tanto* or *nyoi*; the addition of another attacker (two vs. one); and so on.

Competitions

Randori should always be free-flowing and have that essential element of competitiveness that is one of its defining features. However, to fully focus on the element of competition, dojos and federations will also stage less frequent formal competitions where most of the features of modern martial sports are present[83]. These include

82 This is also how *randori* in the first few grading examinations is carried out, with explicit limitations.

83 As seen in Judo, Taekwondo, Karate, and even 'no rules' MMA competitions.

Figure 21 Randori competition (BSKF c1979)

the use of protective equipment (gloves, body and groin protection, head-guards); the presence of a *shimpan* (審判 'umpire') and corner judges, to ensure safety and award points; time limits; a clear matted area; explicit restrictions on certain attack types, targets and excessive or uncontrolled force; and classification by gender and grading rank. The purpose of these additions (relative to normal unstructured practice) is to do the utmost to promote safety for participants, and to enable a fair competition between contestants, so that a winner will emerge who has the best technique, fitness, determination and luck. Note that, in an important way, self-defence training is the exact opposite of this: it is designed to deal with profoundly unfair situations where weaker, vulnerable victims are targeted by experienced (in the successful use of violence, that is) and merciless perpetrators; it then seeks to turn the tables on those aggressors by utilising (within ethical and legal boundaries) as many unfair tricks as possible, such as attacks to weak points and psychological and physiological manipulation. Indeed, it is often the most useful tools for self-defence (such as *kinteki geri* or *meuchi*) that are banned or unavailable in competition *randori*.

Such events can be important learning experiences for all involved; they are an excellent way to promote confidence (though overconfidence must be guarded against) and fitness; they also give a safe outlet for the competitive energy of *kenshi* eager to test themselves against their peers, with the possibility of bringing glory to themselves and their dojos. It is necessary, as in all things, to have a balanced attitude towards competition *randori* – neither disparaging it nor over-emphasizing it, as it has both unique benefits and clear risks.

Other considerations

Protective equipment – *Randori* can and should be practised most often without protective equipment, as its use can subtly but significantly alter the conduct of free sparring, and it is vitally important not to allow such alterations to become embedded as habits or expectations. Gloves that protect the hands from damage can encourage over-reliance on the use of the basic *seiken* (正拳, closed fist) – which could result in a broken hand if applied to the wrong target – and make both *meuchi* and *juho* applications unavailable. Gloves can also encourage a lack of control in striking to the head, which can result in excessive force and potential (micro) concussions that can be dangerous and must be avoided. Body protectors (*do*, 胴), groin guards and head guards also insulate you from the consequences of your errors while offering non-natural targets for attack or counters, as the subtle geography of the torso and its weak points are masked by the plain hard skin of a *do*. However, having said all that, protectors can be both useful and necessary: they allow greater freedom and speed of movement, and are, of course, mandatory in formal competitions. Whatever the situation, be aware of both their benefits and drawbacks and avoid over-reliance on their use.

Juho randori – We typically practise *juho* and *goho hokei waza* separately, and for good reason, since the two different styles of attack – discontinuous contact with strikes, as opposed to prolonged contact and manipulation with grabs – require different approaches and solutions. Similarly, *juho randori* should be practised in a different way from *goho randori*, and it is not generally suitable for a competitive style of contest. This is due to both safety concerns and the fact that the key lessons discussed above are much less well suited to being learned for *juho hokei* in this way. However, a more cooperative style of practice is both possible and valuable and can encourage freedom of movement and thinking; awareness of vulnerabilities and artificial expectations when performing more complex techniques; and learning to recognise and seize the 'gifts' that are presented by a less structured, even chaotic encounter. The beginning of this is to focus on *nuki waza* (抜き技 'release techniques'), and to limit the amount of follow-on *goho* applied. From there, the menu of available actions can be broadened to include throws and takedowns, but only when the opportunity presents itself; in other words, when the attacker has committed to an attack in such a way as to create a vulnerability – a gift – for the defender to exploit.

Go Ju randori – More advanced still is the practice of mixed *goho* and *juho* attacks and defences. Recognising that *Go Ju Ittai* teaches us that there is no clear dividing line between the two systems – that we must think of them as one body of techniques and, thus, practise them together – this type of *randori* is the most difficult

Figure 22 Randori competition (BSKF 2017)

Figure 23 Shakujo (BSKF 2017)

Figure 24 Shakujo and nyoi (BSKF 2014)

Figure 25 Public embu demonstration in London (BSKF 2013)

and rewarding to attempt. However, it is vital that it be conducted in a non-competitive manner and with as few restrictions as possible, the only exception being the requirement for great care and low speed and power. One way to begin exploring this area is to introduce *Go Ju* elements into regular *goho randori*, allowing certain simple techniques to be performed, such as *tembin nage* from *gyaku zuki*, or *sukui kubi nage* from a *mawashi geri* attack.

Weapons – Shorinji Kempo has only limited training in simple defensive and offensive weapons such as the tanto (単刀, short knife), the nyoi (如意, baton) and the shakujo (錫杖, monk's quarter staff). Their use in *randori* obviously introduces a risk of accident and injury that is an order of magnitude greater than regular empty-hand sparring; it should therefore be undertaken only by highly experienced *kenshi,* or under the strict supervision of senior Sensei. However, foam or rubber versions of these weapons are easily available and can offer a useful and relatively safe way to experiment with the techniques and set forms in a free-form environment.

Embu

Embu (演武) is arguably the highest expression of the physical practice of Shorinji Kempo and, as a core form of training, is unique among mainstream martial arts. In *embu*, two (or three[84]) *kenshi* work together to build a set demonstration of the full range of *hokei* techniques they have learned, combining them together in a dynamic and free-flowing sequence that balances *goho* and *juho,* as well as taking turns to initiate or defend attacks. Because of the intense dedication and cooperation that is required to construct and perfect a successful *embu*, the experience of undergoing this often arduous method of training can be transformative for *kenshi* as they progress beyond the initial stages of being a *minarai* (見習 'beginner') towards becoming truly proficient. This applies not just on the physical level of technical excellence, but also on a philosophical and spiritual level.

As regards technical development, *embu* is the only safe context in which to practise many of the more advanced techniques of Shorinji Kempo at full speed and power, as these cannot be safely used in *randori*. The intense, repetitive nature of the practice process is tremendously beneficial in reinforcing and making instinctive the particular techniques used in the embu; indeed, this is a good reason to change them over time, by gradually substituting new techniques for existing ones over the months and years that an embu can take to develop and mature.

Embu as Gyo

When considering spiritual development, we return to the idea of *gyo* as detailed previously (in '*Gyo* – The Discipline of Shorinji Kempo'). The practice and performance of *embu* is particularly well suited to its use as a type of *gyo* (行), or spiritual discipline. The high level of skill and concentration required to pull off an

84 Or a larger group, known as *dantai embu* 団体演武.

impressive (to non-experts) and successful (to trained judges) demonstration is obvious to those who witness it, and such occasions can function as a kind of secular offering to the ideals of Shorinji Kempo and *Kongo Zen*. Indeed, that is why formal occasions within Shorinji Kempo, such as major *taikai* or annual closing ceremonies, often include a dedicatory *ho no embu* ('demonstration of the way'). But, given that the majority of time spent performing any *embu* will be in practice with your partner – a typical *embu* should last no longer than two minutes, while training may span dozens of hours in total, over a period of months or longer – the real work of *gyo* is being achieved in that rigorous and often frustrating process, as limitations are encountered and surpassed, fitness and stamina are built, and speed, strength and *ki* are developed in preparation for the brief chance to exhibit them in one short performance.

Embu as Competition

Embu can take many forms, limited only by the context of the performance and the creativity of the participants. For example, when *kenshi* come together for *taikai* (大会) – periodic gatherings that give an opportunity for students to compete with one another, or simply demonstrate the fruits of their dedicated practice – an *embu* competition is often the highlight. While *randori* competitions are also popular and exciting (to participate in or watch), *embu* provide a unique opportunity to showcase the strength and beauty of the full range of Shorinji Kempo techniques, displayed as they should be, in a flowing and dynamic presentation, at full speed and power. However, in order to enable scoring and fair comparisons, there must be standardization and rules; for this reason, competition *embu* must last a certain length of time (from 90 to 120 seconds), not involve partners of (very) different grades, and conform to several other regulations. Within these constraints, creativity can flourish; however, there is a limit – judges will penalise pairs who construct an *embu* that is overly flashy but devoid of true practical substance. Merely showy or impractical sequences should therefore be avoided.

Embu as Demonstration

With that said, there is a role for showing off the art, and impressing audiences with the same feats of skill and agility that may have attracted many to begin practising Shorinji Kempo in the first place. In the case of non-competitive demonstrations, greater latitude is possible, including variation in the number, grade and role of participants, use of weapons, or other departures from the 'competition standard'.

Ultimately, whatever type of embu is being performed, it should reflect the best of what Shorinji Kempo training has to offer: a concentrated practice which boosts both *jiko kakuritsu* and *jita kyoraku* to produce results that those involved would often have doubted themselves capable of achieving.

Seiho

Seiho (整法) is the healing practice of Shorinji Kempo, and formally includes four groups or branches (of the 25 listed in 'The Structure of Shorinji Kempo'); namely, *seikei* (整経) and *seimyaku* (整脉), which treat central and peripheral meridians respectively; *seikotsu* (整骨), which corrects bone alignment; and *kappo* – resuscitation (活法 literally 'life system'). However, as practised within the wider Shorinji Kempo community, *seiho* often also includes various additional methods for treating common training injuries, relieving pain or tension, or providing longer-term beneficial interventions. Such additional elements include the use of Western physiotherapy methods like fascial release treatment; techniques borrowed from Swedish or Thai massage; and deep or assisted stretching exercises.

In any case, *seiho* is designed to be a holistic therapeutic system, where a 'giver' works on, and with, the body of a partner in order to restore balance, by calming areas of inflammation or stress (*jitsu*) and strengthening the corresponding areas of weakness or flaccidity (*kyo*). It is performed without equipment, normally on the floor (or a mat, or sometimes seated in a chair), and fully clothed; so while there can be a deep contact between the giver and receiver, it is based more on an energetic connection via *ki* than a direct sense of physical (skin-to-skin) touch. The giver must become acutely sensitive to the condition of the patient, and have a confident, fluent technique that causes a natural trust and acceptance to open up in the receiver, so as to be 'allowed in', almost like a visitor to a private house.

Seiho is also, perhaps, the type of training that is most difficult to practise on a regular and consistent basis: it is time-consuming, and the dojo is sometimes not the most appealing environment in which to give or receive it. However, for these same reasons, it is well suited for practice at home, and *kenshi* should take every opportunity to build on the skills they learn (perhaps with only occasional instruction) by offering their services to friends and family, practising those skills repeatedly until they become confident and assured, even if their set of techniques is limited.

History

Seiho has much in common with *shiatsu* (指圧) – the modern Japanese system that grew out of traditional acupressure methods derived from Chinese medicine (*tuī ná* 推拿), via the less overtly medical system of *anma* (按摩). Indeed, many *kenshi* who develop an interest in *seiho* also study *shiatsu* independently, as it can provide a coherent structure and approach, and sometimes even set *kata* that can aid in developing a fluent technique. But its origins lie in the more distant past, with the bundle of Vedic health-promoting practices that may have been (but probably were not[85]) brought by Bodhidharma from India to China in the 5th century CE. Such practices included use of herbal remedies, calisthenic exercises (*ekkin-gyo* 易筋行) and manipulative therapies.

Figure 26 Shiatsu

Seikei 整経 and Seimyaku 整脈

Generally, the first type of *seiho* that *kenshi* will study is the basic use of fingers (normally thumbs) to apply pressure to the easily identifiable meridians of the back. This procedure can relieve tension, help to improve circulation, and speed the removal of metabolites like lactic acid. More importantly, it can act to regulate or balance the flow of *ki* through

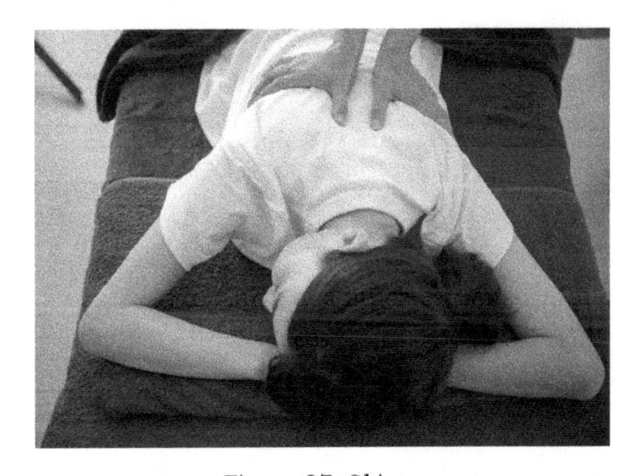

Figure 27 Shiatsu

85 It is more likely that these cultural imports had spread to China at a much earlier stage and had contributed to, and fused with, indigenous (often Taoist) practices.

the main channels of the body. While *seikei* focuses on the channels (meridians) in the centre of the body, *seimyaku* targets those on the periphery; in practice, the two categories are often merged together in a single set of treatments that cover the whole body or large areas.

Seikotsu 整骨

Seikotsu, or bone realignment, includes stretches and 'cracking' manoeuvres[86] which realign skeletal components to improve functional efficiency and reduce the build-up of stress caused by unbalanced or misaligned usage patterns. It also comprises the methods used to relocate dislocated joints (typically shoulders, elbows, fingers or, occasionally, knees), which, while not common occurrences, are not unknown as a result of vigorous martial arts practice. Traditionally, *seikotsu* has also included methods for manually resetting fractured or broken bones, but such methods are very rarely practised nowadays.

Kappo 活法

Resuscitation – bringing an unconscious person back to consciousness quickly and safely – is an important, indeed vital, tool for the responsible and ethical martial artist who spends considerable time learning how to knock people out. *Kappo* aims to bring back to consciousness those who have been stunned or knocked fully unconscious, either by the giver or in their presence[87]. *Kappo* is particularly important as a subject of study alongside the study of *rakan appo* (羅漢圧法) – pressure point methods of attack –which could easily result in such a condition if properly applied. *Kappo* can also be used to help those who have been winded by a strong blow to the torso, causing the diaphragm to spasm and breathing to become difficult. There are even techniques for those who have received an unwelcome blow to the genital area, something that can in rare cases be very dangerous if left untreated.

---

86 Japanese has a charming onomatopoeic phrase for the satisfying sound of joints (especially the spinal vertebrae) clicking back into place – *boki boki* ボキボキ.

87 It is vitally important that they are able to assess whether it is safe to intervene in this way, given the possibility of spinal damage arising from events they may not have witnessed; thus *nokatsu* (脳活) should never be attempted without this first-hand information.

Figure 28 Seiho public demonstration (BSKF 2011)

Tetsugaku

Tetsugaku (哲学) refers to the study of the philosophy of Shorinji Kempo. It comprises listening to and, where appropriate, participating in the *howa*[88] talks given by your Sensei during the course of each lesson. It also involves targeted study of the philosophy topics set for each grade, with a view to answering verbally or in writing the questions that are set, as well as more broadly extending your own knowledge and understanding of all aspects touched on in this textbook and others by pursuing your own research and study with whatever tools you may have available. It is a vital and distinguishing characteristic of Shorinji Kempo that *tetsugaku* is a form of training on a par with the other five physical types, and it must therefore be given due weight and attention, especially by those more naturally disposed to enjoy a good scuffle rather than an abstract debate.

Balance of training

One of the keys to successful study of Shorinji Kempo is balance. Training that is weighted equally to all aspects allows you to make progress in the philosophy and techniques at your own pace, without missing anything. You can use all the tools available to you from this textbook, the instructor's *howa* talks, even discussion with fellow students over a drink (green tea, of course) after training. Don't be afraid to ask questions of anyone else in the dojo; all *kenshi* are there to help one another. It is also vital that you learn to understand the philosophy of Shorinji Kempo on your own terms, in your own words and through your own actions. This means being

88 *Howa* (法話) literally means 'talk of the system / way' so in fact properly only designates talks during class or seminars, not the broader scope of the philosophy as a whole. *Gakka* (学科) is another term sometimes used to refer to the corpus of philosophy topics, and means 'pieces / topics of study' but again just refers to part of the whole.

attentive in class, but also taking time on a regular basis to read through this book and any other valid texts that are available[89]. Mastery of the philosophy will not take any less effort than mastery of the physical techniques, so you must not just assume it will come by letting your Sensei's words wash over you as you sit daydreaming in class; active engagement is required, and, as with any area of training, such effort will yield rapid progress and tangible benefits.

Gakka 学科

One of the key times to test your progress in philosophy is when you are asked to write something on some of these topics as part of a grading (学科 *gakka*), either during the examination, or as homework to be submitted in advance. This is a chance for you to express your understanding (and sometimes your questions too) about these important subjects, and you should try to use your own words rather than copying or memorising sections from this or another textbook. Only then will you be able to get the very best out of the teachings and, in turn, be able to impart the philosophy to more junior *kenshi*. Kaiso made it very clear that he regarded unquestioning acceptance of the pronouncements of any authority as lazy, weak-minded and, above all, dangerous. Therefore, it is up to all of us to put in the hard work of study and thinking so that we may become more fully actualised individuals, able to think independently and make the soundest judgements about what's best for ourselves and others. As Kaiso said, 'Give me Leaders, not Followers!'.

89 Such as the various published works of Doshin So that have been translated into English.

The Five Elements of Atemi

当身の五要素
Atemi no Go Yoso

Atemi refers to striking (*ate* 当) the body (*mi* 身), and Shorinji Kempo describes five elements[90] that contribute to making any strike more effective. No matter how powerful, strikes that ignore some or all of these precepts are unlikely to achieve their goal of taking away an attacker's desire or ability to continue fighting; however, strikes that fully utilise all elements can be extremely effective, even when delivered by smaller, weaker defenders. Therefore, these principles of *atemi* must be studied and practised in order to magnify the results of your strikes; no single element on its own makes for truly effective *atemi*; instead, all five elements must work in harmony to create a powerful synergy.

It is also very important to understand what we are trying to achieve in the first place by striking an opponent's body. Our counter-attacks (see '*Shushu Koju*') are designed with a single, simple goal in mind: to stop violence with the minimum of harm (see 'What is *Budo* and why do we practise it?'). Thus, every element contributes solely to the effectiveness of *atemi* towards that end, and there is no room for purely destructive or punitive action that may violate ethical or legal boundaries without actually making us safer. Bear that in mind during your practice so that, if ever called upon for real, your *atemi* can be used to protect life without causing undue damage (see '*Fusatsu Katsujin*').

But at the same time, do not be under any illusions: in a dangerous (or even life-and-death) situation, you must be mentally prepared to cause another human

90 Mirroring the traditional five elements of wood, earth, water, fire and metal (木,土,水,火,金) in Chinese culture, or earth, water, fire, wind and void (土,水,火,風,空) in Japanese culture.

being potentially significant damage if you are serious about protecting yourself. It is best to work out any qualms you may have regarding that possibility well in advance of actually having to act in such a way (see 'Ethical boundaries' in 'The Eight Stages of Self-Defence').

1. Aim – target weak points

The most important of the elements – and hence its position as first on the list – is that of aim. As mentioned above, the goal of Shorinji Kempo techniques is to end violent encounters by causing immediate but temporary incapacity in an assailant. Being able to accurately strike weak points, or *kyusho* (急所), is essential to this. The central idea of Shorinji Kempo *atemi* is that, if you can strike particular *kyusho* on the body, you can disable an opponent – 'deactivate' might be a better term – without causing lasting damage to flesh, bones or other physical structures. These points can be like light switches: if you find the right way to trigger them, an attacker can be neutralised as easily and with as little effort as flicking off the lights. But accuracy is of paramount importance – even a small deviation from the correct aim will render strikes impotent, no matter how much power is used. Effectiveness depends on delivering a sharp pulse or shock of energy to these pinpoint areas, rather than trying to crush or damage bones or organs, which may or may not stop an attacker in full swing. This reliance on *kyusho* means that anyone – large or small, man or woman – can learn how to defend themselves effectively, as the results are not dependent on strength.

For example, an accurate strike to *suigetsu* (水月, the solar plexus) will cause the diaphragm to spasm, leaving an attacker winded and temporarily unable to regain voluntary control of their breathing. Someone unable to breathe will not be able to press home an attack; on the other hand, somebody who has had their ribs bruised or nose broken by a punch or a kick might not even be aware of it until the adrenaline of combat has worn off some time later.

There are more than one hundred *kyusho* on the human body which are exploited in Shorinji Kempo *atemi*. It is essential not only to know where these lie, but also to practise striking them on a moving target. Another important part of this element is selecting the part of the body (the 'tool') and the method (the technique) you will use to strike. For example, a snap with the backs of the fingers, via *meuchi* (目打), is a more suitable way to strike *ryogan* (両眼, the eyes) than a regular punch with closed fist (*seiken* 正拳).

It should also be noted that many of the *keimyaku* points are not only used for the purposes of attack, but also, when manipulated in a different manner, for healing through *seiho*. In *seiho*, pressure is typically applied gradually with support; conversely, *atemi waza* transfer kinetic energy abruptly to unsupported *kyusho* – the goal being to distract, destabilise and incapacitate.

2. Distance – find the best range

Appropriate distance (*ma'ai* 間合) is essential to *atemi*, and anything other than ideal distance will greatly reduce the effectiveness of your strike. Correct distance depends on the striking method you choose: the longest for *keri* (蹴, kicks); shorter for straight *tsuki* (突, punches); shorter still for *kagi zuki*, *furi zuki* or *hiji ate* (鈎突, 振突, 肘当, hook, swing or elbow) strikes, and shortest for direct pressure-point attacks (*appo* 圧法). For each of these striking methods, there is an ideal distance at which the action develops its maximum speed and momentum, and thus (kinetic) energy which can be focused on the weak point selected. If a strike does not make contact until after this ideal distance, energy will have rapidly dissipated and the strike will be a weak shadow of what it should have been; likewise, if it meets the target too soon, it will not have had the chance to build up the optimal amount of energy[91].

In addition, effective striking distance is not about merely making contact with the surface of a partner's or attacker's body – the strike must penetrate deep enough into the body to activate the *kyusho* being targeted. When we train in Shorinji Kempo using protective equipment such as body armour (*do*), the point of our practice is not simply to deliver greater impact energy to our partner's body as a whole, but to condition ourselves to deliver effective impact energy to designated *kyusho*, by focusing on ideal distance, perfect accuracy and the use of the correct tool (body part).

3. Angle

Each *kyusho* has a very specific angle of attack from which it becomes effective. Attacking at the wrong angle will produce a diminished effect or even no effect at all. A general rule of thumb is that striking (or applying pressure in *appo* or *seiho*) at right angles to the surface of the body, or towards the centre, is best. However, there are multiple instances where this is not the case, and these must be carefully studied and practised[92]. For instance, *suigetsu* (the solar plexus) should be attacked with an

91 These considerations show why correct use of *go no sen* or *sen no sen* in countering can be so successful (see '*Sen*') in reducing the effectiveness of an incoming attack.

92 As mentioned above, we use many of the same points in both healing and self-defence, but occasionally these different applications will require different angles on the same point;

upwards force, but *fushi* (風市, outside of the quadriceps) downwards. These differences can often be understood by the fact that the true location of the weak point is actually inside the body, not on the surface, and if there are intervening protective tissues (such as the ribcage or large muscle groups), then a different angle of penetration will be required to get past them.

Together, these first three elements are concerned with delivering the strike to the right place, which requires aim, distance and angle all to be correct. The next two elements deal with the manner of that delivery – speed and timing.

4. Speed – when striking, faster is better

Speed is another essential element of *atemi*[93]. Rather than relying on brute strength, we maximise effectiveness with speed. By increasing speed, we can increase the amount of kinetic energy transferred into the target. Fast action also makes it harder for the opponent both to determine the exact nature of our attack and respond in time by dodging or blocking. Another consequence of this emphasis on speed is that we do not need to waste time and risk injury by hardening our fists, shins, feet, or any other body parts[94] to make them more formidable at causing damage, for that is not our purpose. Nor do we need to focus on excessive muscular build-up to gain greater strength; indeed, if anything, an overly pumped-up physique makes delivery of effective *atemi* harder, as stiff and bulky limbs are harder to set in motion and accelerate than those that are more naturally developed and conditioned for speed.

Finally, speed does not just refer to the time between initiating and completing an attack; it can also be thought of as the time between your opponent noticing an attack and its impact. In this way, speed is not just for the young and the super fit – a wiser and more experienced practitioner can appear very fast thanks to advanced understanding of timing and disguise.

5. Timing – kyo and jitsu

The most subtle, difficult and effective element of a strike is the timing. Being able

---

for example, the angle required on *gokoku* (合谷) to help with a headache is not the same as that used when attacking the point in the *rakan appo* technique *gokoku zeme*.

93 By contrast, excessive speed can render more sophisticated *juho* techniques ineffective, especially throws.

94 There even exists an art dedicated to the use of the head as a weapon, where conditioning to the repeated impacts of headbutting is practised. Needless to say, Shorinji Kempo views such activities as both foolish and dangerous.

to employ timing successfully depends on awareness of *kyo* (虚) and *jitsu* (実). These two terms literally mean 'emptiness' and 'reality', but as a pair they refer to the complementary strengths and weaknesses of any system. No matter how perfect the stance (*taisei* 体勢) or physical condition (*taishitsu* 体質), there will be some part of an opponent that is weaker than the rest, and it will be matched by one that is stronger. These offsetting areas will also occur not just physically, but also psychologically and even emotionally. By paying attention to subtle differences in form, breathing, facial expression and micro movements ('tells'), we can direct our counter-attacks at those parts which are least able to resist, while avoiding those where our efforts would be brushed aside or endured easily.

This varied distribution of strength and weakness is apparent over the dimension of time as well as that of space, as moments of increased power and robustness will be followed by ones of comparative vulnerability. The most obvious example of this is with the breath: we can withstand considerable impacts when we are breathing out (this is one of the key reasons for performing *kiai*), but are much less resistant when breathing in. Likewise, the moment following the end of an attack, or series of attacks in combination, offers us a great opportunity to strike back, provided we are still undamaged and in the correct position (i.e. in a state of *jitsu*) to take advantage of this fleeting chance.

Note also that *kyo* and *jitsu* can be manipulated: a feint attack can cause a distraction, thus creating an opening (*kyo*) for attack elsewhere; a particular stance can invite a certain attack by making others seem unattractive due to a strong defence in one area (for example, *hasso gamae* overprotects the *jodan* area, thus inviting an attack to *chudan*). So what emerges from this topic is, in fact, the whole arena of tactics and strategy (see 'The Three Levels of Mastering an Art' and '*Ma'ai*').

Sen

先
Taking the Initiative

Sen literally means 'before'[95], and the idea behind the concept of *sen* in martial arts – as well as situations of potential conflict in general – is that if you can be one step ahead of your adversary, you can gain a great advantage. This could, some might imagine, pose a conflict with the strict admonition of Kaiso (not to mention generally accepted legal and ethical norms) to never be the one to start a fight. As Sun Tzu probably did not say, whoever can strike first has a great advantage. This is why violent people use violence so freely and with such confidence: in general, the best way to win a fight is to start one at the moment of your choosing, and they have ample experience of striking first and winning, without undue risk or effort, due to that advantage. But as *kenshi* looking to use *budo* to stop violence and reduce conflict in general, we should not seek out or encourage the kinds of situation where such a solution might seem expedient – we must not start fights. With that constraint in mind, the use of *sen* in the context of self-defence requires the much more difficult task: detecting and responding to an attack that the attacker has already decided on and may be some way into putting into action before you even become aware of it. This requires the ability to see what is happening before or as it actually happens, and just as importantly, the power to act on that information in the most effective way. Hence, *sen* is often translated as 'initiative'; but we must not forget that this initiative must be both taken and taken back from an aggressor who has decided unilaterally to attack.

95 So *sensei* (先生) means 'born before'.

Three types of Sen

Sen is a more sophisticated concept than just 'getting in first'; there are, in fact, three different types:

Go no Sen – accurately identifying an incoming attack and taking steps to avoid or nullify it; then taking advantage of the momentary vulnerability in the attacker (caused by the unexpected frustration of their plan) by counter-attacking decisively to an exposed vulnerable target. Note that this is very different from simply waiting passively for the storm to arrive; *go no sen* requires full alertness and the ability to tactically bide your time – perhaps appearing to be vulnerable, but in reality being at all times prepared and actively engaged in planning to deal with the situation.

Tai no Sen – accurately identifying that an attack has been initiated (but not necessarily knowing precisely which attack is coming), and taking immediate counter-measures (typically involving a simultaneous defence and counter-attack compound movement) to exploit the *kyo* (empty, undefended) areas created by the *jitsu* (fullness, focus) of the attack. *Tai no sen* is difficult at first for beginners, as it requires a high degree of decisiveness – as soon as you see that your opponent has started to move, you must act there and then to counter it, often without knowing exactly what is coming. However, with practice – and in combination with the deployment of a few simple 'universal' self-defence techniques that will work in a large variety of situations – it actually becomes the easiest form of *sen* to master.

Sen no Sen – accurately identifying that an attack is about to be launched, using situational clues and subtle hints of body language (breathing, change in facial expression etc.) and issuing a pre-emptive strike to stop the violence that has been planned from being expressed. Outwardly it looks as if you have initiated the attack (since your strike lands first). The reality, however, is that you have pre-empted your opponent's violence and prevented it from being fully actualised.

The timeline of Sen

These three types in fact lie on a continuum – from late to early – which we can illustrate using a timeline, a visual representation of the sequence of events.

	←	⊗	→
Attack Timing	Attack finished	Moment of impact	Initiation of attack
Defence Timing	Late - wait	Same time - don't wait	Early - anticipate
Type of Sen	**Go no Sen**	**Tai no Sen**	**Sen no Sen**

As we have seen, it is not necessarily a bad thing to be 'late' – that is, to use *go no sen* – since the additional time for observation can yield valuable insights, such as the true intentions of a potential threat. Equally, being 'early' is not always the best idea, for the correct application of *sen no sen* is very difficult and can be prone to error (you may incorrectly judge that an attack is imminent when, in fact, none was planned). However, with these caveats in mind, the sooner you can seize control of the situation – initially, by clearly seeing what is going on or is about to occur, then subsequently putting into action an appropriate response – the better.

Ki no Sen 気の先

Ki no sen refers to the use of *ki* (energy) to perceive not just the actions but the intentions of your opponent. It is sometimes referred to as *mihatsu no sen* (未発の先), where *mihatsu* means 'something that has not happened yet'. In this sense, the idea is that, by mastering control of *ki,* you can read your adversary on a psychological level, thereby gaining the ability to steer the developing situation at an even earlier stage, potentially even forestalling any overt conflict through judicious preventative action. There is also another, broader meaning of *ki no sen*, which is that it is the skill or ability which makes all other types of *sen* possible. By 'reaching out' with your awareness, you can get better at perceiving and identifying the physical and mental status and movement of someone else, and use that sensitivity to inform your decisions.

Ma'ai

間合
Distance and Timing in Defence and Attack

Ma'ai[96] refers to the relationship in space and time between yourself and your opponent. It denotes both the gap which separates you at any one point, and the many ways it can change. It is a simple concept in principle, but very subtle in reality, as this spacing is in constant flux as you both move and as other relevant factors change. The importance of this topic is that, to defend yourself effectively, you need to have studied and (eventually) instinctively mastered both the immediate perception of the opportunities and threats presented by a given configuration, and, as importantly, to have acquired the lightning-fast ability to act on this information without hesitation.

Three distances

The analysis of distance has three basic categories: near, neutral and far.

- Near distance (*chikama*, 近間) – you can execute an attack immediately, without first having to step.
- Neutral distance (*kihon ma'ai*, 基本間合) – a single step is required in order to reach near distance and thus be in a position to attack. Remember, this also means that you are now within your partner's attack distance and are thus vulnerable to an immediate strike.
  Neutral distance is also sometimes described as *issoku ikken no ma'ai,* or 'one step, one fist gap' (一足一拳の間合). This denotes the gap created when two partners' outstretched arms, with hands in fists, touch.

96 Note that 間合 is pronounced in Japanese almost with a 'w', as in *'mawai'*, to separate the two consecutive 'a' sounds; for the same reason, it is written in *romaji* with an apostrophe.

- Far distance (*toma*, 遠間) – you require more than a single step in order to reach near distance and thereby launch an attack.

Self-defence

When confronted by an aggressor, or finding ourselves in a situation where we might need to defend ourselves, the best distance is *toma*. This allows us to read the situation and gives us ample time to react to any attack that may come. Note, however, that 'best' does not mean 'likeliest'. The typical fighting distance we adopt in Shorinji Kempo, when assuming *kamae* with a partner, is just beyond striking range with the longest weapon available – typically, *gyaku geri*. This is *neutral distance*, as either partner will have to close distance to initiate an attack. This habit should then instil an awareness that anybody with hostile intentions at, or inside, this range presents a real threat. In self-defence situations, especially where there is a predatory motive, attackers may attempt to invade your 'personal space' in such a way as to remain undetected until it is too late, or by playing on a culturally ingrained sense of politeness, they may perhaps hope that you will not take the necessary action to frustrate their plan. These situations demand immediate and decisive action, whether that is to calmly re-establish a safe distance; to use verbal means to challenge the intruder (e.g. shouting loudly and assertively to 'back off') and attract attention from others; or to prepare for an immediate physical encounter.

To set expectations in a realistic way, if you are attacked for real, it will be closer, faster, harder and much more surprising than the style of attacks you have been used to in the dojo. Therefore, without sacrificing safety, it is very important to put yourself in disadvantageous positions when practising techniques, to see how well they work for you in more realistic situations. This means particularly focusing on *ma'ai*: you would prefer to be in *toma*, but you must expect to have to deal with what happens in *chikama* when you are least prepared. Having said all that, once a fight is in progress, it is often safer to be at close (or extremely close) range. This will enable you to smother attacks and utilise effective short-range strikes and *juho* techniques to restrain or incapacitate an opponent as quickly as possible.

Ma'ai is fluid and relative

Many things can change *ma'ai* and your ability to control it. You might be in a confined space with little room for manoeuvre, or, worse still, you may have been backed against a wall. The other person may have a weapon of some description: *kihon ma'ai* becomes *chikama* if the person is brandishing a long knife or club. Likewise, height differences can take on significant importance with regard to *ma'ai*. If your opponent is much taller than you, his reach will likely be greater than yours, and so there will be a distance where you are in *kihon ma'ai* – unable to reach him with a strike – while he is in *chikama* – able to strike immediately without stepping.

Ma'ai should be thought of as existing in multiple dimensions: it is not just a unitary concept. In a simple example, a given distance may mean you cannot reach with any hand attack, but you can with *gyaku geri*. And some parts of your opponent will always be closer than others, offering both threats and opportunities. The very point of *tai sabaki* (体捌, body movement) is to create advantageous *ma'ai* in some parts of the overall shared space without changing others; for example, by pulling the mid-section into (relative) *toma* with *hikimi* (引身), while leaving the limbs available for counter-striking. Finally, *ma'ai* exists in time[97] as well as space. Exploiting opportunities in combat is all about seizing brief and fleeting moments of opportunity.

This complexity in a real-life situation is daunting, and no mental analysis can accurately take in all the different aspects of a fast-moving scene whilst being quick enough to respond before things have changed again. Therefore, *kenshi* must try to develop an instinct – *kan* (勘) – for *ma'ai*, developed through extensive and deliberate practice – by learning common patterns, seeing what works and what does not – and by extracting the deep lessons of *hokei* from the very essence of the techniques themselves. Above all, this instinct is developed by *randori*.

Practise seeing and exploiting opportunities in Randori

In a fighting situation or unstructured *randori* practice, we are constantly moving, so the distances are always changing. Opportunities for attack and defence are coming and going in fractions of seconds, and it takes a lot of practice to develop the ability to read the other person's movements, capabilities and intentions. Remember to use *happomoku* to take in all the available information, including from the periphery of your vision, and thereby develop a 'feel' for the overall situation and any parts that demand more attention.[98]

97 間 is often read as *kan*, and normally refers to time, as in *ji**kan*** (時間 'time'), *shun**kan*** (瞬間 'moment'). For a more tenuous connection, it also refers to the length of a *shakujo* (6 *shaku*, or 182cm).

98 *Kendo* (among other martial arts) has many of the same concepts of *ma'ai* as Shorinji Kempo (such as '*issoku itto no ma'ai*'), and also includes the notion of 'teachable' and 'unteachable' *ma'ai*, which roughly corresponds to theory and skill gained from experience, respectively. See *Kendo*: *The Definitive Guide* by Hiroshi Ozawa.

In order to help us capture the subtleties of *ma'ai,* when practising *randori* in the dojo, there are several types of opening (*suki* 隙) that we can look for which may provide a good opportunity for effective interventions such as *atemi* or (*shika-ke*) *juho waza*:

Kamae – stance

- Your partner's stance may be weak or careless, creating an opening for an attack.
- Your partner may be uncomfortable and change stance, and will be vulnerable during the transition.
- Finally, you may lure your partner with a staged weakness in your own stance; for example, by using *hasso gamae*.

Sen – initiative

- Be early – when your partner decides to attack, they will be entirely focused on formulating a plan and carrying it out; at this point, they will be vulnerable to an anticipatory counter-attack (*sen no sen*).
- Match the timing – the moment when the attack attains its full focus and power is also a prime opportunity to deliver your counter-attack: provided your timing is good, and if you can avoid the attack while simultaneously delivering your counter, your partner will be fully committed to their own action and unable to change course in time. Note that, for your counter-attack to reach its target at the same time as the opponent's intended attack, you must start its motion before their attack reaches its focus point (*tai no sen*).
- Bide your time – your partner will eventually run out of ideas, breath, balance or structure after a series of attacks. Before they can regroup, and if you are still standing, an opportunistic counter-attack can end the exchange (*go no sen*).
- Other openings – The above is far from an exhaustive list. Practise hard and often to gain a more complete understanding of the importance of *ma'ai* and its application.

Technical Principles

In 'Guidelines for Effective Training', the fourth point explained the importance of understanding and exploiting the fundamental principles that make the techniques effective. These principles are what allow a smaller, weaker defender to prevail against an attacker who may be bigger and stronger. In almost all cases, an assailant will only launch their attack if they believe they can win, and do so easily. In most of these cases, that confidence is derived from a simple assessment of relative size and strength. This is a capability hard-wired into the nervous systems of all animals when judging the resources of their potential opponents, and humans are no different in this respect. Overcoming this initial disadvantage (together with that of surprise, which may well also apply) requires *kenshi* to use every available trick in the book, maximising their own physical strength through the precise and scientific application of their own energy, and maximising the effect this has by targeting vulnerable places, moments, or even psychological aspects of their opponents. While it may not always be true that you will be attacked by someone apparently more formidable than yourself, it is a fair assumption that this will, in fact, be the case; therefore, it is prudent to plan and train for the worst-case scenario.

Examples of principles and techniques

We will now consider a selection of principles, and mention some common syllabus techniques that rely on their application to be effective. We can also group the principles, as mentioned previously, into three broad groups for ease of learning: those that are purely or mostly mechanical in their action; those that act on the physiology of the body; and those that act on a psychological or tactical level.

Mechanical principles

doryo no ri 動量の理 'principle of momentum'. The generation and control of momentum is absolutely central to the effectiveness of many *waza*. For *goho*, appropriate *ma'ai* (distance) is required to generate the maximum momentum for a strike, and since the masses involved are constant, this means maximising speed[99]. Among the many instances where it can be observed, the technique of *tai otoshi* ('body slam') shows the use of *doryo no ri* most clearly.

hazumi no ri 弾みの理 'principle of the bounce / rebound[100]'. Another application of momentum, *hazumi no ri* is where a rapid change of direction is generated through a bouncing action. This can be seen in the distinctive striking style of *uchi* (打ち), as in *meuchi* (目打), where a strike to a delicate target can be delivered with sharp energy but limited weight or penetration. It is also on display in the lightning-fast rebound from block to counter-strike in *shita uke* or *harai uke dan zuki* (下受・払受段突).

nami no ri 波の理 'principle of the wave'. Several key body actions in Shorinji Kempo involve the generation of power and speed by the build-up of momentum from a wave-like action. This can be seen in the knee block and counter of *hiza uke nami gaeshi* (膝受波返), or, more commonly, in the most basic action of *gyaku zuki* (逆突).

kuzushi no ri 崩しの理 'principle of breaking balance'. *Kuzushi* is slightly breaking the balance of an opponent at the start of a *juho* technique by using subtle manipulations of the point of contact, the distance, and the opponent's own application of force. A classic example of this is at the start of the 'double circle' method of *gyaku gote* (逆小手).

shuho no ri 守法の理 'principle of defensive positions'. *Shuho* are defensive positions within *juho* that consist of a temporary (sometimes momentary) staging point during techniques, but provide protection against various types of pushes, pulls, throws, or attempted joint locks. Examples are *kagite, sankaku, tsuitate, konoha shuho*. (鉤手・三角・衝立・木の葉守法).

---

99 Since p=mv.

100 Another reading of the character 弾 is *hiku*, which means to play a stringed instrument – 'twanging' the strings. So *hazumi* has a sense of not just the energy of bouncing, but also the conversion of that energy into music.

kagite no ri 鉤手の理 'principle of the hooked hand'. *Kagite* is one particular example (and the best known) of the *shuho*, and involves bringing a wrist that has been grabbed close to the body to ensure stability, at the same time as providing an opportunity for *kuzushi*. The shape of both the wrist and the elbow are at this point 'hooked'; further, the hand itself can act as a hook, subtly changing the position and angle of the grabbing hand to your advantage. *Kagite* is often translated as 'locked hand', due to the similarity of the first character to *kagi* (鍵) – a key or lock – and, indeed, the action can also serve the purpose of locking the grabbed arm to the defender's body, which provides stability. However, in more advanced applications of *kagite*, this locking action actually becomes redundant, and its true role as a delicate hook[101] is at the forefront. A good example of this can be seen in the initial defensive position taken in *yori nuki* (寄抜 see photo).

teko no ri 梃子の理 'principle of leverage'. A lever is one of the simplest machines possible, and has the function of multiplying force. We can apply a powerful force through a short distance in order to create a large movement in our opponent (as in *ippon se nage* 一本背投), or apply a light force through a large distance and focus the impact on a particular part of our opponent, as when we release from a strong grip in *kote nuki* (小手抜).

kuruma no ri 車の理 'principle of the wheel'. *Kuruma no ri* is a particular application of the principle of the lever, applied in a circle. This can be seen in the large circular motion required in *furi sute omote nage* (振捨表投), which can create a corresponding smaller but powerful, motion in the shoulder and body of the opponent, allowing them to be thrown with one hand.

tembin no ri 天秤の理 'principle of the weighing scales'. *Tembin* means balance, as in a set of weighing scales or a see-saw. This principle thus refers to the use of leverage in yet another way: to cause rigid structures to move (like a locked arm) by applying force to one part with a fulcrum fixed in place. Examples of this include *maki tembin* (巻天秤) and *tembin nage* (天秤投) techniques.

sankaku no ri 三角の理 'principle of the triangle'. Developed by the late *juho* master Sensei Mori Doki, the principle (or, more properly, the system) of the triangle is a way of understanding the optimal direction to cause an opponent to lose balance,

---

101 *Kagi* (鉤) also means 'fish hook' or 'barb', indicating that you can trap your opponent by using it correctly.

fall, or be thrown, by imagining a triangle with vertices either at the grabbing point and two shoulders of the attacker, or, alternatively, at their two feet and a point in front or behind them.

Physiological principles

keimyaku no ri 経脈の理 'principle of meridians'. Derived from ancient understanding of the human body – and still used in oriental medicine, acupressure and acupuncture – vital points (*kyusho* 急所) can be used for either healing or inflicting pain. In some cases, an accurate strike or application of pressure may cause a limb to become temporarily paralyzed, or render a person incapacitated or unconscious. The use of *keimyaku hiko* (経脈秘孔; literally, 'meridian secret holes') creates maximum effect by causing temporary incapacity without excessive force or consequent long-term damage. *Ude juji* (腕十字) is a familiar example of this principle (with several others) – see photo.

kansetsu no ri 関節の理 'principle of joint locks'. Almost all non-releasing *juho* techniques will utilise the properties of joints in some way. It is obvious that joints work in a particular way, and do not 'like' being manipulated or locked in other ways. Understanding all these different conditions – and the similarities between them as much as the variations – can prove extremely useful for controlling an adversary without having to injure them unnecessarily. Moreover, this understanding can be used as a way of improvising joint locks on the fly in a chaotic fight situation. See photo of *maki gote* (巻小手) for an illustration of *kansetsu no ri* in application.

hansha no ri 反射の理 'principle of reflex reaction'. Some involuntary motor reflexes can be exploited to advantage; for example, when the sudden release of tension in a grabbed arm causes a temporary interruption of the attacker's force ('neutral point principle'), or, more simply, when someone blinks in the face of a feinted attack to the eyes. In other cases, autonomic reflexes such as vasovagal syncope can be activated by strikes to certain pressure points; e.g. *suigetsu* (水月).

Psychological / tactical principles

renhanko no ri 連反攻の理 'principle of immediate counter-attack'. *Renhanko* is practised from an early stage as a follow-on to *hokei* techniques, almost all *goho waza,* and most *juho nuki waza*. This is because of its great effectiveness in keeping an attacker on the back foot once a technique has been successfully used to defend against the initial assault. This effectiveness arises from the difficulty of dealing with multiple overlapping incoming stimuli: the 'OODA loop' overload, as described in 'The Eight Stages of Self Defence' part 6 – 'The Freeze'. What you are trying to do with *renhanko* is to cause an attacker to experience the same state of helplessness they may be used to causing in others with their 'blitz' or 'flurry' opening salvos. That is why *renhanko* should be practised with minimal delay following the initial counter and should continue for at least several moves.

nise no ri 偽の理 'principle of deception'. In general, the more you know about your opponent, and the less they know about you, the better. The use of deception in both single combat and grand strategy is of ancient lineage, and Sun Tzu writes about it extensively. In Shorinji Kempo, a simple example is found in the form of some of the *kamae* (stances), which are designed to either give an exaggerated impression of the defender's size and strength (*manji gamae* 卍構), or, conversely, of concealing their true strength and resolve behind a mild or submissive facade (*tate muso gamae* 立無想構).

kensei no ri 牽制の理 'principle of the feint'. This is a particular variety of *nise no ri* – deception – and involves delivering a diversionary initial attack in order to create an opening (*suki*) somewhere else that can be rapidly exploited. One example would be the initial *hebite zuki* (蛇手突) feint to the eyes in *jun geri chi ichi* (順蹴地一). Note that, for a feint to be effective, it must be believable; thus, it must be noticeable – not too fast and properly ranged.

doji no ri 同時の理 'principle of simultaneous action'. This principle is applied whenever a technique is executed with *tai no sen*; that is, when the dodge, block and counter-attack to an initial attack are all carried out simultaneously. It is also more commonly found wherever a single action (sometimes a compound one) achieves two (or more) aims at once, such as the dodge and counter-punch of *kaishin zuki* (開身突), or the simultaneous block and counter-kick (*doji geri* 同時蹴) of *tsuki ten ichi* (突天一).

Other principles

While this list of principles is perhaps more extensive than those often given in similar guides, it is still far from comprehensive. Therefore, it is up to you as kenshi to examine each technique carefully (and the different ways of doing them that may illustrate or emphasize different principles) to see what principles are at work, asking yourself: why do they work (or not)? How could they work better, either with the application of one of the above principles, or perhaps a completely different one?

Figure 29 Maki gote illustrates the principles of kuzushi, kansetsu, sankaku and kuruma

Figure 30 Okuri gote illustrates the principles of kuzushi, kansetsu, kuruma and doryo

Figure 31 Ude juji illustrates the principles of kuzushi, keimyaku, kansetsu and tembin

Figure 32 Kagite shuho before yori nuki illustrates the principles of kagite, doji, keimyaku and teko

Self-Defence and Violence

Notwithstanding the observation above that violence is, for most of us living in peaceful modern societies, relatively rare, dealing successfully with such violence that we do encounter is nonetheless of great importance. That is why self-defence is one of the three essential components of Shorinji Kempo (see 'The Unique Nature of Shorinji Kempo'). It is both the most visible and obvious aspect of the training, and the reason the majority of new students come to take up the art in the first place. However, it is also the most misunderstood element; for this reason, it is necessary to explore the topic in greater detail to ensure that widespread misconceptions are dealt with at an early stage. There is a vast amount that could be written on this subject[102], so the following discussion should be seen as only an introduction to several related areas.

Types of violence and appropriate responses

It is vital to understand that, if the training and techniques of Shorinji Kempo are the *answer* to a problem – how to respond when we are confronted by violence – then it is of paramount importance to be as clear as possible about the *question*: what forms does violence commonly take in our society?; what does it look like?; where does it happen?; who is involved, and what are the underlying motives or reasons for it? The first point to make is that there are many different types of violence and violent situations. It is, therefore, very important to understand the difference between them, so that you can recognise what is happening and determine the correct response to the threat at hand – responses that can differ almost diametrically, depending on the situation. It is a great mistake to imagine that there is only one type

102 See especially the books and DVDs of Rory Miller, to whom a great deal of the material in this section is indebted, e.g. *Facing Violence*(2011), *The Logic of Violence*(2013).

of violence or dangerous situation, and that therefore a simplistic picture of what you may be faced with is sufficient to guide your preparations for such occasions.

We turn now to a survey of the most common types; but be aware: violence comes in as many forms as there are different people with different cultures, values, emotions and motives, and while there are some universal features, if you think you have seen it all, you are most likely wrong.

Social violence

The first broad type can be called 'social violence'. This resembles the contests between animals of the same species who compete for reproductive dominance by engaging in stylised and typically non-lethal encounters. In human terms, such violence often occurs between young men when they gather in groups (it is meaningless without an audience, as it is predicated on winning status). It almost always follows highly predictable patterns into which, for all their familiarity, it can be very hard to avoid falling: for all our philosophy, we are still animals programmed by evolution to act in particular ways.

Self-defence response – Do not agree to take part in the game; back down and apologise, or do whatever is necessary to avoid getting sucked in. De-escalation and submissive behaviour here will remove the status opportunity for the instigator and leave an easy way for you to walk away safe and them satisfied[103]. However, an aggressive response, such as taking a strong *kamae* and using *kiai*, will lead to mutual escalation and a typically avoidable fight. Such encounters do not really involve self-defence in the moral – or, more importantly, legal sense, since they require both parties to agree to take part, and much more closely resemble the duels we read about from times past. Of course, martial arts techniques can help you win such bouts, but willingly engaging in them is antithetical to the philosophy, indeed, to the whole purpose, of Shorinji Kempo. Having said that, if it is impossible to avoid engagement, a much lower level of force is appropriate, given the typically limited nature of the danger involved.

---

103 This brings to mind a quote erroneously (again) attributed to Sun Tzu: *'Build your opponent a golden bridge to retreat across.'* In fact, he said in *The Art of War* (ch. 7) '**圍師必闕** *To a surrounded enemy, you must leave a way of escape.*' But in both quotes the relevance is clear, even if intended for a different situation; by backing down, you in fact win while making the other person think they have won.

Predatory violence

The second type can be compared to predator-prey interactions in the natural world; that is, inter-species as opposed to intra-species violence, where a predator will seek to gain something from its prey in the most efficient and low-risk way possible. In the human world, these encounters will, unlike social violence, almost always take place in lonely or deserted locales, as the presence of witnesses and thus the risk of getting caught and paying a price is exactly the opposite of what the perpetrator wants. The predator will choose the weakest victim, at their most vulnerable time with least chance of help or escape. Moreover, they will not care about status or winning, as they would in the context of social violence, but only about getting what they want as quickly and easily as possible without getting caught or hurt. The innate socio-genetic barriers to causing serious harm will not operate, which also makes this type of situation far more dangerous. Criminals resort to violence because it works, and they avoid violence when the costs seem too high.

Self-defence response – This is the complete opposite of the previous case: you must be prepared to spring into action with no hesitation and with a fully aggressive counter-response (almost by definition, you will be surprised and at a great initial disadvantage). Any submissive or de-escalatory behaviour will simply confirm to the attacker that they have chosen an easy victim and will not guarantee your safety; rather, it will lead to the opposite. Given the significant nature of the threat and the potential for serious harm, (much) greater levels of force are warranted in response to such situations. However, since the attacker is not committed to the plan at all costs and there is no 'honour' or status at stake, it may be possible to convince them that the costs would be too high, either in terms of the risk of being caught, or the risk of taking unacceptable damage due to unexpectedly fierce resistance. This is where *kiai* (which can also serve to attract attention and help) and aggressive *kamae*, tactics that mimic the actions of threatened animals in the natural world, can be extremely useful.

Group violence

The third broad type can be described as violence that exists due to membership of a group, and is a kind of mixture of the previous two. The best analogy here is with the kind of tribal violence that has been a feature of human group interactions since time immemorial. This is where 'outside' individuals or groups have been subject to extreme levels of violence and brutality, enabled through the psychological process of 'othering' (this also applies in predatory situations). It includes common modern plagues such as football hooliganism, racist attacks, gang violence, terrorism, and even, at the level of nations, war and genocide. Of all the above types, this is the most serious and the most dangerous, and the basic techniques of Shorinji Kempo may have little direct relevance in such contexts, where the situation can be completely asymmetrical in terms of numbers (a mob versus an individual) or weapons (blades, guns or explosives).

Self-defence response – For all types of violence, but particularly here, the use of higher-level thinking, as explained in 'The Three Levels of Mastering an Art (*Gi, Jutsu, Ryaku*)', is of paramount importance. It is much easier and more effective to avoid any of these situations by simply not being there, or detecting the problem at an early stage and taking remedial action. One cannot rely on the uncertain probabilities of physical techniques used in situations that are unfamiliar, terrifying and chaotic. If you nonetheless find yourself in such a situation, and negotiation or de-escalation have not worked or are unavailable, then escape and evasion are your best bet (see 'Avoiding Violence' below).

Types of Self Defence – 'civilian' vs 'military'

What most people think of as 'self-defence' could more accurately be called 'civilian' or 'citizen' self-defence., and, as argued here, training for it should be oriented towards dealing with surprise predatory attacks, insofar as the other most commonly encountered type of violence – in our modern, generally peaceful society – is of the status-seeking social kind which can and should be avoided. Shorinji Kempo has very effective and simple techniques for just this kind of situation, and if training is conducted in the right way, with a clear awareness of the types of violence outlined above and their typical methods and styles of attack etc., then these techniques and training methods can give *kenshi* very valuable tools for surviving such dangerous and difficult situations.

However, Shorinji Kempo, like many martial arts, contains within it more than that: the accumulated insights of generations of masters, not least Doshin So himself, who lived through (by definition, they did not die before contributing their experience to the corpus of knowledge that has been passed on) very different times with very different types of dangers. These masters might have experienced military service in wartime, persecution by a brutally oppressive regime, terrorism or anarchy; some of them could have been professionals (civilian or military, e.g. police officers, security personnel) dealing with again quite different challenges. Thus, it is important not to assume that simply because 'civilian' self-defence, although still rare, is the most likely type we will ever need, it is all we should focus on and all we should bother to preserve and transmit to the next generation of students. Consider the all-too-real example of a 'lone wolf' terrorist who enters a crowded public space with a knife and starts to stab people indiscriminately; such a situation would more closely resemble the sort of mediaeval battlefield encounter on which many traditional Japanese martial arts are based, rather than a typical mugging or sexual assault.

The Eight Stages of Self Defence

When we think of a 'self-defence situation', we are typically only thinking of the fight itself. However, there are in fact many stages both before and after the fight that are equally important to think about and prepare for both physically and mentally. The following eight stages illustrate these often unconsidered but vital elements[104]. All of these are relevant to situations of predatory violence and most (but not all) the other types discussed in these sections.

1. Legal considerations

UK criminal law[105] allows an individual to use 'reasonable force' to defend themselves or others, or to stop a crime from being committed, but this force has to be proportionate to the threat involved, and also be necessary to allow the person under attack to escape the threat[106]. It is also very important to be aware that civil law in the UK and elsewhere has lower standards of proof for a tort claim against someone acting in alleged self-defence, compared with the standard of proof required for a criminal conviction. Thus, it is all the more essential to ensure that your actions are both subjectively and objectively reasonable: that you believed them to be justified and that they were, in fact, justified. You may survive an assault and be acquit-

104 Again, the ideas in this section draw heavily on the work of Rory Miller; read his books and watch the DVDs for a more comprehensive treatment of this subject.

105 See the Crown Prosecution Service website:
http://www.cps.gov.uk/legal/s_to_u/self_defence/; see also this very thorough and interesting discussion of the UK law and its many subtleties:
http://www.bsdgb.co.uk/index.php?Information:Law_Relating_to_Self_Defence

106 Note also that different jurisdictions have slightly different laws in this area, though most are based on similar foundations (for example, different states in the US allow varying reliance on a claim of 'self defense' against a prosecution for assault).

ted of any resulting criminal charges, but still be forced to pay compensation to the 'victim' who sued you, possibly resulting in financial ruin. Truly successful self-defence must take all these possibilities into account and look to avoid them, to ensure both legal and physical protection.

It is also possible that you may be called to account for your actions by the authorities, who will rely not just on your word but on that of witnesses and even the perpetrator. This means that you must be very careful to be able to justify any actions you take with reference to standard types of explanation, such as showing you had good reason to believe you faced a genuine and imminent threat, and that your response was both proportionate and necessary. This requires the skill to articulate what happened, and why you did what you did, and this skill does not come naturally: it must be practised. The following elements are important to include in any account: Did the perpetrator have the intent to do you harm (how could you tell)? Did they have the means (a weapon, size and strength etc.)? Did they have the opportunity (were they close enough)? Did you try to escape or de-escalate the confrontation (what kind of violence was involved)?

One major factor to recognise in advance is the construction and nature of the techniques you may use: do they embody legally proportionate responses to the attacks they are designed to counter? For example, excessive follow-on striking after an opponent has been incapacitated or immobilised may look very poor from a legal standpoint in a court of law, and this includes final strikes after throws or takedowns. Do not train yourself to master instinctive sequences of actions that might put you in prison if you use them. Shorinji Kempo *atemi* are designed to be applied in very specific ways against *kyusho* (weak points) on the body and thus not cause lasting damage; however, control and judgement are still mandatory to avoid unwanted and unhelpful outcomes.

2. Ethical boundaries

What you have the skills and training to do and what you allow yourself to do in a given situation can be quite different: this distinction is referred to as your 'capability' as opposed to 'capacity'. This reflects your ethical boundaries, which must be examined well in advance of being confronted with such decisions for real, in order to resolve any issues or change your planned approach accordingly. If you do not address these questions explicitly now, if you are later in a chaotic and dangerous situation that calls for unhesitating and decisive action to keep you safe, you may experience a 'glitch' – a cognitive freeze that scrambles your ability to perform the actions required for self-defence long enough to be fatal. This freeze is caused by you considering, for the first time seriously, whether you are prepared to do what is necessary in that moment to protect yourself or survive. Such glitches may be caused by the age, size or gender of the attacker: would you use a weapon against an armed assailant? What if they were a child? A girl? They may otherwise be caused by your own reactions to the messiness of fighting: how would you feel about breaking a bone? Drawing blood? You should try to imagine as many such plausible scenarios as possible and work out where your own personal boundaries are; then ensure that the training you are doing either respects those boundaries or works to change them.

3. Context of violence

As discussed above in 'Self-Defence and Violence', violence comes in different types and each requires different – or even opposite – responses. Therefore, to have a better chance of correctly identifying the type of situation you may find yourself in, it is useful to be aware of the context in which each is likely to happen. This includes places, times, participants and tools (weapons).

Social violence usually happens where young people, especially young men, gather, and particularly where they are getting intoxicated. Thus, drinking establishments and their environs are classic flash points, and the danger increases with the amount of alcohol consumed; closing time, for example, can be particularly dangerous. However, these times and places are also correspondingly easy to avoid if you do not wish to be involved in this type of fighting.

Predatory violence will occur more typically at quiet places and times, possibly including car parks, open outdoor spaces, and even the victim's house or flat. Sometimes, a predator will attempt to lure a victim away from a busy spot (such as a bar or club) using charm or a concealed threat, to a place where they have more freedom to conduct their planned assault.

Group violence may often occur at the contested boundaries between rival groups (e.g. urban street gangs) or when such groups come together (e.g. for sporting fixtures or political demonstrations). Dangerous situations may also arise if an outsider enters a key space frequented by a group and proceeds to violate their unwritten 'rules' of conduct or speech.

Finally, a note on weapons: Shorinji Kempo has a limited set of techniques specifically designed to defend against simple weapons, such as short clubs and knives. The way these techniques are presented and practised is typically neutral, in that no specific context (in the sense of the current section) is being envisaged. It is thus up to each sensei and their students to ensure that their practice reflects the kind of situations they may encounter in real life – whether this is a surprise predatory assault or a public rampage – rather than assuming that the stylised 'neutral' version of the technique is the only way it should be practised[107].

4. Avoiding violence

Whether required by law (as in some US states) or not, it is always a good idea to try and avoid violent conflict, either by attempting to de-escalate a heated situation or by physically escaping.

De-escalation comprises both verbal and non-verbal means to defuse a confrontation that may lead to violence. While verbal strategies, such as apologising and admitting ignorance of the 'rules' or of the social hierarchy, are obvious enough (though they may be hard for some to accept in the heat of the moment), non-verbal cues can be just as important and effective. These include submissive body language such as looking down, turning away, and using a softer tone of voice.

However, it should be very clear by now that de-escalation is not appropriate for a developing predatory situation, though it is clearly relevant to getting out of social status contests, and it may be helpful in the more serious group violence scenario, if only as a means to buy time to formulate an exit strategy. In the case of predation, a much more assertive posture (figuratively and literally) is called for, including (if possible) the clear setting of boundaries. Essentially, you must credibly call the attacker's bluff, making them believe the costs of continuing outweigh the gains they may achieve.

In some situations where you are faced with a group of potential threats (this could be an instance of any of the types of violence discussed here; e.g. robbery by a gang), the best (or only) option is to escape through the encircling ring. This – like all the ideas mentioned in these sections – requires practice to be effective, but, with decisive action that comes as a surprise to the members of the group, it can work well. Remember, however, that your aim is not to fight one or more of the potential adversaries, but to get past them and away to safety.

Another option that may be necessitated by a more extreme level of danger, such as a terrorist incident, is that of escape and evasion[108]. It is always a good idea

107 This point applies equally, in fact, to all Shorinji Kempo self-defence techniques.

108 The UK government has recently released a helpful short public information film on how to respond to such situations called 'Run, Hide, Tell'. It is based on, but not identical to, the advice provided by the US government in 'Run, Hide, Fight'. The difference between the two approaches is clear from the titles, although it must be said that the US stance is closer to the philosophy of Doshin So. See: http://www.crisis-solutions.com/run-hide-tell-vs-run-hide-fight/ for a brief discussion.

to take note of the layout of any structure you enter, whether it is somewhere you go every day like an office, social venue or transport facility, or somewhere unfamiliar. Note where the emergency exits are and where they lead. Investigate (if possible) what other doors and rooms are accessible. Take note, even, of the materials used for doors, windows and walls: in an extreme emergency (for example, the kind of mass shooting that is tragically not uncommon in the US) it may be possible and necessary to literally break through a flimsy partition wall or window to escape. Do not discount any avenue for safety.

If you do run, try to make sure that you know in advance where to run to. This means you must always have a sense, always and wherever you go, of the overall layout of the terrain (urban or otherwise), and know which routes will lead to safety (be that somewhere secure, or where there are other people who can help) and which will leave you stuck. Finally, if you hide, make sure your hiding place is as secure as possible (i.e. with walls or objects that could stop a bullet – many thin walls cannot), and keep as quiet as you can, silencing mobile phones, for example.

5. Counter-ambush

In most scenarios in which you may need to defend yourself with the techniques of Shorinji Kempo, the assault will come as a surprise. This is because, as discussed, the kinds of people who use violence this way, and the kinds of reasons they have for doing so, tend towards the use of overwhelming force with the highest chance of success at little risk to themselves. Other kinds of violent encounter can generally be avoided by being sensible. Therefore, it is important to train with 'counter-ambush' tactics in mind. Given the high likelihood that you will freeze after the very short period it takes for adrenaline and other hormones to flood your system, and for the realisation of what is happening to lock your brain (see next section), you need to have a response to being ambushed that is instinctive, giving you the chance to survive for long enough to break that freeze and continue to defend yourself. Such a response can also be highly effective in making the attacker freeze, in turn: as mentioned above, they are used to their initial surprise attack working very effectively to induce this state in their victims, and will thus be unprepared for the surprise of being hit back.

Shorinji Kempo has hundreds of techniques for almost any conceivable attack, but not even the greatest master can summon the perfect customised response to a complete surprise attack every time, let alone an average student with limited training. What we can do, however, is focus on the very simplest and most effective of our techniques – the ones we are taught from our first lessons in Shorinji Kempo – and practise them with such ambushes in mind. Ideally, you should have one or, at most, two basic moves that deal with the vast majority of potential attacks (although not necessarily perfectly), without having to make split-second decisions about which technique to use – which version, which side, the fine details of the type of attack etc. Such techniques must, in one simple movement, protect you (either with a physical block, a dodge, or both) and strike the attacker (or otherwise cause them pain) and be general and robust enough to cover strikes from either side or from hands, feet, heads, knees etc. The list of candidates is short, and includes:

- *Uchi uke zuki* (with variations such as using *kusshin, uchi age uke, hiji ate*, etc.): the key here is that *tai* and *ashi sabaki* takes you off the centre line of the attack; you protect your head somehow whilst delivering a simultaneous counter attack.
- *Mae ryusui geri* (or *Ushiro ryusui* or *Tenshin geri*): again, the key is to move the head away from the attack's focus area, down and to the side, either forwards or back. Counter-kicks will always be more difficult than counter-punches in an ambush scenario as, by design, the assailant will be very close when they launch their attack, so range is likely to be a problem; however, *kinteki geri* can be very useful here, or targets on the leg.
- *Tsubame gaeshi:* more advanced, but more direct; go straight down the middle, leading with *shuto giri* or, as a variation, *hiji* (*sai gaeshi* 犀返) or *kumade*.
- *Kaishin zuki*: also more advanced; step off line and counter simultaneously with *jun zuki* to *jodan*. Not so good for shorter people, who can use *soto uke zuki* instead.

An important consideration here is that different people will have different preferences depending on their build, and even personalities. You must have a clear idea on which of these (or any other technique that satisfies the rather strict requirements above) you wish to focus, and then aim to train until it becomes almost a reflex response to the stimulus of any attack. For example, all the above techniques can work against kicking attacks, but only if performed with sufficiently fast timing (i.e. *tai no sen* or *sen no sen*, see '*Sen*').

Finally, notwithstanding the point about freezing, always practise with *renhanko* – follow-on counter-attacks – so that you do not train yourself to stop after one action that may or may not be effective on its own.

6. The Freeze

In times of great stress and danger, several autonomic processes kick in which can affect the body and mind profoundly. Whilst the idea of the 'fight or flight response' has become established in the popular consciousness, scientists have, in fact, known for a long time that, especially in humans, this should be expanded to 'fight, flight or freeze', with the last option being by far the most common. The reason for this is probably that a physiologically mediated form of 'playing dead' when attacked (as prey) by large predatory animals may have conferred a sufficiently adaptive survival advantage to members of our species for this response to have been 'programmed in' by evolution. Clearly, this does not work so well as a ruse against human predators; nevertheless, it is hardwired and almost impossible to avoid, even for highly experienced professionals long inured to violent situations (who can, however, minimize and shorten its effects so as to appear externally almost unaffected).

There are two linked ways in which the freeze is mediated, physically and psychologically, and, of course, the two are intricately connected (*Ken Zen Ichinyo*). The physical cause is a large 'dump' of adrenaline and other hormones into the bloodstream which instigate notable physical and mental effects. These include auditory exclusion, tunnel vision, clumsiness (inability to access fine motor skills), the withdrawal of blood from the extremities, and often, perversely, insensitivity to pain. On the psychological side – and aside from the sensory impacts of adrenaline – the mind can become locked in a number of unhelpful ways, such as a repetitive and unresolved 'OODA'[109] loop, a fixation on irrelevant thoughts, a 'glitch' (see above, on ethical considerations), a warm sense of well-being and calmness, or simply becoming petrified with fear (that is, 'turned to stone'). Denial or deferral can also be a powerful inhibiting factor to action, with thoughts such as 'this isn't happening'; 'why is this happening?'; and 'I need a plan before I can do anything' being commonly reported in such instances.

If you have been able to execute some – any – response to an initial surprise attack before the freeze fully takes hold (it can take a second or two for the physio-

---

109 The 'OODA Loop' refers to the decision cycle of 'observe, orient, decide, and act', developed by military strategist and United States Air Force Colonel John Boyd. The OODA Loop says that, prior to making a decision (the Decide phase), let alone acting on that decision, the person will first have to get information (Observe) and determine what it means to him and what he can do about it (Orient).

logical effects to really kick in), then you will be in a better position to try to break the freeze. Semi-automatic *renhanko* will aid this effort too, as will *kiai*, as doing anything at all in this situation is the best possible thing. Mustering the will to simply move or shout can seem impossibly hard, but it must be done to force yourself out of the natural mental and physical feedback loops that cause the freeze. In some ways, it is like the tremendous act of will some people report in making themselves wake up from a bad dream.

7. The fight

If you survive both the ambush and the freeze, you are now in a position which more closely resembles a much more serious version of standard Shorinji Kempo practice, be that *hokei waza* or *randori*. The training you have done and the time you have put in will then be your greatest source of strength (*yorube* 寄るべ, from *Seiku* no. 1). However, it should be understood that, far from being at your best, as a result of the adrenaline surge, you may well be operating with limited vision (poor depth perception) and hearing (inability to hear warnings); very poor coordination and manual dexterity (inability to dial a phone); and very limited higher-level cognitive facilities (inability to think tactically). Therefore, it will be the simple, trusty, easy and effective techniques that you should rely on – ones that continue to satisfy the requirements noted above; namely, protecting yourself while simultaneously counter-attacking in order to cause the attack to stop.

Luck and the environment will also play a significant role in the outcome, and you must (if possible) try to play these factors to your advantage. While we normally practise in a safe and sanitary dojo setting – with no obstacles, sharp corners, uneven surfaces or hazardous materials, and with good lighting – the real-life places where violence happens are likely to be very different. The things that can hurt you in any environment – such as a trip or slip hazard, or anything usable as a weapon – can also hurt your opponent, and whether they represent a danger or an opportunity is simply a matter of who sees and exploits them first. Luck more generally will always be a factor, but you can try to introduce randomness and chaos into a situation, or try to exclude it as much as possible, depending on the circumstances. In practice, this means being prepared to take greater risks when you are losing, since any chance is better than nothing; conversely, all your training is typically focused on gaining and maintaining control of an opponent and a situation, so it goes without saying that you should do that when you are able.

8. The aftermath

In the immediate aftermath, it is very important to do the following three things straight away: get to a safe place; check yourself carefully and thoroughly for injuries (you may be quite unaware of them due to the lack of sensitivity to pain mentioned above); and report the crime. This last point circles back to the first topic on legal considerations. It is vital that you are the first person (of those involved in any actual violence) to report the incident to the police, and to do so as the victim. This will set up a presumption on the part of the authorities that you are not the culpable party, and it is far preferable to the situation where your attacker reports the incident first, describing themselves as the innocent victim of your aggression.

If you do have injuries, you may need longer-term treatment beyond any acute first aid, and you may also benefit from therapy. There can be lasting psychological damage for the survivors of violence which causes, among other things, higher rates of addiction and suicide in this unfortunate group. If you find yourself in this situation, seek professional help and do not be afraid to admit to the problem; if there is one thing our training in Shorinji Kempo should give us, it is a sense of humanity's vast potential for resilience, and you should try to never admit defeat; for, even if you win the fight, you can still lose the battle for your life.

Self-Defence and Self Knowledge

The foregoing (very limited and preliminary) discussion of the types of violence likely to be encountered in modern society, and the self-defence responses that would be appropriate to counter them, is necessary for two reasons: first, most decent, law-abiding people are generally quite ignorant of the circumstances in which they occur; and secondly, many martial artists and others hold strong but erroneous opinions on the subject, which can have very negative consequences for the relevance and effectiveness of preparations to avoid such harm. The most widespread misconception is that competitive sparring or combat sports provide a good approximation for this real-life violence, particularly modern competitive MMA disciplines, as showcased in UFC and other 'cage-fighting' arenas. Such activities can be enjoyable, competitive, very effective for fitness, and can teach valuable lessons in discipline, courage and mental toughness; however, the truth is that the ways and places in which violence occurs are very different; thus, preparing for it requires many other skills and training approaches.

Randori in Shorinji Kempo offers these lessons too, but it is always offered as part of a much broader menu of training types that, together, are more effective in preparing *kenshi* for the type of encounters they are likely to face in the real world. For example, the approach of *hokei* training is to isolate one specific – yet wholly committed and single-minded – attack; as such, it may be more representative of a real assault in its most important features than a sparring session with its necessary rules and expectations.

In the end, in the absence of first-hand experience[110], no one can be sure how they will respond to such rare but extreme situations. If your conception of yourself involves a narrative that you are a tough martial artist who can handle rough situations with aplomb, you are likely to face a cruel kind of enlightenment when confronted with the real thing, discovering that you are not the person you thought you were. The teachings of Shorinji Kempo can both give you the tools to deal with such situations more effectively, and also help you to know yourself[111] better, thereby avoiding such self-delusion in the first place.

---

110 Such experience must be repeated multiple times to allow acclimatisation to the uniquely adverse conditions of real violence. But it is the ultimate goal of Shorinji Kempo to help you avoid having such experiences in the first place; thus, this kind of knowledge is unlikely to be gained and not recommended to be sought.

111 Such a project is of ancient lineage; there was an inscription in the Temple of Apollo at Delphi saying *gnothi seauton* (γνῶθι σεαυτόν), 'know thyself'.

Part 5

The Power of Ki, the Bridge between Body and Mind

In this section, we turn to *ki* and explore the many different ways in which an understanding of it can enhance both our practice of Shorinji Kempo and mental and physical effectiveness in all aspects of our lives.

Ki – a Minimalist Interpretation

Ki does not exist

Ki (気, *qì* in Chinese) is a vastly important concept in Asian philosophy, medicine and, of course, martial arts. Its first meaning was 'breath', 'air' or 'steam'; but by extension it has come to mean 'spirit', 'vital force' or even 'energy' in general. In all these senses it is uncontroversial, and it is used very commonly to refer to both air and energy – (*tenki* 天気 means 'weather' in Japanese; *denki* 電気 means 'electricity'). However, it is when the meaning of 'vital force' is taken not as a metaphor, but more literally, that a problem arises, since, in this sense, *ki* does not exist.

In oriental – principally Taoist and Confucian – thought, it is seen as an independent force of nature which may take different forms depending on the level of animation of the host, which pervades all material things, and the understanding and manipulation of which can grant great physical and spiritual powers to the initiated. However, despite the strong conviction that many martial artists and therapists have in the objective reality of *ki*, it is, in fact, a non-scientific, unverified concept which has not been proven to exist in the same sense as, for example, electricity or magnetism[112].

...but Ki is powerful

However, that does not mean that the concept is invalid or serves no purpose. Indeed, treating *ki* as if it does, in fact, exist in this way, proves to be a powerful way to harness the maximum potential of our bodies and minds; thus, its reality can be thought to reside not so much in its being another fundamental force of nature to

112 A US National Institutes of Health (NIH) consensus statement on acupuncture in 1997 noted that concepts such as *qì* 'are difficult to reconcile with contemporary biomedical information'.

add to the four described by modern physics[113], or a different type of energy, but as an emergent effect of the interaction of physical and mental processes. Note that we can think of *ki* in this sense as being akin to both energy itself – like the kinetic energy contained in a flowing river – and the force that that energy can generate, which can spin a turbine or move a boat.

This is a minimalist interpretation of *ki* which will offend many *qì* traditionalists on the one hand, and scientific reductionists on the other; however, in just the same way that Kaiso refused to speculate on the reality of an eternal soul, life after death, or other metaphysical questions beyond his – or anyone's – ability to have definitive knowledge about, we do not need to take an absolute or categorical stance on the issue. Rather, we can simply use the idea of *ki* agnostically, without endorsing or rejecting its supposed existence, as it can help illuminate and enhance many varied aspects of our practice of Shorinji Kempo.

Traditional ideas of ki

However, given that the concept of *ki* has, over time, become quite elaborate – particularly in the realm of Traditional Chinese Medicine (TCM), and in other Chinese Taoist traditions such as Feng Shui – it is helpful to enumerate some of these ideas, in order to see which claims we can justifiably allow and which have no sound basis in science or rationality.

The most basic description of *ki* is of a power which unifies and animates:

> *'It binds energy into matter, which means that without it nothing would hold together and nothing tangible would exist. Ki is therefore a binding, cohesive force at the point where energy is on the verge of materializing, and where matter is at the point of becoming energy. Since matter itself is a form of energy vibration, everything in existence is considered to be Ki. However, it makes for clearer understanding if we limit our interpretation of Ki to be that which animates matter. Therefore beyond its fundamental binding qualities, Ki is also the energy associated with any movement, be it the movement of the sea, wind, blood or of walking. All inanimate and animate things must therefore have Ki to exist, and more Ki to move.'*

Extract from *'The Concept of Ki'* in *Shiatsu - The Complete Guide* by Chris Jarmey and Gabriel Mojay (1991).

113 The strong, weak, electromagnetic and gravitational forces.

This kind of description is, perhaps, vague (non-specific) or even redundant (does it refer to kinetic, potential or relativistic energy, or all of them?). At the same time, however, it can serve as a usefully holistic way to appreciate the physical structure of the universe, as being connected by something fundamentally unchanging, whether on the smallest scale or the largest; something that causes there to be form and structure, rather than just formless energy or cold emptiness.

TCM also introduces the concepts of *jing* (精 'essence') and shen (神 'mind' or 'soul'), which are special manifestations of *qì*. They are, respectively, the nutritive essence required for life, and the energy which is necessary for rational self-consciousness (together, these comprise the 'Three Treasures' or sānbǎo 三寶). The geomancy of Feng Shui goes further, seeing the flow of *qì* through a landscape or a dwelling as being shaped by physical features – a flow that can be deleterious in some circumstances, but which can be moulded and improved by the skilled manipulation (for a fee) of elements like water in a garden or mirrors in a house.

Ki as emergent force

The minimalist position is that – if nothing else – the concept of *ki* can be useful in understanding the subtle interactions between physical and mental processes in a person. Moreover, when efforts are made to integrate and unify these two seemingly very different aspects, the resulting gains in power, efficiency and clarity can appear to constitute a novel source of energy that was not evident in the absence of such coordination. In this sense, *ki* can be seen as the bridge between body and mind (心身一如 *shin shin ichinyo*) and can also be described as an emergent effect of this synergistic integration. Very high levels of skill can result in effects that can seem almost magical in their potency or ease; in areas such as martial arts, however, where the smallest differences can have the greatest impact on the success or failure of techniques – and where an almost ethereal sensitivity is required to accurately sense how, when and where to act for maximum effectiveness – such an impression is not, in fact, surprising.

To summarize: *ki* may well be, indeed is likely to be, not a single, unique and distinct form of energy or force whose existence Western science has, so far, mysteriously failed to corroborate; nonetheless, it is still tremendously powerful as a concept and tool for bringing out the power that comes from truly integrated thought and action. So can *kiai* make you both stronger and braver? Yes. Can someone push or pull you from a distance without contact using only *ki?* No. Can *ki* be a useful guide in diagnosis and treatment of certain medical conditions? Yes. Can *ki* be a useful guide in the siting or design of your house or office, either to gain prosperity or avoid disease? No. With these caveats in mind, we proceed to explore the many manifestations of *ki* in Shorinji Kempo.

Breath & Physical Power

Ki's original, fundamental meaning is 'breath', from which it derives all the other connotations to do with energy, vitality and power; for without breath, we quickly die, and spending energy will cause us to demand more oxygen to replace the stores that have been depleted. Therefore, the first and most obvious place to look for the power of *ki* is in the breath, and in the effects that controlled and deliberate breathing techniques can have on the body and on physical performance.

Chosoku

Chosoku (調息) means to regulate the breath. The first part (*cho* 調) can also mean 'investigate', and additionally both 'musical pitch' and 'tempo'. This implies that the process of *chosoku* is one of becoming aware of your own respiration, then harmonizing it with the needs of your body and mind, like the conductor of an orchestra. This basic act of unifying – in this case, adapting the rate, depth and type of breathing to the demands being put on your system – has the obvious effect of improving your ability to maintain a high level of physical exertion or control, with the secondary effect of calming the rational and emotional mind. *Kenshi* should strive to breathe deeply and evenly whenever possible, and to harmonise this with their movement and actions. When out of breath from strenuous exertion, attempt to bring down the rate of breathing (and thereby the heart rate as well) as quickly as possible through conscious effort. Try also to breathe through the nose with mouth closed when recovering. This style of breathing has a clear connection to the various types of conscious breathing exercises practised in traditional yoga (e.g. Ashtanga) – collectively known as *pranayama* – and *ujjayi* breathing[114] in particular. During *zazen* meditation, *chosoku*

114 *Ujjayi* breathing has a characteristic rasping 'ocean sound', and means 'victorious breath' in Sanskrit.

breathing serves to literally recharge your energy supplies (e.g. glycogen in the muscles and liver) by drawing energy – *ki* – from the environment in the form of oxygen. This is used to bring body and mind into closer alignment, promoting the release of physical tension and mental preoccupation. Imagining the flow of *ki* from without, passing through the body and back to the rest of the universe, can be a powerful visualization tool to accelerate and deepen this process.

Kiai

An important type of *chosoku* is *kiai* (気合), as discussed previously. Unlike the *ujjayi* style of breathing (through the nose only) used during *chinkon-gyo*, normal *kiai* involves an explosive release of breath through the mouth, together with a given action, to reinforce and magnify the effects of that action. This is achieved through *kiai*'s power to bring together the multiple different and subtly important elements of any specific movement into one unified whole, with one intended result and one overall feeling. This is why it is called *kiai* – to unify (*ai* 合) the *ki* of the various parts of mind and body, and to do so by using *ki*. The techniques of Shorinji Kempo range from the simple to the complex, but even the most basic of the movements of *kihon* require tremendous coordination of intention and motor processes: you must be able to marshal not only large muscle groups – for example, in the legs and torso – to generate speed and power, but also smaller muscles that control and direct the action, so that the intended result is achieved, not least, successfully striking a moving target at exactly the correct point. Furthermore, the ability to allow groups of muscles that are not participating in (or needed by) a given action to fully relax to their lowest state of *tonus* can vastly enhance speed and effectiveness; however, this is a skill that is very hard to master in practice. A sense of the flow and balance of *ki* in your body – through the sharp and clarifying mechanism of *kiai* – can help to sense this difference: which parts need to strain, and which should relax. When successfully performed in this way, the role of *ki* can seem to greatly magnify the effects[115].

Finally, the importance of *kiai* in gathering a *kenshi*'s spirit and focusing it on the task at hand cannot be overstated, whether that be joining in with total enthusi-

115 Several articles in academic research journals support the idea that *kiai*-type breathing increases power and efficiency in sports. See Journal of Strength & Conditioning Research: July 2014 - 'Grunting in Tennis Increases Ball Velocity but Not Oxygen Cost' and February 2016 - 'The Effects of Forced Exhalation and Inhalation, Grunting, and Valsalva Maneuver on Forehand Force in Collegiate Tennis Players'.

asm in a packed class, training in the rigours of *kihon*, or confronting a sudden and unexpected act of aggression. *Kiai* not only unifies the mind and body, the action and purpose of the individual, but also the individuals of a group into one cohesive whole; as such, it is one of the great tools we have to help us in our training. Especially when we are struggling with low energy or reduced motivation, *kiai* can give us an energetic bridge to the enthusiasm of our comrades.

Fukumi giai

Kiai begins with a shout, but it is the focus of energy which is ultimately most important. This leads on to the idea of *fukumi giai* (含み気合) – literally, 'contained' or 'bottled up' *kiai*[116]. This is when you execute the coordinating process of normal *kiai* without the loud and obvious movement of breath; a breath is still required to perform *fukumi giai*, but it is contained, and released through the nose, with mouth closed, and with minimal noise. This practice is subtler and more advanced: the large and boisterous action of *kiai*, which can serve as an easy way for the beginner to gather physical strength and mental focus into a single action, is now transformed into something equally powerful but much more restrained. To successfully perform this method, and to a much greater extent than with regular *kiai*, a feeling for *ki* – its sources within and without the body, and the way it seems to flow through the body in sync with various actions – is essential. However, the results can seem all the more impressive due to the lack of apparent (and real) effort, and this almost magical boost in efficiency is perhaps one of the reasons people have attributed wondrous properties both to *ki* and to those who can master its use.

Kisei and Kihaku

Kisei (気勢) and *kihaku* (気迫) both refer to the state of vigour, preparedness and determination possessed by a body full of *ki*. The difference between them is subtle (and arguably not so important): *kisei* may be used more in reference to the physical state of 'fully charged batteries', while *kihaku* can refer more to the mental condition of spirited resolve. This condition manifests itself externally in several ways – it can affect the facial expression, eyes, voice, posture, and overall impression given by a person – and is literally the force of *ki* being revealed by these outward clues. It is generated in the same way as *kiai*, but in a more sustained fashion, drawing on the

116 It also has the sense of something implied, a hidden meaning.

body's reservoir of resources, built up through past hard training over a long period. Each breath contributes to the build-up and maintenance of *kisei*, by first drawing in air, then briefly holding it as the feeling of power and energy from the *ki* is released and permeates the body. The slow controlled release of breath allows the cycle to be refreshed without exposing you to a sudden emptiness which would leave you vulnerable and unbalanced. *Kihaku* is a state of mental strength: alert and decisive, but also open and without prejudging the situation at hand. When confronted with a person clearly displaying *kisei* and *kihaku*, many potential opponents will sense this latent strength and be profoundly unsettled, deciding not to go ahead with their planned aggression without necessarily being able to articulate why. Once again, this is the power of *ki*.

Protective ki

One other important feature of the build-up of bodily *ki* seen in *kiai, kisei* and *kihaku* is that the tension and focus involved creates a momentary protective effect, making the body less vulnerable and sensitive to impact. In extreme examples, devotees of such disciplines as 'iron shirt' kung fu or Shaolin *qigong* methods can render themselves insensitive to genuinely hard blows from fists, feet, or even clubs and sticks. Without questioning the dedication and impressive achievements of the most advanced practitioners, Shorinji Kempo does not teach or recommend such practices, considering them time-consuming, unnecessary and unhelpful in real-world self-defence: the condition of 'invulnerability' is not constantly or instantly available, but must be summoned with lengthy preparatory exercises – something that is unlikely to be practical in any real attack. Furthermore, such a condition renders the user at least temporarily immobile – the very antithesis of Shorinji Kempo's fighting tactics, which emphasize speed, agility and fluid movement. However, the characteristic *kiai* of Shorinji Kempo does provide an instantaneous (although admittedly much less protective) version of these body-hardening feats – another useful application of the power of *ki* in the art.

Mental & Spiritual Power

The preceding section covers some of the ways that the concept of *ki*, and mastery in its manipulation and management, can contribute to physical power, stamina, resilience and control. But as we have already noted, if *ki* can be described (among other ways of doing so) as a bridge between body and mind, the power of *ki* is also manifested in ways in which it can enhance mental and spiritual capabilities, notably courage, calmness, initiative and intuition.

Tanryoku – Courage

When faced with situations or thoughts that evoke fear in our hearts, we need courage to face that fear and take the necessary action regardless. Fear itself is a natural emotion, a helpful evolutionary response designed to maximise reproductive success; thus, like all feelings and emotions, it is essentially neutral, neither good nor bad; it is how we respond to fear that can be positive, helpful and praiseworthy or their opposites. Far from betraying cowardice, it is the person who is afraid but still does what must be done that is truly courageous. Conversely, some who are apparently unafraid may simply not understand the true nature of the situation they are facing.

The Japanese term for the visceral kind of courage required to act in the face of fear is *tanryoku* (胆力), and means literally 'gall bladder strength', although 'guts' might be a more natural translation. In English, we speak of people who have 'the gall to complain' or who don't have 'the stomach for a fight', in each case equating courage with a physical sensation or condition located in the middle of the body. This is surely because the hormone rush caused by the strong emotions – not only fear, but also anger and excitement – associated with a dangerous or confrontational situation has a direct effect on the digestive system, as well as the other effects discussed earlier in the section on Self-Defence (especially 'The Freeze'). That's why we feel fear 'in the pit of the stomach' or experience 'butterflies' of excitement, and all the many other expressions across different cultures referring to the same sensations.

In any case, to say that there is a physical as well as mental aspect to the experience of fear is only to restate the fundamental idea of *Ken Zen Ichinyo* for this particular context. Likewise, overcoming such feelings is also something that can have a physical as well as a mental aspect, and this is where *ki* again comes into the picture. Indeed, by taking deliberate action to boost our access to *ki* – the reservoir of which we may feel in our core, and its flow as we breathe – we can directly bolster our courage and resolve by reversing the causality. That is to say, by deep (but, more importantly, conscious and deliberate) breathing, we can begin to reverse some of the hormonal, physical effects of the fear cascade; in so doing, our minds are correspondingly calmed and made more resolute, as they sense a lessening of the usual feelings and responses that accompany panic or terror. When we draw in breath deep within us to the *seika tanden* (臍下丹田 navel area) or *hara* (腹 belly), the *ki* – which we can imagine as being collected in our very centre, near the organs most affected by those hormones, notably the heart, lungs, stomach and bowels – radiates this calming and strengthening influence outwards into the body, and thereby into the mind and spirit as well.

There is also an intellectual aspect to the ability to summon courage in the face of fear: once you have experienced for yourself the power of action mediated and enhanced by *ki*, your memory of such an occasion can provide confidence that you have the resources to prevail. On the flip side, trained, automatic responses to the threat or presence of danger can also kick-start the process of taking positive action to blunt the effects of fear (for example, by taking control of the breath and consciously centring oneself), thereby helping to stop the negative feedback loop of mental and physical distress that can lead to uncontrollable panic.

Heijoshin – Calmness

'Normal heart' is as much a physiological description as a psychological one. *Heijoshin* (平常心) is just that: the ability to maintain 'everyday', usual conditions in both body and mind, when faced with difficulties or even potentially life-threatening peril. It is the result of the application of *tanryoku*, in the sense that repeated exposure to (and overcoming of) challenging or fearful situations results in an acquired capability to stay calm under fire, to not lose (so many) fine motor skills or the capacity to make sensible decisions when under pressure. Therefore, the key to *heijoshin*, as to *tanryoku*, is the development and maintenance of *ki*. Just as the act of breathing is a circular process when viewed from the perspective of *ki* and energy flow, the development of *heijoshin* is a circular process with the exercise of *tanryoku*. This is because *heijoshin* both develops courage and requires it in order to be developed further.

There are two contrasting ways that we can seek to engage in this process of recursively building calmness and courage: either by facing small difficulties or meeting great challenges. Regular Shorinji Kempo practice in the dojo is an excellent source of these repeated small difficulties, whether it be memorising unfamiliar names in Japanese, mastering a tricky movement, increasing fitness or flexibility or facing an intimidating opponent in *randori*. For some, the moment they are asked for the first time to lead part of the class, be it *taiso* or *chinkon*, can be a terrifying experience, leaving otherwise strong and confident brawlers brain-locked and sheepish. Overcoming such reactions, refusing to give up, and facing the difficulty can be a very rewarding experience which builds a broader base of self-confidence and resourcefulness. It goes without saying that the practical means to achieving this starts with *ki*: breathing, mental and physical centring, and the build-up of positive energy that results from those actions.

Naturally, such occasions also present themselves regularly outside the dojo, though we often structure our lives with a view to avoid difficult situations (not unreasonably) and, in so doing, deprive ourselves of further opportunities for growth. That is one of the great gifts of Shorinji Kempo training: having made the decision to come along, for all the obvious positive reasons, you also gain the benefits of submitting yourself (albeit unintentionally, perhaps) to a mild dose of (self-) discipline and hardship that you might have chosen to avoid were it not inseparably bound up with the more pleasant aspects. Therefore, whether inside the dojo or in your life, try to seek out judicious opportunities for growth, through facing uncomfortable, arduous or stressful experiences.

If you find your regular training does not present these opportunities, consider what you can do to change that, either by putting in more effort, doing extra practice on your own or with *sempai* (先輩 your seniors), or even finding other occasions or places to train. However, as many *kenshi* have seen or experienced for themselves, if you put great effort into training, you can reap great results and make rapid progress; therefore, the only thing typically holding back our growth and development is our own level of commitment and effort, not some structural feature or problem with the training itself. On the other hand, if you find everything difficult, don't despair – whatever you find challenging will, by its very nature, make you stronger for having tackled it.

Finally, the second method of developing *heijoshin* is either to dive into the deep end or be pushed. This means occasionally facing much more significant challenges;

for example, a violent confrontation, a public Shorinji Kempo demonstration or competition, or a crucial presentation at work. In the case of violence, particularly, if you find yourself facing such situations repeatedly (and not in a professional context, such as law enforcement or private security), it is possible that, maybe without being fully aware of it, you are living your life in such a way as to invite such encounters. Of course, it may merely be the result of a difficult or dangerous environment; in any case, something at the level of *ryaku* (strategy) needs to be done to avoid further trouble – rather than continuing to rely on good *gi* and *jutsu* (technique and tactics) – no matter how developed your *heijoshin*. In normal life, these more extreme challenges do not come around so often (unless you seek them out), and that is exactly how it should be. Just be aware that, for all their seriousness (and in some cases, their potential to have a very negative impact on your life), overcoming them successfully can have a disproportionately positive effect on you. In many ways, they can lead to significant enlightenment[117] about who you really are beneath the tangle of stories you tell yourself to construct an outward identity, and this self-knowledge is a truly precious treasure, the goal of seekers after wisdom throughout history[118].

Zanshin – Focus

Zanshin (残心) is the state of mind – or, perhaps better, quality of mind state – to which *kenshi* should aspire at all times, but particularly at times of danger or action, where absolute focus and concentration is required. It is used particularly to refer to the concentration required after you have finished an action or completed a task, to ensure that you do not let down your guard and become careless, thinking you have achieved your goal and have nothing further to be concerned about. The phrase means 'left-over spirit', implying you must keep your mind focused on the task at hand (*gi*), the surrounding context and environment (*jutsu*), and your overall

117 This idea of the two sources of progress in *heijoshin* is similar to the Zen tradition of 'small enlightenment' versus 'big enlightenment'; i.e. a quotidian (everyday) series of small gains in awareness, versus a single (or occasional) big event of discovery.

118 The popularity of (Rinzai) Zen amongst the Samurai class during the *sengoku jidai* (戦国時代 the civil war period from 1467) and *Tokugawa bakufu* period (徳川幕府 the Tokugawa Shogunate from 1603-1867) in Japan is a testament to the power of this idea; it was not so much they were attracted to the teachings because it helped them deal with the possibility of facing death on a daily basis, so much as that those experiences brought them to an understanding of themselves and the world that is a type of enlightenment in itself, and they found this reflected in Zen.

purpose (*ryaku*) to ensure that you do not 'snatch defeat from the jaws of victory' through inattention.

In regular Shorinji Kempo training, this means keeping strong *kamae*, eye contact and full readiness after completing a technique; in *randori*, you must not let your guard down even if you believe you have scored a point; and, of course, in a real-life self-defence situation, you must be extremely careful that an attacker who has been fought off or subdued in some way will not renew their attack when you turn away or relax your defences. The most obvious instance of *zanshin* is during an *embu* performance (indeed, it is one of the criteria used by judges in their scoring of *embu* competitions). Here, both participants (or all, in the case of larger groups) must maintain *zanshin* at all times, from before the initial *gassho rei* until after the final one, as well as in the pauses between sequences of attack and defence. This *zanshin* is visible as *kisei* and *kihaku* in the electric, almost tangible tension produced by the very best embu performers. However, as noted already, *kenshi* must try to cultivate this ability for use in all their training and, indeed, in their everyday lives[119].

In all these cases, *ki* is again the source and mediator of the power to focus, but whilst being a strongly mental instantiation of this energy, it is still distinctly visible to an observer through expression, posture, and other signals. In a way, it is redundant to point out that you must be focused while executing a technique or when preparing to face an adversary; such a mental state is entirely natural, provided you haven't seriously underestimated the situation you are in, or are otherwise not in a fit state to judge correctly. Instead, the danger may more often arise from complacency after you have finished; it is then that you must summon your *ki* – no matter how exhausted or battered you may be – to continue to focus and be ready to act, with your 'left-over spirit'[120].

Ki no Sen

The topic of *Sen* – initiative – has been more fully covered previously. Here we need only focus on how the ability to maintain an accurate picture of a developing and

---

119 In kyudo (弓道), traditional Japanese archery, *zanshin* refers to 'follow through'; that is, the act of mentally pointing to the target after the arrow has been released. For, even though there is no physical way of affecting its trajectory once in the air, the mental focus involved in following through conditions the action that preceded it in such a way as to make it more accurate and certain.

120 Zan (残) is also used in compounds that denote cruelty and harshness; perhaps there is a hint of that in the injunction to not 'go soft' on an opponent before you are absolutely sure they pose no threat.

fluid situation, together with the capacity to act at the best moment in response to that information, is enhanced and mediated by *ki*. As already discussed, the essence of *sen* is decisiveness, and the foundation of that ability to act at the appropriate time is information. Both of these features can be seen to be enhanced by the presence and application of *ki* energy at the moment of action; hence, *ki no sen* (気の先) – *sen* that is directed by *ki*.

When faced with an imminent attack, if you can be level-headed enough to accurately read the body language and 'tells' of your opponent, you have a chance of knowing what they are about to do before or as they do it. Such an ability is hard-won through lengthy and rigorous practice, with much trial and much error (that is to say, repeatedly getting it wrong and getting hit or thrown, but learning from the experience); when it is in place, you can develop an almost instinctive feel for what is about to happen. However, such a refined perceptual ability is also dependant on being calm enough to see properly (recall how adrenaline can physically affect field of vision, auditory exclusion and fine motor skills), and on being cool-headed enough to match the pattern you see with what you have learned to anticipate and, equally importantly, what you should do in response. In addition, a command of your own *ki* can allow you to enter into a state of openness, with regard to the signals you are receiving from the environment (sight, sound, touch, even smell and taste), that can increase the acuity of your perception. Such an experience causes some to suggest you can 'reach out' with your *ki* to touch that of another, thereby divining their intentions even before they act; this may be going too far, but it is true that an almost uncanny ability to 'read' another person can be developed through the kind of arduous practice described.

Finally, when in possession of the relevant information, you must act decisively for it to be of any use. For this, *ki* is once again required, perhaps in the form of simple *tanryoku* to overcome terror, or the willpower to break a mental freeze or semi-involuntary act of denial ('head in the sand syndrome'). Indeed, the true application of *go no sen* – 'waiting sen' – requires considerable *sang froid*, in that you must consciously decide to wait for a better opportunity, even though you may be aware that an attack is about to be launched.

Kan – Intuition

The skill of reading an opponent as described in the above section on *ki no sen* is one instance of a broader ability called *kan* (勘), or intuition. We talked of an 'instinctive' feel for what is about to happen, but 'intuitive' would actually be a better descriptor. This is because instinct refers to something with which we and all other animals are born – part of the phenotype expressed by our genes – whereas intuition is a cultivated ability (although, as with any other basic human capacity, individuals will initially possess it in varying degrees) that we can learn and improve with practice. Essentially, *kan* reflects processing carried out by our brains below or outside the scope of our conscious awareness. The fact that its mechanisms are invisible to us does not make it any less effective, or even rational in a broad sense of the word. Indeed, despite the fact that the successful use of *kan* can seem almost magical – a gift someone may seem to exercise spontaneously, innately and without effort – it is merely the result of lots of hard work being done by your brain, but at a subconscious level. Your brain is a sponge for data, and is particularly adept at seeking out patterns and inferring connections.

Kan can also be cultivated, encouraged, and prompted; for, although we don't have direct access to its workings, we can first seek to expose ourselves to as much interesting and challenging input as possible, then try to retrospectively analyse why certain events turned out the way they did. Despite this analysis being conscious, the act of 'seeing' the connection from cause to effect can help train the intuitive faculty and kick-start further useful, hidden ruminations.

In a parallel way, researchers at the forefront of today's revolution in artificial intelligence use a similar kind of process to train neural networks, and other deep learning systems that are beginning to produce extraordinary results in various fields, by exposing them to huge amounts of often unstructured data about the world and letting them learn for themselves how one thing relates to another. Interestingly, these researchers are often no longer able to specify either why a system has reached a particular correct solution, or the means by which it arrived at the answer – the mechanisms of the 'thought process' are opaque to them. This does not mean, however, that these machines are magic; they are simply processing and using information from the external world in massively complex ways that may be obscure to outside – or, indeed, any – analysis, but still produce robustly good results.

In the relatively predictable event space in which Shorinji Kempo is usually practised – where normally empty-handed fighting training is conducted in a mostly uniform environment, with norms and expectations about what can happen and when – the opportunity to cultivate *kan* is highly available, and *kenshi* can quite quickly feel that their ability to operate within the controlled chaos of *randori* has improved markedly from when they first attempted it. This can give an immediate sense both of the power of *kan*, and your own ability to develop that power simply through repeated exposure to, and proper processing of, the lessons gained through practice. But *kan* goes far beyond *randori* – beyond the dojo – and can be important in all aspects of life.

Kan is the most purely mental of the *ki*-mediated skills and powers, and is therefore in some ways one of the highest and most important; but just as with all the others, the quality of the physical experience you are having has a significant bearing on the ability of *kan* to surface at the right time. Have you ever had the experience of needing to remember a name or some other fact, and not being able to, only to find it popping into your mind at some later point when you are no longer straining to think of it? Or when solving a crossword clue – the answer which resisted a full-frontal assault suddenly occurs to you when attempting another clue? The operations of our subconscious and unconscious minds are indeed (still, currently) mysterious, but it is clear that a necessary condition for this sort of often surprising insight is to be relaxed, to have stopped grasping for an answer; that is, to allow *kan* to work its non-magical magic. And this kind of physical and mental ease – openness, flow, lack of anxiety or tension – is precisely what *ki* can help to bring about.

One final thought: *kan* has nothing to do with our egos, our pride, our hopes and fears. It is therefore, in some sense, a purer form of processing than supposedly rational conscious thought, whose accuracy can be undermined by so many hidden flaws. It is a mode that is less distorted by our mental biases and hang-ups (confirmation bias, selection bias, anchoring, groupthink, among others), though it will certainly reveal our unconscious prejudices if that is the data it has been fed, if those are the experiences we have had. Therefore, you should trust it. It is not trying to protect your honour or hoping that things will turn out alright; rather, it is simply reporting what it has learned – that B mostly follows A – based on the input it has received, and that information could save your life.

Healing & Nurturing Power

Seiho

Seiho (整法) can be both understood and practised in two complementary ways that can also overlap. First, it can be seen as a physical intervention to manipulate the body on a physiological level – releasing tension, improving circulation and helping to flush out impurities and metabolites; correcting skeletal misalignments, or even dealing with more acute problems like joint dislocations and loss of consciousness. Secondly, it can be viewed from the perspective of *ki*, as an exercise in restoring balance and harmony both to the body's reserves of *ki* and the network of channels or meridians through which it runs. From this viewpoint, the giver will not only fix problems in the same way that a sufficiently advanced piece of equipment could (in theory), but actually utilise[121] their own *ki* to enact the calming or revitalising treatment required by a particular patient. The idea of *kyo* and *jitsu* is central to this understanding, as is the notion that, to fully and accurately sense these imbalances and fluctuations, a therapist must themselves be tremendously sensitive to the condition of the receiver. This sensitivity is enabled by *ki*[122].

Nurturing, Teaching, Leadership

For all the reasons stated above, *ki* is also a vital ingredient for success in many important life-skills, such as nurturing (parenting), teaching and leadership. *Ki* can

---

121 Not utilise as in 'transfer', for that is not normally understood to be how the beneficial effects of *seiho* are achieved (i.e. by draining energy from the giver), but in the sense of using as a tool or a sensor, in order to better understand what is required to be done.

122 This is one reason that it is inadvisable to give *seiho* treatment if you yourself are unwell: not only can it be tiring and draining, but your sensitivity will be compromised and, thus, the effectiveness of the intervention.

enable us to understand better and empathise with those who rely on us for support and guidance – this is the 'sensor' function of *ki*, in a manner of speaking. It also gives us the confidence and energy to step up and lead – this is the 'power supply' function. These two aspects are never far apart; indeed, they can be seen to operate in a circular way, like a feedback loop. Most (although sadly not all) parents and teachers will tell you that they have benefited immeasurably from their experiences in those roles; indeed, in the context of Shorinji Kempo, the only reliable way to continue the long process of self-improvement beyond a certain intermediate point of progress is to teach others, and, in so doing, continue to learn in ever new and unexpected ways. Considering this benefit from the perspective of *ki* can illuminate the process: *ki* is visible not only in the bond that good teachers (and parents) develop with their charges, but also in the energy and force of personality that is necessary for leaders to believe in themselves sufficiently to be trusted and respected by those in their care.

The Power of Integration

As humans, we have various kinds of strength to draw on when meeting the challenges of our everyday lives, or when faced with more serious threats or opportunities. The first that comes to mind is our physical strength, which can be seen in more than just the ability to lift heavy weights or overpower others, but also in our stamina and physical resilience or toughness. In Japanese, this is *tai ryoku* (体力). The second kind is mental strength – *shin ryoku* (心力) – and, analogously with *tai ryoku*, this can take several forms, such as problem-solving ability or having a good working memory[123]. These are akin to having well-developed 'mental muscle', on the one hand, and persistence and willpower – which resemble physical stamina and toughness – on the other. It will come as no surprise by now to hear that these two kinds of strength, while not identical, are inseparably linked; however, like any of the relationships to which we draw attention in Shorinji Kempo philosophy, the fact that there is an underlying unity and a strong link does not mean that the two aspects are equally developed, or function smoothly in a unified fashion. This requires both careful attention to balanced training of each side, together with the ability to deploy the two aspects in practice.

Shin Ki Ryoku no Icchi

This balancing function is the role of *ki*. As we have seen with all the examples given above, its function can most often be seen as that of a force which unifies, focusing

123 Recent scientific research has shown that, contrary to long-held assumptions, a person's basic level of intelligence as measured by IQ (for example) is not a fixed quantity and can be raised by certain, admittedly arduous forms of mental training, often focused on improving and extending working memory. It is certainly clear that IQ can be lowered by other activities. See also 'The Growth Mindset'.

disparate elements of a system and bringing them together, making them more harmonious and thereby more effective and powerful as a result. The ability to do this is called *ki ryoku* (気力), and when it is deployed, we may feel a surge of power resulting from this alignment of physical and mental energy with that elusive quantity we have identified as *ki*. This, again, is something like the energy that is created[124] by the synergy of otherwise disjointed parts, and is called *shin ki ryoku no icchi* (心気力の一致) – 'the union of mind, *ki* and strength', or, more memorably, 'The Power of Integration'.

124 Not from nothing – you could also say it is the energy not wasted or dissipated through a lack of integration.

Part 6

The Structure and History of Shorinji Kempo

This section covers the extended history of Shorinji Kempo, from its origins in the fighting and healing traditions of ancient Vedic India to the present day. It also describes the overall structure of Shorinji Kempo and its extensive array of sub-disciplines, together with some other topics of historical interest.

Bodhidharma, Zen and the Shaolin Temple

Bodhidharma

Bodhidharma was a Buddhist monk who lived probably in the early 5th century CE. He is traditionally credited as the transmitter of *Ch'an* Buddhism from India to China (in Japanese: *Zen* 禅), and with developing the Shaolin Temple (*shorinji* in Japanese, 少林寺). He is also said to have taught the monks there a system of body-conditioning exercises to improve their health and fortify them to endure rigorous spiritual practices. Whilst he was very likely a real historical figure, over the ages he has attained a semi-mythical status, and accounts of his life have collected layers of wishful thinking and hagiography ('writing about the Saints') that make most serious modern scholars doubt whether we can now ever confidently know the true facts about him. Regardless, the legends serve a powerful and useful purpose: Doshin So drew great inspiration from this figure, naming his new art after the temple Bodhidharma made famous, and even modelling his own image, to a certain extent, on the popular picture of a bushy-bearded, irascible (but also wise), compassionate and

Figure 33 Bodhidharma, Ukiyo-e woodblock print by Tsukioka Yoshitoshi, 1887

martially adept monk. This was not only a clever branding exercise which appealed to ancient historical lineage and authority, but also embodied clear philosophical messages taken from the legend of the iconoclastic and ascetic monk who, at the end of his long pilgrimage, taught the misguided and flaccid Chinese monks he encountered to be healthy, happy, and not easily taken advantage of or cowed by adversity.

Zen

Bodhidharma's chief mission was to revitalise the stagnant state of Chinese Buddhism. This had grown sclerotic and distanced from the true path of Buddha almost one thousand years after his death, and several centuries after the first introduction of Buddhism from India along the Silk Roads. Superstitious rituals abounded, as did the purchase of 'merit', in which the wealthy would attempt to circumvent the iron law of *karma* and attain *nirvana* without honest effort or true understanding of Buddha's core ideas. Bodhidharma preached a pared-down, radically simple form of Buddhism: dispensing with most ritual and focus on scripture, it instead focused on the practice of meditation, or *dhyana* in Sanskrit. This word was rendered into Chinese as *ch'an*, and then into Japanese as *zen*. One other key feature of Zen was its focus on the tasks of daily life in providing an opportunity for all (not just holy men or monks) to 'polish the mirror' of their hearts, and thus obtain *satori* (悟),or enlightenment.

Ekkin-gyo

Legend states that, as well as a completely new take on the philosophy and practice of Buddhism, Bodhidharma was concerned by the physical condition of his Chinese acolytes, and saw fit to also introduce the body-conditioning exercises known as *ekkin-gyo* (易筋行, detailed in a text called *yijin jing* in Chinese), which can be translated as 'discipline to ease / change the muscles and tendons'. Another interpretation may be that he realised that if he encouraged the monks to adopt a religious practice which involved a lot of sitting down, it was also necessary to

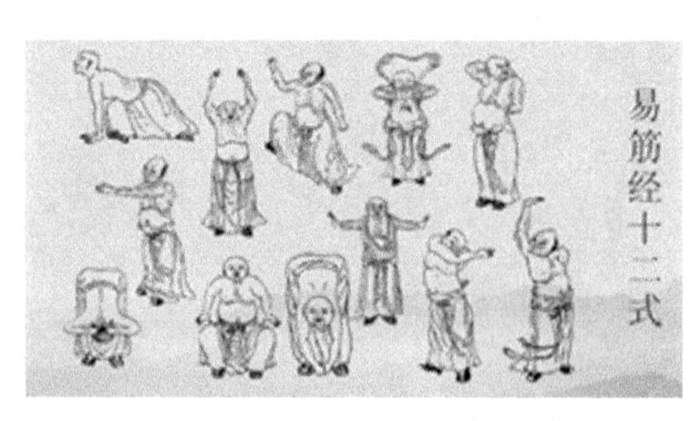

Figure 34 Detail from the Yijin Jing manuscript

balance this with a vigorous training regime to counteract the debilitating effects on the body of too much inactivity[125].

In its original form, *yijin jing* appears to be only a set of calisthenic-type exercises promoting strength, stamina and flexibility; similar to the *qigong* exercises widely known today, they have a clear lineage in Indian yogic practices. Thus, it did not have any explicit martial or self-defence content; instead, it was more of a preparation for those fighting activities. However, in Doshin So's interpretation, the subject is viewed more broadly to include not just the body conditioning, but also the fighting techniques and practices themselves. This association of Bodhidharma with martial arts is, in fact, probably a rather late (19th century) addition to the corpus of the legend[126]; however, as mentioned above, the composite picture has a strong resonance with the ideals of Doshin So and Shorinji Kempo and, thus, the literal truth of the story is, perhaps, of only secondary importance.

The Shaolin Temple

The Shaolin monastery has become inextricably entwined in the popular consciousness with Chinese martial arts, and is seen as the origin of much (or all, depending on the source) of the later myriad styles of Chinese martial arts (*wushu*, Japanese *bujutsu* 武術). This idea is clearly inaccurate, as historical accounts starting from as early as the 5th century BCE prominently mention martial arts theories and practice[127]. Nonetheless, the Shaolin style of *kung fu* can still be regarded as the first 'institutionalized' form of *wushu*. While there are some scattered early historical references to fighters from Shaolin engaging in battles to defend the monastery[128], it is not until the 16th century that martial arts activity there is independently attested. For our purposes, again, what is important is the symbolism of the story, which

125 There is a modern scholarly consensus that Bodhidharma did not compose the *yijin jing* (though he may well have introduced Vedic practices for fitness and self-defence), and that the current text was authored by the Taoist priest Zining, writing in 1624.

126 E.g. Lin Boyuan, *Zhongguo wushu shi*.

127 See, for example, the *Spring and Autumn Annals* (5th century BCE), which mentions a hand-to-hand combat theory that integrates notions of 'hard' and 'soft' techniques. In addition, a combat wrestling system called *juélì* or *jiǎolì* (角力) is mentioned in the 'Classic of Rites', including techniques such as strikes, throws, joint manipulation, and pressure point attacks.

128 A stele from 728 CE attests to two occasions: a defence of the Shaolin Monastery from bandits around 610 CE, and their subsequent role in the defeat of Wang Shichong at the Battle of Hulao in 621 CE.

brings together the spheres of physical health, self-defence skills and spiritual development. Whenever in its long history this synthesis was, in fact, fully implemented at Shaolin[129], it offers an ideal of the true meaning and purpose of martial arts (see 'What is *Budo* and why do we practise it?'), and it was this ideal that Doshin So was both appealing to and helping to strengthen when he named his system 'Fist Method of the Shaolin Temple', or Shorinji Kempo.

Figure 35 The Mountain Gate (built 1735) at the Shoalin Temple, Henan Province

Later history and development

Over its history, the temple was destroyed and rebuilt many times, starting in the 14th century until as recently as 1931. While many of the 19th-century martial-arts-based secret societies in China created dubious origin stories based around such events, the truth is probably that, by the beginning of the 20th century there was little formal

129 For a thorough, if mostly unsubstantiated, account of the history of Shaolin – both the temple and the monastic order – see *The Shaolin Grandmasters' Text: History, Philosophy, and Gung Fu of Shaolin Ch'an* (2008).

wushu activity at the site. In any event, a young Doshin So was able to study as a disciple under the grandmaster of the *Giwamonken* school (*Yihemenquan* in Chinese, 義和門拳), Wen Taizong, who (it is claimed) formally passed the title of grandmaster to him at a ceremony in the grounds of the Shaolin temple in 1936[130].

Figure 36 Mural from the Shaolin temple (early 19th C)

130 This version of events is strongly contested by martial arts historians such as Donn Draeger, who argues that, "[f]or Nakano to suggest that he, a foreigner, could succeed to a position of leadership over a Chinese martial arts tradition is to deliberately ignore Chinese tradition and to insult the intelligence of those whom he would have believe his claim"

3 Vessels, 3 Systems, 25 Groups

三鼎・三法・二十五系
Santei, Sampo, Nijugokei

This topic describes the incredible breadth and depth of Shorinji Kempo. Doshin So divided his overall programme for self-improvement and world peace (see 'Establish Yourself, Live in Harmony with Others') into 3 broad areas, which he called 'Vessels' – *tei* 鼎 or *ding* in Chinese. A *ding* is a 3-legged Chinese cauldron – hence, 'vessel' (see picture) – and the imagery is of a container that holds a great store of knowledge. The three areas are Heart (*shin* 心), Body (*tai* 体) and Intellect (*chi* 智); we could also translate these in a more familiar way (but in a different order) as Mind, Body and Soul. He then further subdivided 'Body' into the 3 practical Systems (*ho* 法, as in *juho*, or *po,* as in Kempo) of Hard, Soft and Healing (*Goho* 剛法, *Juho* 柔法 and *Seiho* 整法), giving further divisions of those Systems into Groups (*kei* 系). Examples of these groups are strikes and defences in *Goho* (*tsuki waza* and *bogi*); throws and pins in *Juho* (*nage waza* and *katame waza*); and skeletal realignment and resuscitation in *Seiho* (*seikotsu* and *kappo*).

Figure 37 A ding in China

In total there are 25 Groups (sometimes translated as 'branches') which together enumerate the dizzying variety of Shorinji Kempo techniques. However, it is important to note that these 25 Groups are just elements of one third of the whole practice: the realm of the body; physical techniques, in other words. When we consider the realms of *shin* (heart[131] / spirit) and *chi* (wisdom), it is clear that a lifetime's worth of material for the student to study is encompassed in the holistic discipline that is Shorinji Kempo.

Variety is the spice of life – and training

This breadth and depth of material is very important to our practice because it gives us, as students, a truly rich seam to mine, for an extended or even indefinite period. Why does this matter? Because it keeps our training ever interesting and fresh; for example, it allows even long-experienced and senior *kenshi* to still feel a great curiosity about so many areas of that whole that they have yet to fully investigate, let alone master. It is vital for teachers to consider themselves students – still growing and learning as they continue to pass on the fruits of that study to others – as this prevents them from getting stale or complacent, and sets an invaluable example of dedication to lifelong learning and continuous improvement to their followers.

We can draw a comparison between Shorinji Kempo and some other activities that offer similar benefits in some respects, like fitness and physical training, or sports. There is no doubt that these bestow clear positives to those who take part in them, but very often these are not fully realized or sustained, as most people find it hard to continue over extended periods of time. This occurs for different reasons in each case, but in general we could say it is because the activity loses its relevance in one way or another. Fitness-type regimes, for example, simply become boring or routine, and the initial, entirely laudable goals (e.g. looking and feeling better) lose their potency with familiarity. In addition, as the body becomes habituated to a particular type of movement, the challenge diminishes and, thus, eventually becomes uninteresting. For most amateur sports, the thrill of competition (against oneself or others) also declines in line with physical strength and capability, as being better normally requires simply better physical condition, rather than ever-increasing skill. Shorinji Kempo, on the other hand, is rich and deep enough to offer the continuous opportunity to challenge oneself and to improve at techniques, *randori* (sparring),

131 In Far-Eastern thought, the heart is the seat not so much of emotions in general, as in the West, but of courage, and specifically the will. Compare our use of phrases like 'lion hearted' or 'losing heart'.

embu (demonstrations), *Seiho* or philosophy, while all the time reaping the physical benefits of strength, stamina and flexibility conferred over years and decades of regular practice.

Furthermore, many of the most basic ideas and techniques of Shorinji Kempo, while startlingly simple, are very hard to implement in practice, whether it be the ability to apply a basic self-defence technique like *uchi uke zuki*, or the fundamental prescription to live 'Half for your own happiness, half for others". Thus, what is required to master such basic but subtle ideas is simply persistence, prolonged practice and many repeated experiments, including both successes and failures. If we limited training to just the basic but vital elements, we too would risk getting bored long before we came close to achieving mastery; however, it is the variety of approaches and avenues used to get us closer to achieving the goal of self-actualization (*jiko kakuritsu*) that keeps us coming back for more, whether we fully comprehend the broader effects of the practice on our lives or not.

Symmetry between the Vessels

If we look at the structure of the whole, we can see that, of the three main 'Vessels', only one (Body) has been further subdivided for us into the three Systems with whose various Groups most *kenshi* are familiar. It is therefore possible to imagine that the other Vessels have a similar degree of complexity and depth which is not listed in explicit detail here. Moreover, we can also reflect on the potential symmetry between the different branches of the tree. For example, we could think of *Goho* as somehow representing the Body Vessel, *Juho* the Vessel of Wisdom, and *Seiho* that of the Heart. With this perspective, we can also try to imagine what the Systems (*ho*) within *chi* (for example) that correspond to *Goho*, *Juho* or *Seiho* might be: strongly rational argument, humble acknowledgment of others' views, and talking therapy respectively, perhaps. In a similar vein, what Groups of techniques or approaches exist in the broad area of the study of developing one's *Shin*, or Heart / Spirit?

Explore the unfamiliar

Within the long list of technical items, there are many rare elements listed that we don't often come across in our regular training or syllabus techniques, but they are there to be explored. For example, few are familiar with *fusemi uke* (an extreme form of *kusshin* where you flatten yourself to the floor). We do not practise it as part of our normal techniques, but it can come in very useful when unarmed, as a response to a mid-level swing with a *shakujo*. Alternatively, we might consider *age kage zuki* (side uppercut to the body) or *nai sokuto gari* (sweep using the inside of the foot arch).

The main point to note here is that there are endless possibilities, as varied as the different aspects of any human being, both physical and mental, logical and emotional, instinctive and rational. Yet most of these are not even mentioned in this long list of Groups, let alone in the syllabus that most think of as containing the totality of Shorinji Kempo teaching. A good example is when students ask, 'Does such and such a strike / block / escape exist in Kempo?'; the answer is almost always that anything that can be done which makes physical or tactical sense in a self-defence context should be thought of as included, whether there is a common technique that incorporates it or not. Note that one place where such possibilities can be explored is within *kumi embu*, though be aware that over-elaborate or impractical moves may not be looked on favourably by the judges. The other moment to explore the boundaries of what is possible or useful is during *randori* – both *goho* and *juho* – where unconventional attacks and defences can enrich our understanding of the core principles, alongside the basic techniques of our core curriculum.

Further thoughts

When considering the bewildering variety of Shorinji Kempo techniques, systems and focus areas, the following points are important to remember:

- Think of the big picture – consider how our practical self-defence techniques are just one part of a larger body of teachings about how to become a better person and lead a more enjoyable and fulfilling life.
- Become proficient in the main areas – practise the basics, not forgetting that this includes *Seiho* (*tai*), philosophy (*chi*) and trying to 'polish the mirror of your heart' (*shin*).
- Master the syllabus – work to familiarize yourself with, and then master, the full set of *hokei* techniques, *kata*, *gakka*, and all the other elements required for progress through the grades.
- Investigate the items listed in the textbook (the 25 Groups) – ask, practise, explore.
- Think out of the box, looking beyond the list – What is implied but not explicitly listed? What can you think of that is completely novel?

- Try to refresh your practice continually by returning to each of these ideas on a regular basis, always believing that there is more to learn, if only you can manage to 'never forget your beginner's heart' – *shoshin wasuru bekarazu* (初心忘るべからず).

If you can draw from this multifaceted tradition a source of ongoing inspiration and fascination, you can easily continue your practice for a whole lifetime – through doubts, difficulties, and obstacles – and eventually look back on many years of training as just the beginning of a great journey of discovery.

Santei, sampo, nijugokei

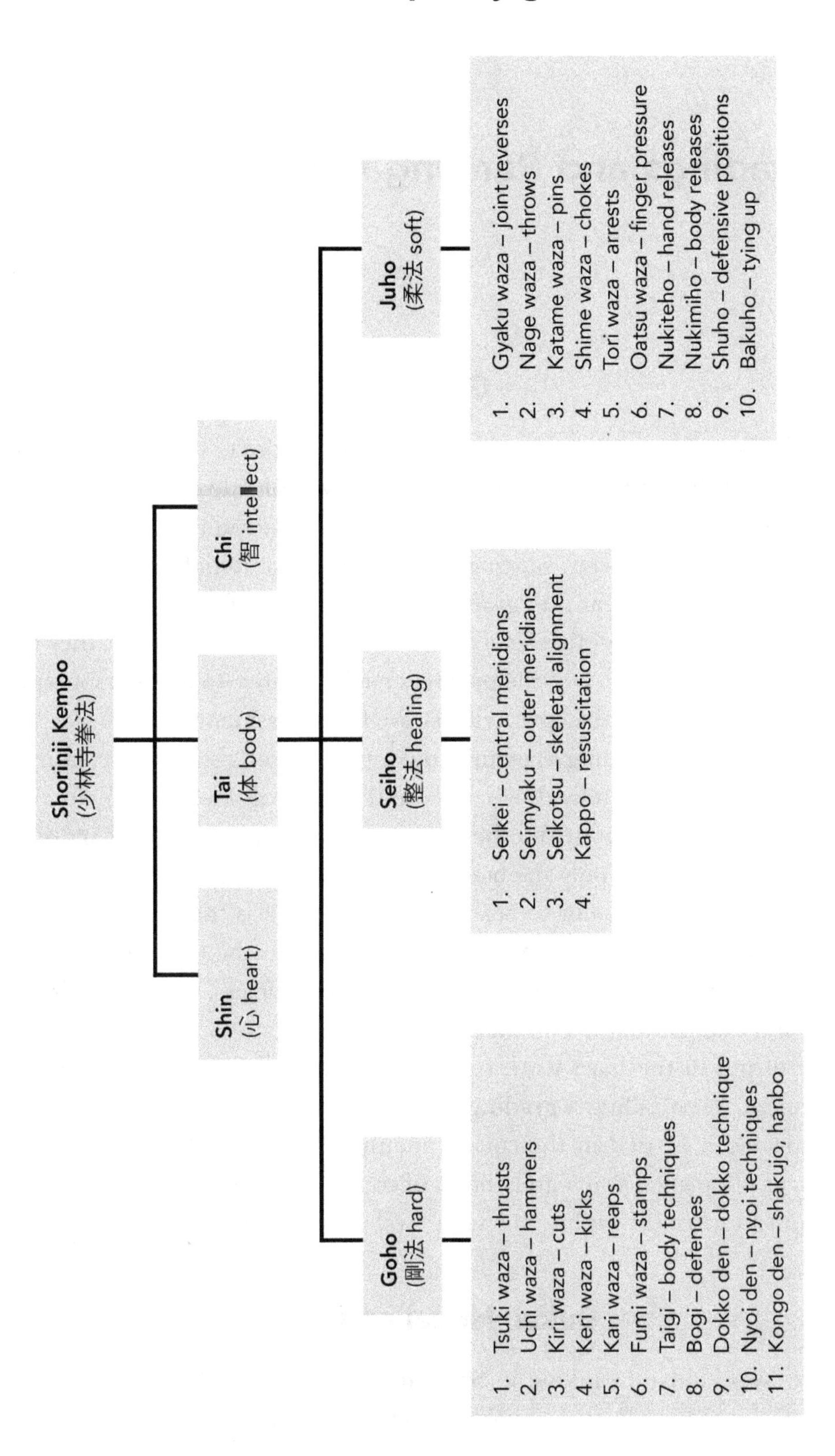

Gradings and Ranking in Shorinji Kempo

Gradings

The syllabus of Shorinji Kempo is divided into grades to enable learning to proceed in an incremental and cumulative way. This idea of steady progress is called *zen zen shugaku* in Japanese (漸漸修学 'gradually advancing education'). Given that everyone has a different starting point in terms of initial physical and mental attributes, it should be clear that grading examinations are not meant to determine a wholly absolute and objective level of attainment in a student, but rather measure the amount of work put in and the progress made, relative to that person's previous state. Having said that, objective criteria for the assessment of technical skill and philosophical understanding are applied, so that there is still a necessarily strong correlation between an individual's rank and their skill level; it is neither wholly divorced from comparison with others ('everyone gets a medal') nor merely based on competitive ranking ('only the best fighter makes it through to the next level').

But the important point to bear in mind is that it is the work put in towards gaining a new colour belt (or a new *dan* grade) that has the true value, rather than the superficial status boost of the award itself. Nonetheless, motivation is very important, and maintaining it over an extended period is vital to ensure that you can continue to put in the hard work required to make long-lasting and deep-seated improvement. Even failing a grading can ultimately be a positive learning experience, provided it is used in the correct manner. However, there is no doubt that passing a grading gives you a great boost of confidence and enthusiasm which helps power your practice through to the next level and the next grading.

Bukai, Hokai and Sokai

There are two kinds of ranking in Shorinji Kempo: *bukai* (武階) and *hokai* (法階). These refer respectively to technical achievement and philosophical progress. A third kind of ranking – *sokai* (僧階) – relates to progress within the formal religious organization of Kongo Zen Sohonzan Shorinji, and is given to people who enter the *soseki* (僧籍), or priesthood.

Bukai ranks are divided into 6 *kyu* (級) grades, from *minarai* (beginner) to 1st *kyu*, and then 9 *dan* (段) grades, from the first black belt (*shodan* 初段) on to 9th *dan*. Ranks are awarded based on performance at regularly scheduled grading examinations, with additional requirements for minimum time having elapsed since the last grading, along with attendances at regular classes and, at higher levels, special events and seminars. In the early *kyu* grade stages, gradings can be taken every three months, but as *kenshi* advance through the higher *dan* grades, intervals stretch out to periods of five years or more.

Hokai ranks start at the time *kenshi* achieve *shodan* – the first black belt – and are awarded automatically, together with the corresponding *bukai* rank, from 1st to 4th *dan* (*jun*- 'provisional', *sho*- 'small', *chu* 'middle' and *sei*- 'proper' -*kenshi*). From 5th *dan* onwards, a separate examination is required to attain the higher *hokai* ranks of *daikenshi*, and *jun*-, *sei*- and *dai-hanshi* ('big kenshi' and 'provisional', 'proper' and 'big professor' respectively). See Appendix 5 for a table of *Bukai, Hokai* and *Sokai* rankings.

History of the BSKF

The British Shorinji Kempo Federation is the organization in the UK that groups together Shorinji Kempo clubs around the country. Its origins trace back to 1974, when Tameo Mizuno arrived in the UK, coming to live in London from his native Aichi Prefecture in Japan. He had previously obtained the rank of 3rd Dan in 1969, having started training in 1963 at the Meiho Doin[132]. When he arrived in London in 1974, without a single personal connection or knowledge of the English language, he immediately established what is now the BSKF's oldest branch at the Polytechnic of Central London, which has evolved over the years to become the present-day City University Dojo.

In 1975, Sensei Mizuno opened a further dojo in Finchley Road. At around the same time, Toshiaki Yoshida and Benny Wang opened branches in Bournemouth and Glasgow respectively; Sensei Yoshida came from a university club background and held the rank of 3rd Dan at that time. They were soon supported by Soon Keat Jee (Abbey Dojo) and Paul White (Richmond Dojo). These early branches formed the British Shorinji Kempo Association (BSKA) and, in 1976, the first All-Britain Taikai was held. The BSKA was accepted into the Martial Arts Commission (MAC) in 1977. The BSKA became the British Shorinji Kempo Federation (BSKF) when the MAC disbanded in 1989. Sensei Mizuno is quoted as saying at the time: 'We believe that we are taking the path that Kaiso called on us to follow, to build an ideal society by taking single steps, each in the right direction. To make Shorinji Kempo an Organization is to be more capable of influencing society.'

Sensei Mizuno's efforts to promote the aims and objectives of the martial art of Shorinji Kempo in the UK were rewarded in 2000 by the then Japanese Ambassador

---

132 In Japan, *doin* (道院) is the term used for a private dojo – i.e. one not based in a public institution, such as a school or college – and refers specifically to a religious foundation or institution (in this case, tied to *Kongo Zen*).

to the UK, Sadayuki Hayashi. On November 16, Sensei Mizuno was awarded a 'Year 2000 Ambassador's Commendation' at the Japanese Embassy. The award was made in recognition of his achievements, throughout many years of effort, in fostering Anglo-Japanese friendship. Sensei Mizuno was one of eight people honoured at the event, and the BSKF was the only martial arts organisation so recognised. Whilst attending the BSKF 25th anniversary celebrations in July 1999, the Ambassador said, 'It would seem that people from most fields could benefit from the important lessons of mutual co-operation enshrined as fundamental principles of Shorinji Kempo.'

In 2010, BSKF severed relations with the World Shorinji Kempo Organisation (WSKO) due not only to a dispute over the encroaching commercialisation of the art, but also to a widely shared belief that the true teachings of Kaiso were no longer the priority of WSKO. Since then, the BSKF has played a leading role in the creation of the International Kempo Association (IKA), which aims to replicate the benign functions of the former international grouping. It does this by organizing international study sessions and competitions, encouraging communication and enabling visits between members of different clubs in different countries, and maintaining the consistency and quality of technical instruction across the various member federations. In 2019, IKA included eight independent groups from five national federations, and continues to welcome new member federations under its umbrella.

The Manji and the Meaning of the BSKF Logo

Manji

Doshin So chose the *manji* as the symbol for Shorinji Kempo when he created the art in 1947, seeing it as a powerful way to encapsulate many of the most fundamental ideas of both the system and of *Kongo Zen* in one familiar (to his initial Japanese audience, at least) and memorable figure. *Manji* is the Japanese name for the ancient Indo-European sign of the *swastika* (a Sanskrit word meaning 'good fortune'). This symbol has been used worldwide for millennia, including widely in Europe and America before WWII; for example, to promote consumer goods, or as good-luck talismans on British airplanes in the First World War. For obvious reasons it is now impossible to use it naively following its perversion by the Nazis and its indelible association with fascism and the horrors of genocide. However, the concepts it truly represents are fundamental to the core ideas of Buddhism, and of

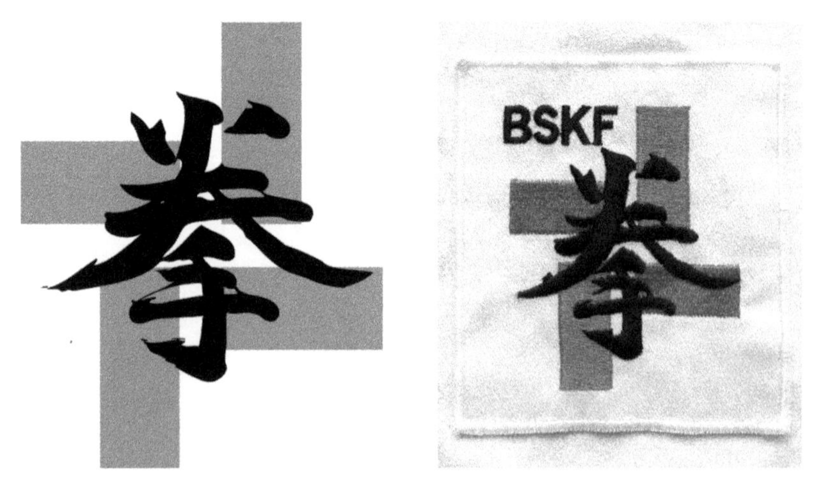

Figure 38 The BSKF logo (left) and as used for the sandan and yondan chest badge (right)

Zen in particular. In the UK, the BSKF has redesigned the ancient but tainted figure into one that illustrates these same ideas, but in a visually distinct way (see picture, which incorporates a simplified manji together with the character *ken* 拳, 'fist', superimposed). Indeed, many versions of the basic shape have been used over the centuries, and can be seen in swirling patterns from both East and West, such as the classic 'yin/yang' sign from China, or the repeating geometrical reliefs of the ancient Greeks.

Unity of Opposites

So what are these ideas? In brief, the *manji* symbolises the unity of opposites in a simple diagrammatic form, by connecting trailing 'limbs' across the centre to partners on the other side. These connected pairs are then imagined to be spinning, creating a sense of motion, and ultimately blurring to form a unified circle. The interpretation is that, not only are the opposed pairs connected by being features of a deeper unified reality, but also that the universe and everything in it is in constant motion, thus eliminating the illusory differences between such categories since everything is always changing into something new. Some simple pairs to fit into this framework would be *Ken* & *Zen* (body & mind), *Go* & *Ju* (hard & soft), and *Riki* & *Ai* (strength & love). Ultimately, all these dualities are linked by the concept of *chudo* (中道) – the Middle Way – which refers (among other things) to the idea that the space between apparent extremes is where true reality of things is to be found (see 'The Middle Way').

Omote and Ura

One of the key features of the *manji* is that it is a physical representation of a very subtle philosophical idea. But this representation exists not just as a written symbol on the page: it can also be rendered in 3D, as an object that can be viewed from the front or back, which is common in wood or stone carvings in Buddhist temples. This forcefully conveys the idea that the *manji* can face and spin either way, depending on from which side you are viewing it. The 'front' side conventionally spins clockwise, and is called *Omote Manji* (表卍), representing *Ai* (愛, 'love / compassion'). The 'back' side – Ura Manji (裏卐) – represents *Riki* (力, strength and power); indeed, it has been suggested that the character for *riki* derives from an abridged version of *ura manji*. It is significant that the perverted use to which the Nazis put this ancient sign focused entirely on the facet that symbolised power and will, ignoring the vital corresponding facet of compassion and empathy[133].

> *'Through change, ten thousand endings. But only through one theory - the union of opposites' attrib. to Ueshiba Morihei, founder of Aikido*

Figure 39 Manji patterns in the balustrade at Tofukuji, Kyoto

133 See http://www.bbc.co.uk/news/magazine-29644591 for further interesting historical perspective.

The History of Ken Zen Ichinyo

While the phrase 'fist and Zen are one' (拳禅一如) was coined by Doshin So, the origins of the phase *ken zen ichinyo* are much older[134]. Its original formulation was as 剣禅一如, meaning 'the sword and Zen are one'. The Zen monk Takuan Soho (1573-1645) is generally credited with its creation in this form.

Figure 40 Painting of Takuan Soho

Takuan explores the idea that Zen has a role to play in mastering the sword arts through his correspondence with the famous swordmaster Yagyu Munenori (1571-1646), collected together in his work *Fudochi Shinmyoroku* (不動智神妙録 'the mysterious record of immovable wisdom'):

> *'There are many instances where the martial arts and Buddhism are in accordance, and where the martial arts can be understood through Zen. Both especially abhor attachment and stopping at things. ... No matter what kind of secret tradition you may inherit or what kind of technique you use, if the mind stops at that technique, you will lose in the martial arts. Regardless of your opponent's actions, cutting or thrusting, it is an essential discipline that the mind does not stop at such a place.'*
>
> —*Takuan Soho*

134 Indeed, even the 'fist' version is by no means unique to Shorinji Kempo; it can be found in use in other contemporary martial arts such as Karate, and its meaning is relevant to all 'empty hand' styles.

In response to his correspondence with Takuan, Munenori developed this idea further in his master text, *Heihoka Densho* (兵法家伝書 'book for the art of war'[135]), where he describes how Zen brings to martial arts the idea of 'not dwelling'. By this he means that, if, at the moment you complete a strike, you allow your mind to become fixed on the completion of that movement, you will be distracted from what the opponent may do next (see the section on *Zanshin* for more on this idea in Shorinji Kempo). If all your awareness is directed at the point of the strike, you will be stopped and easily open to a counter-attack:

Figure 41 Wooden figure of Yagyu Munenori, at Hotokuji, Nara

> *'...if you strike with your sword and think, "I've struck" the mind that thinks "I've struck" will stop right there, just as it is. Because your mind does not return from the place you struck, you will be distracted, struck by the second blow of your opponent, and your initiative will be brought to nothing.'*
>
> —*Yagyu Munenori*

Although originally explored in the context of sword arts, the concept is of course relevant to all forms of martial arts practice. Both Munenori and Takuan emphasise the importance of staying unattached and open-minded, of not allowing the mind to dwell anywhere (or everywhere). By remaining detached from all individual actions in this way, there can be no distraction, and the mind and body are free to move as one.

135 Both texts are available in good translations by William Scott Wilson under the titles *The Unfettered Mind* and *The Life-Giving Sword*, respectively.

Part 7

Kongo Zen and Buddhism

In this section we describe *Kongo Zen*, its key ideas, and its relationship to Buddhism as a whole. We also give a brief overview of the central concepts of Buddha's teaching which underlie *Kongo Zen* and the philosophy of Shorinji Kempo.

Introduction to Kongo Zen

Kongo Zen and Shorinji Kempo

Doshin So, the founder of Shorinji Kempo, was an ordained Zen Buddhist monk. He eventually created his own school of Zen – which he named *Kongo Zen* (金剛禅) – to sit alongside Shorinji Kempo as a method to help students achieve a better understanding of their place in the world and so attain happiness, or even *satori*: enlightenment. In that sense, *Kongo Zen* is distinct from Shorinji Kempo as a technically free-standing religious denomination, but it is arguable that this original formal distinction was made at least as much for legal and economic reasons as for spiritual or philosophical ones[136]. In practice, the philosophy of Shorinji Kempo is simply the body of teachings of *Kongo Zen*, and the practice of *Kongo Zen* is just Shorinji Kempo training: *ekkin-gyo* and *chinkon-gyo*.

Religion

Shorinji Kempo is not a religion. However, the philosophy of Shorinji Kempo draws deeply from Buddhism, which, although primarily a fount of practical wisdom and teaching about how best to live, is nevertheless conventionally understood to be one. If Shorinji Kempo and *Kongo Zen* are not properly separable, this is not because Shorinji Kempo is in fact a religion in the traditional sense, but rather because *Kongo Zen* is not. *Kongo Zen* is a stripped-down form of an already stripped-down version of Buddhism – Zen. It is a religious practice with no gods or supernatural elements, limited scripture or liturgy, and almost no emphasis on assertions of dogma, origin stories or the personalities of founders, prophets or saviours. In the radical (the

---

136 Religious organizations enjoy advantageous tax and legal status in many countries, including Japan.

root) sense of the word, Shorinji Kempo practice is religious (in the same way that Zen is). It involves a 'binding' (from the Latin *religo*[137]) of oneself to a set of actions and principles that one believes are true, just, and above all helpful. In other words, it is a discipline (*gyo*). But whilst not endorsing or rejecting the claims of other great faiths[138], it is very far removed from the most common types of theist movements (both monotheist, as in the Abrahamic faiths, and polytheist, as in Hinduism[139]). If *Kongo Zen* can be seen as representing the *shin* (心) and *chi* (智) sections (*tei* 鼎) of the overall structure of Shorinji Kempo (see 'The Structure of Shorinji Kempo 3 Vessels, 3 Systems, 25 Groups'), then it is not a religion in the normal sense of the word, but a practical system of humanistic philosophy designed to promote a happy, fulfilling life and, ultimately, a peaceful society and world. Zen in general, and *Kongo Zen* in particular, are best seen then as 'paths' – 'ways of life', or *do* (道) (note the connection made previously between *gyo*, meaning 'to go', and *do*, 'path'[140]).

Origins of Kongo Zen

Kongo is a highly evocative word with layers of meaning and a rich history, and Kaiso chose it for the name of his new philosophy for several overlapping reasons. Its basic meaning is 'hard metal', but this is extended to mean something supremely hard, tough and resistant. Thus, the primary sense Kaiso intended it to convey is of a truth that is adamantine, eternal and unshakeable[141], as opposed to flimsy, contingent and unreliable. The next most common, everyday association is with *kongo seki*

---

137 The original meaning of *religo* is 'I tie again [and again]' or 'I keep on tying'; compare also the word 'ligament'.

138 Or, indeed, of the many other theist belief systems that have fallen by the wayside over the course of history, such as the classical Greek pantheon, the Viking gods of Valhalla, or the beneficent god of the Zoroastrians (Ahura Mazda).

139 A case can be made that the experience of *anatman*, 'not-self' (see below), and the conviction that you are in fact not separate from the rest of the universe, is also at the mystical core of both the Abrahamic faiths and Hindu traditions like the *Advaita Vedanta*. But such mystical cores are often invisible to the regular folk who are encouraged to worship a personalised and separate godhead.

140 In Chinese this character is read as *tao*; so, while differing in the specifics of views about the nature of the universe and the optimal practices to achieve harmony with it, Taoism in its purest, philosophical form can be seen as an approach very similar in spirit to that of Zen.

141 The family of pinning techniques in Shorinji Kempo is called *Kongo Ken*, to reflect this uncompromising nature.

(金剛石): diamond. This is seen as not only supremely hard, but also pure and very valuable. However, it is its powerful association with Buddhist teaching, and the cultural heritage of Vedic India more generally, that Kaiso had uppermost in mind when naming his new system.

Kongo is the Japanese rendering (via Chinese) of the Sanskrit *vajra*, which, as well as carrying the meanings noted above, was also used specifically to refer to a thunderbolt – the weapon of the sky god Indra – and to the traditional hand-held object known as a *dokko* (独鈷), which can both have ritual significance or be used as a defensive weapon (also known as a *kongo sho* 金剛杵).

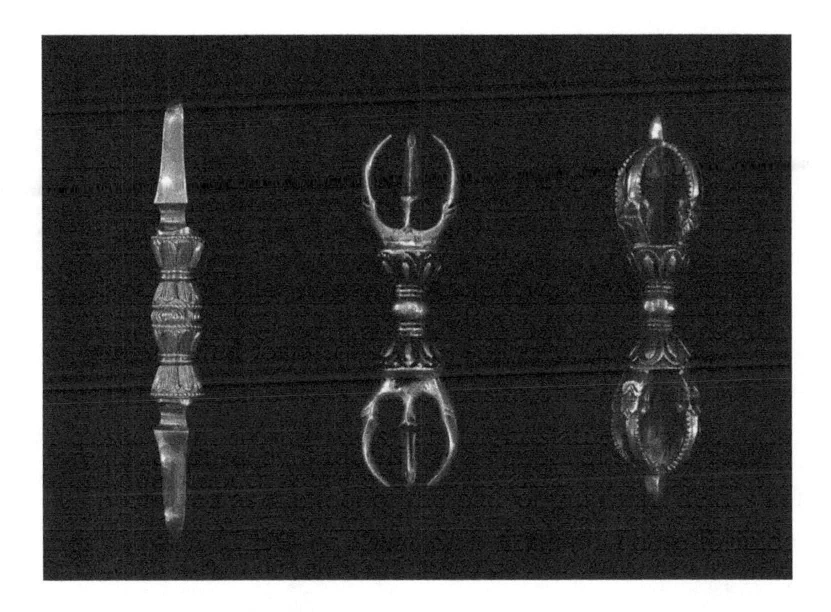

Figure 42 Three types of kongo-sho – dokko, sango and gokko

Even before its adoption by Buddhists as a symbol of indestructibility and power, the *vajra* was portrayed as the tool of the pair of guardian deities known as the Two Deva Kings (*Nio-son* 仁王尊 or *Kongo Shin* 金剛神). These formidable figures stand guard at the gates of many Buddhist temples, adopting complementary poses that are, in fact, exaggerated forms of stances still used in Shorinji Kempo (*nio gamae*); note that each is, in some ways, the opposite of the other, with mouths and hands open or closed in mirroring ways. The right statue is called *Misshaku Kongo* (密迹金剛), and his open mouth represents the vocalization of the first syllable of the Sanskrit Devanāgarī alphabet (अ), which is pronounced 'a'; this is also the first sound in the Japanese syllabary あ. The left statue is called *Naraen Kongo* (那羅延金剛), and his closed mouth represents the vocalization of the Devanāgarī consonant म्, which is pronounced 'm' and is the last sound of the Japanese syllabary ん. The pairing of first and last letters (a-m) symbolizes 'everything' or 'all creation'; as such, it is strongly reminiscent of 'Alpha & Omega' in the Christian tradition[142]. The contraction of both is *aum* (ॐ), which is the sacred syllable of Hinduism, and refers to *brahman* (a concept that is akin in many ways to that of *dharma*, see below). Apart from the obvious symbolism of the strength of these two mythical warriors, standing in evidently martial arts stances (the legendary art they represented was known as *tenjiku nara no kaku,* 天竺那羅之捔), Kaiso was also drawing on a more subtle association: the physical embodiment in the persons of the *Kongo Shin* of the principle of the *Manji*, the 'Union of Opposites' (see also 'The Middle Way', below).

Figure 43 Naraen Kongo (left) and Misshaku Kongo (right) at Ogawaji, Tokyo

142 It may also refer to the birth and death of all things: creatures are supposedly born making the 'a' sound with mouths open, and die making the 'n' sound with mouths closed.

The final significance of *Kongo* is from The Diamond Sutra (Sanskrit: *Vajracchedikā Prajñāpāramitā Sūtra*; Japanese: *Kongo Kyo* 金剛経), one of the most influential and important Mahayana[143] texts and a key scripture for many schools of Zen. In a nutshell, the sutra deals with the idea of the illusory nature of our perceptions of reality, and particularly our sense of self. This idea – that the concept of the self or ego is not only a dangerous illusion, but the key obstacle to seeing things as they truly are and thus gaining the peace of *satori* – is called *anatman*, and it is closely related to the concept of *sunyata*: 'emptiness'. In this sense, 'emptiness' does not mean that there is not something that exists in the world, but rather that the word or the concept we attach to that reality is not the same as – or in any sense as real as – the thing itself.

Focus on reality

The entire focus of *Kongo Zen* is on the world in which we live and the creation of an 'ideal world' by changing ourselves, in the first instance, rather than the world. This sets it apart firmly from the twin types of extremist belief system alluded to in 'Doshin So and the Founding of Shorinji Kempo': secular totalitarianism and religious fundamentalism. Totalitarian ideologies view the current state of affairs in the world as in need of radical engineered change, attempting to change that world by forcing people to behave in ways that are fundamentally unnatural. Because of this, they are ultimately doomed to failure, but not before unimaginable suffering has been inflicted as a result of their society-level experimentation in trying to create a 'new man' (consider Hitler, Stalin, Mao or Pol Pot). Religious Fundamentalists view the world as corrupt and, in some sense, unreal, compared to the imagined glories of heaven; thus, they direct their activities to either violent imposition of their views on non-believers, or the hastening of a dearly wished-for apocalypse to cleanse the stain of sinful humanity from the face of the earth.

Kongo Zen is quite different. It encourages us to calibrate our expectations to the reality of existence, not to some fantasy of intellectual or spiritual purity. It asserts that we are the authors of our own happiness – or the opposite – and that we can, and should, take active measures to improve our lot and that of those closest to us. In so doing, we will have the best chance of creating the ideal world sought at such a cost by these other absolutist systems; however, it will be impos-

143 One of the three main branches of Buddhism, the others being Theravada and Vajrayana.

sible to specify in advance what it will look like, for it will be different for every person. If there is no single monolithic truth to which all must bow down to achieve utopia, and if ideas of an afterlife or reincarnation are an unsound basis on which to build a philosophy of living this life, then the approach of *Kongo Zen* makes perfect sense: that ideal world is here, now, beneath our feet, ready to be built by our own efforts from the grass roots up, not imposed on everyone from the top down.

Kongo Zen and Buddhism

As already stated, the practical activity of *Kongo Zen* is Shorinji Kempo training. Thus, it is fairly obviously distinct from more conventional types of Buddhism – either the traditional institutionalised forms of East Asia, or the more modern mediation-focused versions now growing in popularity in the Western world. It has none of the ritual[144] or superstitious cosmology of the former, while, compared to the latter, the time spent on actual seated meditation is minimal and can appear cursory. Nevertheless, *Kongo Zen* and Shorinji Kempo together are a practice that is designed to help people live better lives and ultimately learn to perceive the world more truly, thereby getting closer to enlightenment – *satori*, *nirvana*, liberation from suffering (*dukkha,* see below), call it what you will. This, despite their outward differences, is what the various traditions that are offshoots of Buddha's teaching are all trying to achieve. It was Kaiso's belief that the combination of physical training, intellectual analysis and zen meditation that he promulgated was just as valid a path to this ultimate goal as any. *Kongo Zen*'s first principle is *Ken Zen Ichinyo* – The Unity of Ken and Zen, of Kempo and mindfulness – and this sets the course for the path to take to spiritual liberation, as opposed to traditional Buddhism; that is, the practice of Shorinji Kempo training as opposed to seated meditation or ritual actions. The mind is still an important arena, hence the strong emphasis on philosophy and intellectual understanding, but the core work of 'polishing the mirror of your heart' happens mainly not in seated *dhyana* meditation, but in fighting practice.

---

144 Kaiso was particularly offended by the basely commercial descent of the Japanese institutional Buddhism of his day into a money-making enterprise based on providing weddings, funerals and other key socio-religious rituals.

Figure 44 Buddha statue at Mahabodhi Temple, Bodhgaya, India, said to be the location where the Buddha gained enlightenment

The Key Elements of Buddha's Teaching

With that said, it is crucial to understand the key elements of Buddha's teaching, his insight into the human condition and how to fix the fundamental problem of conscious beings: the illusory nature of reality and the suffering that that causes. Therefore, the next part of this chapter will briefly deal with those key elements as an introduction to this deep and broad field of psychological and spiritual enquiry. Topics addressed are *Dharma*, Fate (*engi)*, Karma (*innen*), The Middle Way (*chudo*), The Four Noble Truths (*shishotai)*, The Noble Eightfold Path (*hasshodo*) and Emptiness and Non-Self (*ku* and *muga*). These are followed by brief discussions of the relationship of Buddhism to morality and science.

Inevitably in such a brief treatment, much is left unsaid; moreover, what is said is only one interpretation of a tradition that has, over its 2,500 years of ever-evolving existence, included many varied and sometimes hard-to-reconcile perspectives. But ultimately – and this is uniquely true of Buddhism as a practical and spiritual path – this brevity (even shallowness) need not matter so much, for the deepest teaching and the most important lesson of the Buddha was that it is up to each of us individually to confirm the truth of his ideas for ourselves, and this must be in practice – not just in theory, by listening to or reading the words of another, even of Buddha himself. Whatever form of teaching, whichever *dharma* (see below) achieves that best, or even at all, is the one you should use, and it may – indeed, must – differ for different people, from different cultures, backgrounds and ages. *Kongo Zen* is Doshin So's method for helping people take this journey and come closer to the goal of *satori*, and it will not appeal to (or work for) everybody (or even the majority), but for those who find a fit with its unique prescription of a lot of training and thinking mixed with a good dose of Zen meditation, it can be a great resource.

Buddha famously compared his teachings to a raft[145]: a man who builds and uses a raft to cross a river to safety has no need to carry it on his back, as he continues his journey on dry land when he reaches the other side. Whilst there are several overlapping interpretations of this story, one clear implication is that the teachings are merely a tool for getting to 'the other side' – to safety, or *nirvana* – and that they are not special or holy in themselves. If even a brief exposure to the key ideas is enough to trigger enlightenment (or the beginning of the process of becoming enlightened), then that is enough! *Kenshi* are encouraged to use the following brief summary as an initial introduction to concepts and ideas that will repay much further investigation, but, as Buddha said repeatedly, it is in the practice that the work of enlightenment is done, not the theory.

145 The raft parable appears in the *Alagaddupama* (Water Snake Simile) Sutra of the *Sutta-pitaka* (*Majjhima Nikaya* 22), and is also referenced in the Diamond Sutra.

Dharma

The concept of *dharma* has a central place in Buddhist thinking, but it can be difficult to grasp fully. This is partly because it is a fundamentally subtle idea, but also because, over time, the word has been used in different ways and by different people to express sometimes quite different things. In a nutshell, it means 'the law of the universe', in something akin to the way we talk about 'the laws of physics'. However, it is a broader and more inclusive idea than particular scientific laws, as it encompasses the process by which everything changes and occurs –both the fact of it happening, and the means or force by which it happens. Thus, it can be seen to include not only all basic physical laws, but also abstract formulations such as principles of *engi* (cause and effect) and *innen* (*karma*), together with higher-level ideas like the generative force of life. To add to the confusion, it can also refer to the method and teachings of Buddha. To get a better sense of this sometimes elusive concept, it is helpful to look at the historical use of the word to see what it meant before it was adopted by Siddhartha Gautama, the future Buddha.

Origins of dharma

The original meaning of *dharma* (Pali *dhamma*) was 'a fundamental law of life for gods, humans and animals alike'[146]. This concept was already common in Vedic thought (the pre-Hindu and pre-Buddhist traditional religious and cultural system of the Indo-European Aryans) by the late 6th or early 5th Century BCE, the time at which Buddha is thought to have lived and taught. The environment in north-eastern India in which he emerged was a ferment of religious and spiritual enquiry and experimentation, not to mention social, political and economic upheaval. Many schools and sects split off from the dominant Vedic mainstream to pursue various

146 Karen Armstrong, *Buddha*, 2000.

goals or avenues towards 'liberation', 'enlightenment' or *nirvana* (Pali *nibbana*) – a state of cool and peaceful quietude (literally, 'extinguished', as in a fire or a fever). Most often, these groups would adopt an ascetic lifestyle, rejecting all comfort and the support of traditional structures such as family, homes, and sometimes even possessions, living by begging for alms in the streets, as they moved between the towns and villages of the crowded and fertile Ganges plain[147]. Striving as they all were for the best recipe for spiritual release, they would greet each other as they passed on the roads with the cry: 'Who is your *guru*? What *dharma* do you follow?'. In this usage, *dharma* had come to mean 'law' or 'system' (a sense very close to that of the *ho* of Kempo), and simply referred to the set of practices and beliefs adhered to by a particular group in the belief that it would foster spiritual progress.

This is a much more limited meaning than either the original usage – 'fundamental law' – or its later expansion to encompass both that concept and the system or path taught by Buddha. However, it does help to clarify what can otherwise be a confusingly multifaceted (even muddled) concept by giving a clear sense of the progression of meaning and scope, from something abstract to something quite tangible, and from there to its later significance as an idea that included both previous usages. To add new layers of meaning to the word, *dharma* was subsequently translated in Buddhist teaching from its original meaning – signifying the method of seeking enlightenment (the path) – to signifying the view of the universe that an enlightened being would gain; that is, as totally interconnected and always changing. This hybrid nature – it is certainly difficult to translate with a single word – is one of the reasons many struggle to get to grips with *dharma*.

Kongo Zen and dharma

From the perspective of *Kongo Zen*, the important point to understand about *dharma* is that it is nothing less than the way the universe works. It is the truth behind the often misleading picture of reality fabricated by our over-busy and over-analytical intellects, and a true appreciation of its working – a true clarity in seeing how it functions – can be a precious gift for us. This is particularly true because a failure to see

147 This lifestyle was considerably enabled by the prevailing popular belief that charity, in the form of giving alms to itinerant holy men, was a means of gaining 'merit' which would benefit the giver in the quest to escape the endless wheel of birth, death and reincarnation (*samsara*). The comparative lack of such a cultural basis for alms-giving in the West or Japan perhaps explains why the dominant religious traditions in those regions coalesced around monasteries or temples (respectively) rather than wandering ascetics.

– to really see – how it operates can lead to consistently self-sabotaging behaviour. This is because the connectedness of all things means that negative causes – that is, bad decisions and actions – will inevitably have negative effects that rebound on the actor in some way or at some point. This is true even if the complexity of these interactions (and the veil of ignorance that obscures true understanding of our connections to the universe and all those around us) often makes it not at all obvious how or when those negative consequences actually come to pass (see below on '*Karma*').

Kongo Zen also places central importance on the concept of *dharma* as a way of appreciating the true preciousness of human life[148]. This is because *dharma* is, in some sense, most intense and most apparent in its role in creating life, awareness, consciousness and individual human spirits. The fact that distant galaxies spin and evolve is something we can attribute to the workings of this universal law, but it is of scant relevance or importance to us in the here and now compared with our own lives, or the fates of those with whom we share the world[149]. Every person is a unique instantiation of *dharma*, regardless of race, gender, wealth, status or talent, and is correspondingly irreplaceable and precious for that very reason. The potential inherent in all of us is a vast resource that must not be squandered, suppressed or taken away prematurely; thus, we must learn to live our lives in such a way as to maximise that potential in ourselves and help to foster it in others.

Note: Daruma dolls

Dharma or *Daruma* (達磨) is also used in Japan as shorthand for Bodhidharma, and stylised dolls depicting the ancient monk are widely available for sale at temples around the country. When purchased, the figure's eyes are blank and unpainted. The buyer will then think of a goal or wish, and paint in one of the two eyes. Once the desired goal is achieved, the second eye is filled in, signifying the completion of the task or ambition. The shape of the doll also carries meaning: it is round and weighted at the bottom in such a way as to never fall over onto its side. This symbolises the indomitable attitude of the Zen patriarch, in that he never gave up in the face of adversity, but picked himself up after setbacks and continued on in his ef-

148 And to lesser degrees, non-human life, the environment, and everything else that makes up the world.

149 As with 'Half for your own happiness…', proximity is very relevant to our concerns, for although all things are connected, the connections are not by any means equally strong or direct.

forts. This famous phrase captures the spirit: *nana korobi, ya oki* (七転び八起き) 'fall down seven times, get up eight times'.

Figure 45 Daruma dolls

Fate and Free Will

Perhaps the most fundamental insight of Buddhism is the dual observation that everything is interconnected (*shoho muga* 諸法無我) and that therefore nothing stays the same (*shogyo mujo* 諸行無常):given that something is changing, then everything must be. This is an ancient view of the universe that has been validated by modern theories about the deepest levels of reality underlying the everyday world, in which our common-sense view of things as distinct entities dissolves into a probabilistic realm of quantum fuzziness, entanglement and constant change.

Engi

The fact that causes have effects (and that everything which happens is the result of previous causes that were, themselves, the result of earlier causes) is called *engi* (縁起の法則), the Law of Dependent Co-origination[150]. One way of interpreting this idea is that everything that happens in the universe is – in some sense, at least – pre-determined, and that we are therefore the puppet-like victims of an impassive fate that grinds on, heedless of the will or independence of humans as actors and agents of their own destiny. In this scenario, you might as well resign yourself to that fate and give up hope of changing anything for the better[151]. It should be clear from the life and writings of Doshin So that he did not regard such an interpretation as warranted; indeed, his whole argument is that, by our own efforts, we can improve both ourselves and our surroundings; we can create an ideal world, one constructive thought, choice and action at a time. Such positive steps are our choice and

150 Literally, 'connected awakening', Sanskrit: *pratītyasamutpāda*. Also often translated as 'conditioned arising'.

151 Indeed, in Japanese, *engi* has the everyday meaning of 'fortune' (good or bad) or 'luck'. An *engimono* 縁起物 is a talisman or lucky charm.

could just as easily be left undone, but in either case, they form part of the matrix of connected events which constitute the ever-changing tapestry of reality. The principle of *engi*, then, amplifies the consequences of such actions and omissions, good or bad, into long-tailed causes that ripple outwards, away from the point of action both in time and space.

Free Will

The fatalistic interpretation above rests on the assumption that, given a precise specification of pre-existing conditions and causes, the resulting decisions and actions of people can be precisely known or predicted in advance, or, in other words, that free will does not exist. While at some ultimately reductionist level of analysis this may (or may not) be the case, given the vast complexity, non-linearity and chaotic nature of the connection between causes and effects in the real world – even in the relatively simpler realm of physical interactions, let alone the mental sphere of thought, belief, reason and emotion – in reality, we as humans are effectively free to make our own decisions and act on them, thus sowing the seeds for future causes and effects based on the quality of those decisions and actions. In other words, our free will is an emergent property of the complexity of the relationships that determine our actions, whether or not it is strictly true that we live in an ultimately deterministic universe. Decisions and actions will sometimes have obvious causes, but this does not mean that they were entirely determined by those same few specified causes, or that they would be exactly replicated if those causes could somehow be reproduced (the fact that they cannot is the core of the idea of *ichigo ichie*).

Because of the possibility of free will, the pervasive law of cause and effect (*engi*) does not trap us into an unchangeable sequence of preordained actions and events, but leaves open the possibility of an infinitely variable future, which we have the power to influence.

Karma and Destiny

None of this is to say, however, that we are not influenced by people or events, or that we do not influence other people and later events in our turn. This is, indeed, precisely why it is so important for us to set those causes over which we have some influence – for which we have some responsibility – on the right track, in order to produce good effects in their turn. This idea of the connection between past and future actions and results is the true meaning of *karma*, or *innen* in Japanese (因縁 – *in* means 'cause' and *en* as before means 'connection').

Therefore, if we live in an interconnected world where we are subject to all sorts of pushes and pulls, but nevertheless have constant opportunities to steer the course of events one way or another (rather than merely being victims of Fate) we can think of ourselves as the authors of our own destiny. This 'destiny' is some (normally positive) state of affairs that we can help to bring about through our efforts, but which won't happen without our active participation; where we are neither entirely free to accomplish wholly unrealistic daydreams – born, as we are, with our advantages and disabilities, talents and failings – nor entirely prisoners of impersonal forces, since we have the power of free will and the ability to act. This means we should seek to make the best of the circumstances in which we find ourselves in order to better our own condition and that of those whose lives we touch.

What goes around

Returning to the idea of interconnectedness (*shoho muga*), we can see that these good or bad causes will, at some point (or, alternatively, immediately), but with different degrees of intensity, rebound to affect us as well; this is where the popular conception of *karma* (as something that enforces 'what comes around, goes around') springs from. However, as noted above, the complexity and lack of one-to-one correlation between obvious causes and explicit effects at macroscopic scales means that the connection between our choices and the results they produce is seldom obvious beyond their most immediate impact. For someone truly aware of the negative effects on themselves of bad actions, 'avoiding evil' (*Seiku* 2) would be as easy as avoiding eating rotten food or putting a hand into the fire, something obvious and instinctive that requires no conscious decision to 'do the right thing'.

Clear vision

But this is clearly not the case in everyday life, and this failure to see things clearly for what they are – both the fundamental connection of self to the rest of the universe, and the propagation of causes to effects that connect, at some point or in some way, the deed to the doer – is at the root of all unhappiness and evil in the world. On the other hand, the effort to clarify one's vision sufficiently in order to not just understand these things, but feel and believe them to be self-evidently true, is the whole point and purpose of the project of Buddhism: to attain enlightenment not as a way to somehow separate from the ills of the world, but to understand the way it works at the deepest level so as to be able to choose wisely, to build a happy and fulfilled life and a peaceful society. This insight is *satori* (悟)[152], also known in Zen doctrine as *nehan seijaku* (涅槃静寂) – the quiet stillness of *nirvana*.

152 *Satori* is the broader, longer-term understanding that comes from *kensho* (見性), which are particular experiences of 'seeing into one's true nature' (and fully appreciating what is seen).

The Middle Way

The Middle Way is a very important idea in Buddhism; indeed, it can be seen as the starting point for the insight gained by Buddha himself which allowed him to discover his method for transcending the flawed and unsatisfactory (*dukkha* – see below) nature of perceived reality. In many ways, his realisation of its importance paved the way for his subsequent innovations in thought and practice that were later encapsulated as the Four Noble Truths (*shishotai* 四聖諦) and the Noble Eight-fold Path (*hasshodo* 八正道). In Japanese, this way of the 'golden mean' is known as *chudo* (中道)[153].

Buddha's journey

Buddha's original insight was simply that the various extreme ways of life he had practised right up to the point immediately preceding his enlightenment were not the solution to his long quest for understanding, or the release from *dukkha* – that is, the unsatisfactoriness of the world that led to suffering, not just (or even mainly) physical discomfort, but also disagreeable mental states such as dissatisfaction, disappointment, jealousy and frustration. In his long quest to find an answer to the problem of suffering (a question all major religions strive to address, with varying degrees of success or credibility), he had first rejected the life of hedonistic excess which his father, in a misguided attempt to shield him from any knowledge of the pain of existence, had bestowed (or imposed) on him. Following his 'going forth' into the world as an itinerant and aspirant ascetic (*bhikkhu*), for six years he tried various different *dharma*'s – notably, an extreme form of yoga discipline –, and when

153 It can also be read as *nakamichi*; it is not known whether Doshin So's given and family names of **Naka**no **Michi**omi (中野道臣) were intended to evoke this resonance.

that failed to fully satisfy him, he tried an even more extreme form of physical self-mortification that almost killed him. It was the realisation that none of these harsh or unnatural practices and states would lead him to salvation which set him on the path to achieving *satori* shortly thereafter. This idea was then developed further into the Noble Eightfold Path – the means by which anyone could achieve the same state of release from suffering as he had.

Figure 46 A bhikkhu monk meditating

Looked at in this context, *chudo* could be seen as just an absence of action – in the sense of merely avoiding extremes – but Buddha's insight included an equally important positive component. Instead of merely avoiding negative actions, he resolved to actively pursue positive but moderate goals. Thus, 'Right Speech' means not telling falsehoods, but it also means striving to say things that are 'reasoned, accurate, clear and beneficial'; likewise, 'Right View' means avoiding prejudging anything you see, but also striving to uncover the true nature of things, to see things as they really are.

Kongo Zen and Chudo

In Zen thought, the Middle Way has been developed as an idea closely related to the concept of the 'union of opposites' seen in many parts of *Kongo Zen* philosophy. As described in the chapter on 'The *Manji*', it can be seen as a unifying concept – the idea that the space between apparent extremes or opposites is where the true reality of things is to be found. Or, to put it another way, the true nature of things inhabits the parts inside (in the middle of) the external surfaces, even though those surfaces are often all we can see or be aware of directly.

In a less abstract and more helpful (if prescriptive) vein, *Kongo Zen* philosophy advocates adhering to *chudo* by seeking harmony in both your training and your life. Thus, the sixth 'Guideline for Effective Training' recommends seeking balance between many of these apparently opposed pairs – left / right, hard / soft, and body / mind – and the seventh encourages us to train moderately, with respect for our limitations, and not go heedlessly beyond them. It goes without saying that the extreme forms of ascetic and punitive self-mortification practised by misguided (at least in Buddha's view) seekers after redemption from his time forward, are to be avoided as unhelpful (they do not, in fact, bring you closer to the ultimate spiritual goal of understanding) and dangerous[154]. Rather, what is most helpful and fortifying is a change of focus from self-mortification to moral self-discipline. Such a posture brings you to a type of behaviour towards self and others which is characterised by the 'golden mean'[155] – the directive to seek balance and harmony in all things.

Ahimsa – Do No Harm

One final way to think about this broad and far-reaching idea is from the angle of *ahimsa*, the Buddhist doctrine of non-violence. This idea is normally thought of as applying to our conduct towards others, but it is just as relevant when thinking about the way we treat ourselves. Either extreme neglect or extreme indulgence can be seen to be harmful to oneself in the same way that it can be to others, and the

---

154 See also the note on 'waterfall austerities' in '*Gyo* – The Discipline of Shorinji Kempo'. In yogic practice, such austerities were called *duskara-carya*, and *tapas* in Jainism.

155 The idea of the Middle Way is not just restricted to Buddhist thought. Among the many philosophers and religions that have promulgated such a view are the ancient Greeks (Pythagoras, Plato) and the Abrahamic faiths (Judaism, Christianity and Islam). Indeed, a famous inscription at the Oracle of Delphi in ancient Greece said simply *meden agan* (μηδὲν ἄγαν) 'nothing in excess'.

middle path between these two poles can be seen as a caring approach where you do no harm[156]. This prohibition on causing harm should operate in both the physical and mental spheres, and suggests avoiding practices that will injure the body (austerities, hedonism, excess, neglect) and those that will degrade the mind (laziness, indulgence, fanaticism, obsession, despair).

156 An interesting contrast with Buddha's Middle Way is shown by the historical practices of some sects of Jainism (a religion that arose roughly contemporaneously with Buddhism in north-east India), where an extreme form of *ahimsa* involves elaborate measures to avoid any accidental damage to any creature (for example, ants under foot, and even plants) accompanied by violent self-mortification and privation.

The Four Noble Truths

四聖諦
Shishotai

The Four Noble Truths – better translated as 'the Four Truths for the Noble Ones' – contain Buddha's original basic insight into the nature of reality, the problem of suffering, and what to do about it. Though they may seem unusual or strange to some modern eyes, in Buddha's time the first three would have been entirely uncontroversial among those many itinerant seekers of spiritual salvation of whom he was but one; arguably, the only true innovation that he brought was the last truth – the actual enumeration of a practical method whereby anyone, not just *brahmin* priests or yogic supermen, could attain release from the shackles of dependence on the ego, and the suffering caused by such a state.

Dukkha

The key to understanding not only what the philosophers of 5th-century BCE India apparently agreed on (whilst disagreeing vehemently about what to do about it), but also the power and clarity of Buddha's solution, lies in the meaning of *dukkha*. This word was originally translated into English as 'suffering', but that term more recently fell into disfavour as being overly narrow and restrictive, and has variously been rendered as pain, anxiety, distress, frustration, unease or unsatisfactoriness; however, as argued below, 'suffering' (as opposed to 'pain') does work well as a nuanced translation.

For the aspiring holy men of ancient India and others, life was permeated by, and saturated with, *dukkha*. This meant not just physical pain and suffering, but – to a much greater extent – painful mental states, ranging from anguish to sadness, to things as mild as boredom or disappointment. It seemed to dominate their outlooks, and overwhelmed any enjoyment derived from the positive aspects of life, particularly as the ultimate end of all life's experiences would inevitably be death. But they sensed that this did not have to be the case – that there was a way of being whereby this suffering could be alleviated or, better, removed entirely. It was in this great quest for a solution to the problem of suffering that they were all engaged, devising and trying out different *dharma*'s to see if they truly worked to set them free from this ever-present unsatisfactoriness, and the ultimate foreboding of the pain and sorrow of death. Some chose punitive asceticism; others believed that the furthest reaches of yogic trance could take them to psychic realms where they would be immune to all negative feelings[157]; others even preached a kind of agnostic acceptance of fate, but with a focus on goodwill and ethical action, just to be on the safe side[158].

Returning to *dukkha*, we can understand this single-minded, almost obsessional focus on it if we draw a distinction between pain and suffering. Pain is a physical sensation caused by damage to the body of one kind or another; as such, it is an indispensable aid to the survival of any organism, as it provides vital information about states or situations that need immediate attention if the creature is to stay intact, or even alive. Indeed the disease 'Congenital Insensitivity to Pain' (CIP) – in which a person cannot feel physical pain – is an extremely dangerous condition; it is common for people who suffer from it to die in childhood, due to injuries or illnesses going unnoticed (burn injuries being amongst the most common). On the other hand, we can define suffering as the mental state caused by awareness of negative conditions – one of which might be physical pain – but which can also include all the other sources of distress noted above.

Given the emphasis elsewhere in the philosophy of *Kongo Zen* on the unity of body and mind (*shin shin ichinyo* 心身一如), it may seem contradictory to draw a clear distinction between the two types of unpleasant sensation, and it is absolutely the case that each type can 'cross over' and cause the other. But there is still a crucial difference between them, and likewise, between their sources and the ways of alleviating them: suffering is essentially a consequence of our mental states, and more specifically of how we think and feel about things, and can thus be controlled or even eradicated by thinking or feeling differently. This is what is meant by *dukkha*. In the memorable words of Buddha from his first sermon following his enlightenment under the Bodhi tree:

157 Buddha's first *guru* was Alara Kalama who taught a form of the innovative *Samkhya* philosophy; he was also a highly advanced yogi.

158 This is a very abbreviated version of the *dharma* of the Materialists, led by the sage Ajita.

'Birth is suffering, aging is suffering, illness is suffering, death is suffering; union with what is displeasing is suffering; separation from what is pleasing is suffering; not to get what one wants is suffering.'

Pain, on the other hand, just happens. It can never be entirely avoided – nor should it (see above) – though it can be effectively managed with medications, if necessary. However, the extent to which we suffer (in our particular definition) is, in fact, up to us; moreover, the vast majority of our pain or suffering is mental rather than physical. Indeed, much physical pain caused by injury, disease, ageing or dying is vastly amplified by the mental anguish that can accompany it.

So the core insight of the Indian sages, and the solution offered by Buddha, is to eliminate the kind of suffering that, in essence, we cause for ourselves. If we can do that, we will not be entirely free from pain, but we will be able to achieve a truly balanced state of natural harmony, where our minds are not tipping us constantly into chronic states of worry, anxiety, frustration or despair[159].

Tanha

The final piece of the puzzle, before turning to the Four Truths themselves, is *tanha*: 'desire' or 'craving' (Japanese *katsuai* 渇愛). This is the craving for things that can never be attained (and contrasts with *chanda*, 'the desire for things that is proportionate and can be satisfied'). They cannot be attained because they are not real; thus, the craving is not in harmony with reality. Rather, it is the result of a blind refusal to see the world as it truly is, and thus it produces *dukkha* – a sense of dissatisfaction. Essentially, we (our egos) want what we can't ever fully have. This does not mean that the objects of our desire are not real – the status symbol, attractive partner or sweet revenge on a rival – but rather, that which makes us desire them is not their true natures but something we attach to them – a feeling, meaning or interpretation that is most likely incomplete or totally fictitious. Note that *tanha* is not the

159 The subject of the natural balance between positive and negative thought patterns has been the subject of much recent academic research. In brief, negative experiences or thoughts affect us several times more strongly (perhaps five times) than positive ones, due to the presumed evolutionary survival advantage of learning from bad experiences (which could be immediately fatal) relative to good ones (where effects are slower to show). This means to overcome the 'negativity bias' we should actively focus on positive thoughts and practices (e.g. gratitude) to restore balance. See also: https://www.theatlantic.com/health/archive/2013/10/how-to-build-a-happier-brain/280752/

only possible cause of *dukkha*; as mentioned above, physical pain can equally give rise to mental suffering. But importantly, it is a cause that we have the power to affect directly; thus, it can be seen as the most important cause from our perspective.

Tanha is also seen as a kind of fire: not the good kind that gives energy and warms us, but a destructive force – something that consumes and burns, causing pain. To snuff it out is to experience the cooling balm of *nirvana*. The other feature of fire is that it spreads – it causes more fire – and one of the key consequences of *tanha* is that it perpetuates *samsara*, the endless cycle of birth, suffering, death and rebirth to more suffering. It is not necessary to believe literally in the truth of reincarnation[160] – a topic on which Doshin So was studiously silent – to see the sense of this concept. *Samsara* means 'going around', and its true significance is the endless cyclical nature of unsatisfied desire leading to more suffering, leading in turn to further unsatisfiable desires. It is in this sense that the unreal and illusory self (ego) is constantly reborn – reinvented – as it turns from one frustrated desire to the next, because, in a deep sense, the ego *is* desire (see 'Emptiness and Non-Self').

苦集滅道 kujumetsudo

The Four Noble Truths, then, are centred around *dukkha*: the fact that it seems to be omnipresent; an explanation of where it comes from; the idea that it can be overcome; and the method by which to achieve this. These four ideas can be compressed into the short phrase *kujumetsudo* (苦集滅道), with one character for each truth.

1. The Truth of *Dukkha* / 苦諦 *kutai*

   As discussed above, *dukkha* is suffering, and because we use our minds to filter all our conscious experiences, they are always at risk of being infected with, at the very least, 'unsatisfactoriness'; at worst, they can be invaded by acute mental anguish on a constant basis.

2. The Truth of the Causes of *Dukkha* / 集諦 *jittai*

   Dukkha is (principally) caused by *tanha* – craving – which is to say that it is caused by the fact that reality does not match our expectations, and so we are left unsatisfied by everything.

160 It is possible to reinterpret the literal beliefs in *karma* and reincarnation that are inherent in East Asian thought in a universalist and rationalist framework: *karma* is simply the fact that causes have effects, and rebirth is the constant renewal of mistaken perception that causes suffering.

3. The Truth of Overcoming *Dukkha* / 滅諦 *mettai*

   If you govern and ultimately extinguish *tanha*, you can do away with *dukkha*.

4. The Truth of The Way / 道諦 *dotai*

   By following the Noble Eightfold Path, you can master and ultimately eliminate the flames of *tanha* and, thus, be free from *dukkha*.

The Noble Eightfold Path

八正道
Hasshodo

The Four Noble Truths are centred around *dukkha*, and state that if you can eliminate *tanha* – its cause – you can set yourself free. The Noble Eightfold Path[161], then, gives the method by which this desire or craving can be managed, governed, and eventually removed altogether. Attaining this state of 'extinguishing' – *nirvana* (Japanese: *nehan* 涅槃) – requires very precise conditions which several of the eight paths are designed to create; in a nutshell, their aim is to foster an environment where there will be no distractions to trick the ever-restless mind back into its perversely preferred state of illusion and misinformation, and they do this via a set of habits and recommended ways of life which all contribute to this end. The paths that foster this type of 'correct thinking' are Right Vision (*shoken* 正見) and Right Thought (*shoshii* 正思惟). Vitally important to the quest is the commitment to behave ethically, treat other people fairly, and refrain from harming the self or others. These paths are Right Speech (*shogo* 正語), Right Conduct (*shogoh* 正業), and Right Livelihood (*shomyo* 正命).

The other three paths deal directly with the work of gaining the insight required to directly perceive reality as interdependent (*shoho muga* 諸法無我) and impermanent (*shogyo mujo* 諸行無常), to understand the illusory nature of the self (*anatman*, see below) and thereby to extinguish *tanha*. These paths are Right

161 Again, the 'Noble' should really be translated as 'for the Noble Ones'. It is also interesting to note that these noble ones are in fact 'Aryans', and that this word describes not a separate ethnic group of fair-skinned overlords, but the group of accomplished and enlightened sages; identifying Aryans as some kind of master race was yet one more mistake the Nazis made about pre-Indo-European culture.

Effort (*shoshojin* 正精進), Right Mindfulness (*shonen* 正念) and Right Meditation (*shojo* 正定).

1. Right Vision / 正見 *shoken*

   Avoid pre-judging things you perceive, making assumptions, or simply fabricating stories about reality; do try to see things for what they really are, beneath the veil of language and limiting conceptual frameworks.

2. Right Thought / 正思惟 *shoshii*

   In the original teachings, this meant taking the decision to renounce normal life, to leave home and dedicate oneself to the pursuit of spiritual liberation, and to commit oneself to *ahimsa* and goodwill towards all. In a more secular modern framework, it means the resolve to consider what is good for oneself, others and society in general, and to decide correctly what should then be done to further those goals.

3. Right Speech / 正語 *shogo*

   Avoid falsehoods, but also promote positive communication – words that are truthful, reasoned, helpful and supportive.

4. Right Conduct / 正業 *shogoh*

   Do not take life (of any kind), steal, or engage in sexual misconduct. Do help others whenever possible.

5. Right Livelihood / 正命 *shomyo*

   Serve others or society through your profession; avoid harmful or exploitative ways of making a living. For the original wandering *bhikkhu*, this meant living only by accepting alms, and not taking any more than was needed.

6. Right Effort / 正精進 *shoshojin*

   Never give up. Fight against distraction, doubt and weariness.

7. Right Mindfulness / 正念 *shonen*

   Be aware of the core teachings of Buddha, and recognise that all sensations, perceptions, mental states and phenomena are insubstantial and do not possess a reality in themselves.

8. Right Meditation (*Samadhi*) / 正定 *shojo*

Dhyana / *zen* meditation is necessary to pursue the deepest level of understanding. The previous seven steps are all seen as leading up to, and contributing to, the success of this most important stage. *Dhyana* is also significant because it requires a physical discipline – *pranayama* (breathing) is essential for proper meditation – to complete the otherwise wholly mental exercise of seeking enlightenment[162].

162 In the ascetic *Ashtanga* tradition of yoga, all the sub-disciplines (yama, niyama, asana, pranayama, etc.) are similarly seen as preparations for, and preludes to, the final act of meditation – *dhyana* – which leads to *samadhi*.

Emptiness and Non-Self

Concluding this partial selection of the core teachings of Buddha, we turn to a brief discussion of the idea of emptiness (Sanskrit: *sunyata*, Japanese *ku* 空) and non-self (*anatman*, Japanese *muga* 無我[163]). We have already mentioned the key role these concepts play in the Diamond Sutra, although, as it happens, the word *sunyata* itself is not used there. They also feature prominently in another well-known text – the Heart Sutra (Sanskrit: *Prajñāpāramitāhṛdaya*, Japanese: *Hannya Shingyo* 般若心経). This *sutra* is perhaps more familiar to regular (non-Buddhist) *kenshi*, as it is read out in full in Japanese during the closing ceremony of each branch at the end of the year:

舎利子色不異空 *Sha-ri-shi-shiki-fu-i-ku*
空不異色 *ku-fu-i-shiki*
色即是空 *shiki-soku-ze-ku*
空即是色 *ku-soku-ze-shiki*
受想行識 亦復如是 *ju-so-gyo-shiki-yaku-bu-nyo-ze*
舎利子是諸法空相 *Sha-ri-shi-ze-sho-ho-ku-so*

'Shariputra[164]*, form is no different from emptiness*
Emptiness is no different from form
That which is form is emptiness
That which is emptiness is form
Feelings, perceptions, impulses, consciousness, the same is true of these
Shariputra, all dharmas are marked with emptiness'

---

163 無我 *muga* is the same phrase used in the more general *shoho muga* (諸法無我).
164 Shariputra was an early disciple of Buddha, and probably a historical figure.

Emptiness

Both texts deal with the idea of the illusory nature of our perceptions of reality, and particularly our sense of self. *Anatman* suggests that the concept of the self or ego is not only a dangerous illusion, but the key obstacle to seeing things as they truly are, and thus gaining the peace of *satori*. *Sunyata* does not mean that there is not something that exists in the world that we are talking about, but rather that the word or the concept we attach to that reality is not the same as, or in any sense as real as, the thing itself. What is 'empty' is the word or concept; yet we easily mistake it for the thing itself and, in so doing, adopt and cling to an incomplete and inaccurate view of it (the Sanskrit *sunya-* comes from the word for 'hollow'). Part of the reason for this inaccuracy is that a concept is fixed and static; thus, we attribute fixity, permanence and a separate, unaffected existence to its referent (what it refers to), whereas the thing in question is inherently transitional, connected to everything else by the web of *engi*, and thus participating in the constant flux and change of the fabric of reality. This means it cannot be fully or truly grasped solely by means of such words or concepts but, rather, can only be experienced 'directly'.

Language as both enabler and prison

Whilst everything in the real world lacks a clear, independent existence, this is not the case in the imaginary representation of the world that we construct with our self-conscious declarative intellects. The capacity to carry out this world-building is the very thing that goes on to make us intelligent and rational: the ability to plan, to abstract, to predict and to perform all the other higher mental faculties which are unavailable, as far as we know (in their entirety, at least) to any other conscious animal. This ability has arisen in tandem with, and (crucially) as a result of, our use of language as a symbol-creating tool to represent things both in the world and in our minds as objects of thought, and which has allowed us to manipulate those symbols to produce the stunning effects of our intellectual talents. Without this ability to create concepts, we would have no direct means of making sense of the jumble of data we receive about the world from our senses. However, such a development has also created an inherent problem with our experience of reality: it has interposed a powerfully plausible layer of symbols – an illusion – between us and the raw nature of that reality, and we are inevitably seduced by that illusion. As a consequence, we experience an unshakeable sense of *dukkha* in direct proportion to the amount of time we spend consumed with *tanha* – the desire for things that the universe is not (cannot be) set up to satisfy. To escape from that illusion is not to be free from all pain or misfortune, but it can serve to eliminate the great proportion of suffering we impose on ourselves through our own misguided and unfulfillable cravings.

Non-Self

Thus, the central project of Buddhism can be reduced to the idea of expanding one's awareness to the actual truth of things underlying our constructed representation of the world – to retain the fabulous benefits of rational self-consciousness, but freed of its limitations and inherent pitfalls. Because *sunyata* is really the mental state of not ascribing solid reality to our concepts and words – that is, of recognising such concepts as 'empty' or 'hollow'[165] – the key to this change of view is to recognise that the sense of self is as much a constructed concept (with no unchanging, independent reality) as any other, and that the ego – the 'I' that suffers; that wants all the things it craves and tries to avoid all things it does not like – is also fundamentally unreal. This, then, is *anatman*, and only once it has been accepted on a profound, direct level can the liberation of *satori* truly be experienced.

165 A subtly different interpretation is that *sunyata* is a mode of perception which is 'empty of the presuppositions we usually add to experience to make sense of it' (Thanissaro Bhikkhu).

Buddhism and Morality

Much of the preceding discussion has been about the psychological aspect of *Kongo Zen* and Buddhism; that is to say, about the true nature of reality and how perceiving it directly can lead to a happier and more successful and fulfilled life. However, inextricably woven into Buddha's teachings on those subjects is the constant theme of moral behaviour. There are several interrelated reasons for this, chief among which seems to be Buddha's view that behaving ethically removes distractions that would otherwise make it harder to make the kind of progress he was advocating. Such moral actions and omissions all tend towards the creation of an environment that is conducive to the calmness of mind and clarity of vision that is both necessary for, and part of, the very experience of enlightenment. The underlying mechanism here is that of *engi* and *innen* (*karma*): everything is connected; you are connected to those around you; and bad causes (both thoughts and actions) have counterproductive effects. Thus, behaving badly in any way harms you directly – which is precisely why the behaviour can be called bad, once the true extent of the harm is clearly understood – and makes it harder to attain the kind of simple peace that is a necessary precondition for effective progress towards liberation, be it via meditation or another clarity-promoting practice. The words of the second part of *Seiku* put it concisely:

> *'By committing evil you defile yourself; by avoiding evil you attain purity'*

The Golden Rule and the Middle Way

Taking the Middle Way in one's treatment of the self and others (avoiding excesses of indulgence or harshness); behaving altruistically; not lying to, cheating, stealing from or harming others; and all the other universal precepts of the common core of morality, as promulgated by the great faiths and philosophies since time immemorial (that is, what is left after the specifics of supernatural metaphysics, origin stories and particular cultural practices are stripped away); all these actions could be aptly summed up by the precept of the Golden Rule: 'do unto others as you would have them do unto you'. When the doctrine of the non-existence of the self is added – or, equivalently, the lack of a true boundary between the self and the outside world (of people and things) – this precept also includes the Buddhist insistence on behaving well towards oneself as much as towards others. The Golden Rule is more than just a recommendation: it has almost the status of a fact (though it still bears repetition and constant reinforcement); the reason for acting ethically is not because some authority figure (supernatural or temporal) has commanded it, or the result of abstract devotion to some kind of utilitarian concept of the universal good, but because it directly benefits the actor, whether or not they have the unshakeable conviction that such is the case or not. The ease with which they are able to act in such a way is directly proportional to the degree to which such a truth has become self-evident to them through their own practice and efforts.

Self-Control

Self-control is close to the heart of all systems of morality: it is our sense of self as unique, separate and uniquely privileged that leads to actions which harm others, thus violating the Golden Rule. Therefore, according to a rather simplistic view, if we can control or resist these base urges, we are capable of acting more morally. However, it may seem strange to advocate controlling something whose existence has just been completely denied: the self. In the Buddhist context, self-control does not mean battling bad thoughts with virtuous ones; instead, it means coming to see the very feelings and desires (*tanha*) that animate such behaviour as essentially contingent, even misguided; not part of who we really are, and not really helping us beyond the momentary satisfaction of an ultimately unslakable thirst. Controlling the self in fact means seeing it for what it is, and thus reaching a state of not being ruled by emotions with which we choose not to identify. Ultimately, it means coming to see the self as a sometimes dangerous illusion that traps us in chains of selfish behaviour and obscures the understanding of what will make us truly happy.

Altruism as selfishness

Taking the idea of *anatman* (not-self) further leads to the idea of altruism as essentially selfish behaviour, albeit selfish in a good or natural way. If you are not truly separate from others, helping them makes perfect sense; indeed, it is natural behaviour which should take no conscious effort. This feeling is familiar to many parents who instinctively help or promote the interests of their children (at the same time as feeling their pain as if it was their own); the challenge of Buddhism is to extend this shared feeling[166], evolved through natural selection, beyond the limits of close kinship, to everyone else – indeed, to all sentient beings. This is not to say, however, that those closest to you (either genetically, socially, or through ties of shared cultural attributes like language) should not rank higher in your concerns than those further away. As mentioned before, whilst everything and everyone is connected, the strength and directness of those connections are by no means all equal; we simply have a larger effect on, and more potential to create good or ill for, those closer to us than those more distant.

One consequence of putting this attitude into practice in everyday life is the possibility to score 'free *karma* bonus points' from small everyday acts of kindness or consideration. These may include helping people with heavy bags navigate stairs or public transport; giving up a seat or holding open a door, or simply offering to help a lost tourist find their way. In themselves, it is hard to see how such small acts of goodness would be able to benefit the doer, but when viewed from Buddha's perspective, it is clear that the most obvious and immediate effect is on oneself. Without allowing a feeling of smug self-righteousness to intrude, the small glow of satisfaction gained from a helpful deed, when reinforced repeatedly, can be a powerful contributor to better mood, self-confidence and decisiveness.

Charity

Widening the circumference of your concern from those in your immediate vicinity – be they family, friends, or just those you happen to bump into on the street – we come to charity. This can be defined as altruistic action that is more organized and can be channelled through local, national or international institutions. There are several ways to participate in charity, from simply donating money to offering your time as a volunteer. One of the most powerful methods, which encompasses both the ways referred to above – that is, in terms of benefit to self as well as to others – is to group together with like-minded friends or colleagues and stage or participate in some event, raising money which is then donated to the designated worthy cause. Among Japanese Shorinji Kempo dojos, there is a tradition of holding such events

166 The word 'empathy' derives from ancient Greek meaning 'feeling / suffering together', an etymology that directly points to the shared experience of another's feelings.

on 'Kaiso Day' in May each year, around the anniversary of Kaiso's death. Other groups have developed different traditions, with the BSKF having organized many successful 'Martial Aid' public demonstrations to raise money for charities including the Red Cross and Cancer Research UK. It is also possible to organise events on a smaller scale, such as a single dojo's 'sponsored kick' in aid of disaster relief, or an individual's participation in such events as marathons or gruelling obstacle-course races. All these actions can help raise money for (and build awareness of) those causes and, of course, they also help the participants in numerous ways.

The important thing to remember is how beneficial it is to occasionally come together with others in a common purpose for the good of strangers. Such great efforts do not need to be made on a daily or weekly basis; rather, in the same way that the strength of body and mind that is a key goal of Shorinji Kempo training (*jiko kakuritsu*) is built up through a variety of efforts (both small and regular, and great but infrequent) so, too, our efforts to help others should follow a similar pattern, with small acts of kindness becoming an everyday habit, and more significant charitable endeavours an occasional challenge.

Buddhism and Science

To conclude this chapter on *Kongo Zen* and Buddhism, we will refer to an important contribution to the literature on Buddhism in the modern world – a recent book by Robert Wright with the (somewhat provocative) title: *Why Buddhism is True* (Simon & Schuster, 2017). *Kenshi* and other readers are encouraged to read this comprehensive but very readable book for themselves, since it offers an overview of all the key concepts of Buddhism from a modern scientific perspective, including much current neuroscience and psychology (particularly evolutionary psychology). The approach focuses on the effects of meditation on the minds, affective states and behaviour of committed meditators. In this respect, it describes a type of Westernized Buddhist practice that will be more familiar to most people than Kaiso's unusual prescription of *Ken Zen Ichinyo*. Nonetheless, it is a masterful and generally successful attempt to justify and support the 2,500-year-old claims of Buddhism, using modern science.

Wright includes a helpful précis at the end of the book, which summarises his main arguments in twelve paragraphs, with reference to key Buddhist ideas, and a condensed version is given here. Within each chapter, extensive examples and references are given, relating to the latest research in relevant areas.

- **Right Vision (正見 *shoken*), Right Thought (正思惟 *shoshii*)**

  'Human beings often fail to see the world clearly, and this can lead them to suffer and to make others suffer.'

- ***Tanha* (渇愛 *katsuai*)**

  'Humans tend to anticipate more in the way of enduring satisfaction from the attainment of goals than will, in fact, transpire. This illusion, and the resulting mind-set of perpetual aspiration, makes sense as a product of Natural Selection.'

- ***Dukkha* (苦諦 *kutai*)**

  Dukkha is a relentlessly recurring part of life as ordinarily lived... Organisms, including humans, are designed by natural selection to react to their environments in ways that will make things 'better' (in Natural Selection's sense of the term). This means they are almost always, at some level, scanning the horizon for things to be unhappy about, uncomfortable with, unsatisfied with.'

- ***More on Tanha***

  'The source of *dukkha* identified in the Four Noble Truths makes sense against the backdrop of evolution. *Tanha* is what Natural Selection instilled in animals so they wouldn't be satisfied for long.'

- **Right Mindfulness (正念 *shonen*)**

  'The two basic feelings that sponsor *dukkha* – the two sides of *tanha*, a clinging attraction to things and an aversion to things – needn't enslave us as they tend to do. Meditative disciplines such as mindfulness meditation can weaken the grip they exert... It's important to emphasize that becoming less enslaved by craving and aversion doesn't mean becoming numb to feelings; it can mean developing a different relationship to them and becoming more selective about which feelings to most fully engage with.'

- **Not-Self (*anatman*, 無我 *muga*)**

  'Our intuitive conception of the 'self' is misleading at best. We tend to uncritically accept all kinds of thoughts and feelings as 'ours', as part of us, when in fact that identification is optional. Recognizing that the identification is optional and learning, through meditation, how to make the identification less reflexive can reduce suffering. An understanding of why Natural Selection engineered various feelings into the human mind can help validate the idea that we shouldn't uncritically accept the guidance of our feelings and can help us choose which feelings to accept guidance from.'

- **Interior *Anatman***

  'The idea 'that there is no CEO self, no self that is the 'doer of deeds,' the 'thinker of thoughts' – is substantially corroborated by modern psychology, which has shown the conscious self to be much less in charge of our behaviour than it seems to be. A number of psychologists, including in particular evolutionary psychologists, subscribe to a 'modular' model of the mind that is quite consistent with this view that there is no CEO self. All told, the 'interior' version of the not-self experience... draws validation both from experimental psychology and from prevailing ideas about how Natural Selection shaped the mind.'

- **Exterior *Anatman***

  'The 'exterior' version of the not-self experience – a sense that the bounds surrounding our self have dissolved and were in some sense illusory to begin with – is not empirically and theoretically corroborated in the same sense that the 'interior' version of the not-self experience is corroborated. At the same time, considerations from evolutionary biology suggest a distinct sense in which the bounds of the self can be thought of as arbitrary.'

- **Morality**

  'Where a sense of the dissolution of the bounds of self leads to a less pronounced prioritization of 'my' interests over the interests of others, does that move a person closer to a moral truth? Considerations from evolutionary biology support an affirmative answer to that question.'

- **Emptiness (*sunyata, ku* 空)**

  'The intuition that objects and beings we perceive have 'essences' is, as the Buddhist doctrine of emptiness holds, an illusion. Specifically, it is an illusion engineered by Natural Selection to identify the significance of things with respect to the Darwinian interests of the organisms doing the perceiving. An 'essentialist' view of other people and groups of people can lead us to countenance or intentionally cause their suffering. So awareness that essence is a perceptual construct, not a reality, can be valuable, especially if paired with a meditative practice that dampens the sense of essence or permits selective engagement with it.'

- **Right Conduct (正業 *shogoh*)**

  'Not seeing the world clearly can lead not just to our own suffering but to bad conduct in the sense of making others suffer needlessly... There is a close enough association between the psychological dynamics that make us suffer and the psychological dynamics that make us behave badly towards people that the Buddhist prescription for lessening or ending suffering will tend to make us not just happier but better people.'

- ***Innen* and *Engi***

  'Many Buddhist teachings could be lumped under the rubric of 'awareness of... causes'. Mindfulness meditation involves increased attentiveness to the things that cause our behaviour – attentiveness to how perceptions influence our internal states and how certain internal states lead to other internal states and to behaviours. This attentiveness includes an awareness of the critical role feelings play in these chains of influence – a role shaped by Natural Selection, which has calibrated feelings as part of its programming of our brains. Importantly, the meditative practices that bring awareness of these chains of influence also empower us to intervene and change the patterns of influence. To a large extent, that's what Buddhist liberation is: a fairly literal escape from chains of influence that had previously bound us and, often, to which we had previously been blind.'

Conclusion

Wright's book is just one of many attempts to 'explain' Buddhism, and derives from a very particular perspective – one that is compatible with, but quite different from, the general approach of *Kongo Zen* and Doshin So. *Kenshi* may find it useful to triangulate their own experiences of personal development with the scientific explanations and personal anecdotes contained in the book, especially if they are of a more rationalistic bent, and find vague or self-contradictory pronouncements from spiritual 'authorities' which do not stand up to close logical scrutiny unsatisfactory. Another perspective, alluded to previously in the discussion on *dharma*, is the historical perspective; by studying what is known of the environment in which Buddha and his ideas arose, it is possible to gain a more nuanced and emotional understanding of the problems he was trying to solve and the solutions he proposed. Ultimately, it is invaluable for all students to keep as open a mind as possible about the different types of *gyo* – different rafts for crossing the river – that may lead to the same destination of *satori*. Doshin So's way is just one of these, and a broader appreciation of the range of alternatives that have been tried throughout the millennia since Siddhartha Gautama's enlightenment under a tree in North East India 2,500 years ago can enrich your own practice and help to cultivate a more tolerant and open way of thinking in general.

Afterword

It is difficult to summarise the broad scope of Shorinji Kempo philosophy as introduced in this book. The topics covered range from the practical details of studying and mastering a martial art, to some of the most hard-to-grasp concepts of Buddhist metaphysics. However, there is a unifying conception which lies behind it all: Doshin So's unique formula of *Ken Zen Ichinyo*. Its uniqueness resides not so much in its call for mindfulness and spiritual training in order to become a more effective martial artist or warrior – such a conjunction had been made centuries before by the likes of Takuan Soho and Yagyu Munenori, as detailed previously. Rather, its uniqueness lies in Kaiso's belief and assertion that you can use martial arts training to become a stronger, happier, and ultimately more enlightened person, and thereby contribute to the building of a better society and a peaceful world. Essentially, he is offering a new *gyo*, or discipline – a means to pursue the path to liberation first indicated by Buddha 2,500 years ago.

If this practice is to be effective, then one feature of the teachings assumes central importance and is a recurring leitmotif in almost all the separate topics here; namely, the primacy of being skilful (Pali: *kusala*). This means that you must strive for accuracy and correctness in all your actions, thoughts, and even emotions. Accuracy of vision and judgement is none other than Right Vision (*shoken*); it is the antidote to self-deception caused by believing things that are untrue or unreal. Accuracy of technique is essential in combat, where even the smallest elements can make the difference between success and failure. But in both spheres – *Ken* and *Zen* – another form of skilfulness is required which transcends the basic mechanics of thought or action. This is the ability to arrange your life, as far as you can, to make things as easy as possible for yourself, whilst at the same time preparing for when things are not easy. This is a two-pronged strategy: avoid negativity – thoughts, emotions, situations, people – as much as you can, by learning to discern the true character of things (and their true effects on their environment) and acting accordingly; at the same time, build up your strength – both physical and spiritual – for those times when such neat arrangements are not possible, or have been swept away by events. This kind of 'True Strength' is what the path of Shorinji Kempo is particularly effective at cultivating, and results in a character and resolve that are truly adamantine – diamond-hard, and just as rare and valuable: *Kongo*.

Appendix

The Appendices to the book contain summarised information that will be useful for *kenshi* in their study of the philosophy syllabus. Items included are the full text of the Dokun in English and Japanese, a selection of useful lists, the technique families or *kenkei* of Shorinji Kempo, a table of *bukai*, *hokai* and *sokai* rankings, and the current version of the full BSKF Philosophy Syllabus requirements by grade.

Appendix 1: Kyoten 教典

The Dokun 道訓

Seiku 聖句

1. Rely on yourself and not on others; no one is as reliable as your own well-disciplined self.

   己こそ己の寄るべ、己を措きて誰に寄るべぞ、良く整えし己こそ、まこと得がたき寄るべなり

   onore koso onore no yorube, onore wo okite dare ni yorubezo, yoku totonoeshi onore koso, makoto egataki yorube nari

2. By committing evil you defile yourself; by avoiding evil you attain purity.

   自ら悪をなさば自ら汚れ、自ら悪をなさざれば自らが浄し、浄きも浄からざるも自らのことなり、他者に依りて浄むることを得ず

   mizukara aku wo nasaba mizukara kegare, mizukara aku wo nasazareba mizukara ga kiyoshi, kiyoki mo kyokarazaru mo mizukara no koto nari, ta no mono ni yorite kiyomuru koto wo ezu

Seigan 誓願

1. In acquiring this art, we pledge to honour our founder and not betray our masters, to respect our elders and not slight the young; as comrades, we pledge to help each other and to co-operate for the accomplishment of these teachings.

一、我等此の法を修めるに当り、祖を滅せず師を欺かず、長上を敬い、後輩を侮らず、同志互いに親しみ合い援け合い、協力して道の為につくすことを誓う

hitotsu, warera kono ho wo osameru ni atari, so wo messezu shi wo azamukazu, chojo wo uyamai, kohai wo anadorazu, doshi tagai ni shitashimi ai tasuke ai, kyoryoku shite michi no tame ni tsukusu koto wo chikau

2. We pledge to leave our past aside and to devote ourselves to mastering the art as plainly and naively as infants.

一、我等一切の既往を清算し、初生の赤子として、真純単一に此の法修行に専念す

hitotsu, warera issai no kio wo seisan shi, shosei no sekishi to shite, shinjun tan itsu ni kono ho shugyo ni sennen su

3. We pledge never to perform our art for selfish reasons, but for the benefit of all mankind.

一、此の法は、済生利人の為に修行し、決して自己の名利の為になすことなし

hitotsu, kono ho wa, saisei rijin no tame ni shugyo shi, kesshite jiko no meiri no tame ni nasu koto nashi

Shinjo 信条

1. We are grateful that we are endowed with our souls from Dharma and our bodies from our parents; we determine to make every effort to return their blessings.

一、 我等は、魂をダーマよりうけ、身体を父母よりうけたる事を感謝し、報恩の誠をつくさんことを期す

hitotsu, warera wa tamashii wo dharma yori uke, shintai wo fubo yori uketaru koto wo kansha shi, ho'on no makoto wo tsukusan koto wo kisu

2. We love our country and determine to better the welfare of our people[167].

167 The translation shown here is the form of words in use at every BSKF dojo and has been unchanged since it was first introduced. However, the original Japanese text (not shown here) referred specifically to Japan, and has more recently been adapted by the World Shorinji Kempo Organization to refer to 'world peace' rather than solely the advancement of Japan.

一、我等は、愛民愛郷の精神に則り、世界の平和と福祉に貢献せんことを期す

hitotsu, warera wa aimin aikyo no seishin ni nottori, sekai no heiwa to fukushi ni koken sen koto wo kisu

3. We love justice, respect humanity, observe courtesy, keep the peace and determine to be true and brave.

   一、我等は、正義を愛し、人道を重んじ、礼儀を正し、平和を守る真の勇者たることを期す

   hitotsu, warera wa seigi wo aishi, jindo wo omonji, reigi wo tadashi, heiwa wo mamoru shin no yusha taru koto o kisu

4. We strive to master the art and discipline the body and soul; we love our comrades and help each other; we co-operate and endeavour to establish an ideal world.

   一、我等は、法を修め、身心を練磨し、同志相親しみ、相援け、相譲り、協力一致して理想境建設に邁進す

   hitotsu, warera wa, ho wo osame, shinshin wo renma shi, doshi ai shitashimi, ai tasuke, ai yuzuri, kyoryoku itchi shite risokyo kensetsu ni maishin su

Dokun 道訓

道は天より生じ、人の共に由る所とするものなり、その道を得れば、以て進むべく、以て守るべく、その道を失すれば、即ち迷離す、故に道は、須臾も離るべか　らずと、いう所以なり、人生れて世にある時、人道を尽すを貴ぶ、まさに人道に於て、はずる処なくんば、天地の間に立つべし、若し人あり、仁、義、忠、孝、　礼、の事を尽さざれば、身世に在りと雖も、心は既に死せるなり、生を偸むものとゆうべし、凡そ人心は、即ち神なり仏なり、神仏即ち霊なり、心にはずる処な くば、神仏にもはずる処なし、故に一動一静、総て神仏の監察する処、報応昭々として、毫厘も赦さざるなり、故に天地を敬い、神仏に礼し、祖先を奉じ、双親　に孝に、国法を守り、師を重んじ、兄弟を愛し、朋友を信じ、宗族相睦み、郷党相結び、夫婦相和し、人の難を救い、急を援け、訓を垂れて人を導き、心を至し　て道に向い、過を改めて自ら新にし、悪念を断ちて、一切の善事、を信心に奉行すれば、人見ずと雖も、神仏既に早く知りて、福を加え、寿を増し、子孫を益 し、病い減り、過患侵さず、ダーマの加護を得られるべし。

Raihaishi 礼拝詞

謹みて天地久遠の大みちから、ダーマを礼拝し奉る。我等、無始よりこのかた、煩悩にまつわりて造りたる、もろもろの罪とがを、悉く懺悔し奉る。　我等、この身今生より未来に至るまで、深く三宝に帰依し、み教えに従い奉る。願わくば良き導きと加護を垂れさせ給え。南無、ダーマ。

Appendix 2: Useful Lists

The Key Teachings of Shorinji Kempo

少林寺拳法の特徴 shorinji kempo no tokucho

Ken Zen Ichinyo – The Unity of Ken and Zen

Riki Ai Funi – Strength and Love are not separate

Shushu Koju – Defence before Attack

Fusatsu Katsujin – Do not kill, but help others to live

Go Ju Ittai – Hard and Soft form one whole

Kumite Shutai – Pair-form training is at the heart of Shorinji Kempo

Fuhai Shoju – You must not lose; winning is secondary

Guidelines for Effective Training

修行の心得 shugyo no kokoroe

Purpose

Order

Basics

Principles

Repetition

Balance

Level

Never give up

The Three Levels of Mastering an Art

拳の三要 ken no san yo

Gi – Techniques

Jutsu – Craft

Ryaku – Essence

The Three Stages of Learning a Skill

拳の三訓 ken no san kun

Shu – Protect

Ha – Shatter

Ri – Be Free

The Five Elements of Atemi

当身の五要素 atemi no go yoso

Aim

Distance

Angle

Speed

Timing

List of Technical Principles

Mechanical principles

hazumi no ri 弾みの理 principle of the bounce / rebound

doryo no ri 動量の理 principle of momentum

kuzushi no ri 崩しの理 principle of breaking balance

tembin no ri 天秤の理 principle of the weighing scales

teko no ri 梃子の理 principle of leverage

kuruma no ri 車の理 principle of the wheel

kagite no ri 鉤手の理 principle of the hooked hand

shuho no ri 守法の理 principle of defensive positions

nami no ri 波の理 principle of the wave

sankaku no ri 三角の理 principle of the triangle

Physiological principles

keimyaku no ri 経脈の理 principle of weak points

kansetsu no ri 関節の理 principle of joint locks

hansha no ri 反射の理 principle of reflex reaction

Psychological / tactical principles

renhanko no ri 連反攻の理 principle of immediate counter-attack

kensei no ri 牽制の理 principle of the feint

nise no ri 偽の理 principle of deception

doji no ri 同時の理 principle of simultaneous action

The Four Noble Truths

四聖諦 shishotai / 苦集滅道 kujumetsudo

The Truth of *Dukkha* / 苦諦 *kutai*

The Truth of the Causes of *Dukkha* / 集諦 *jittai*

The Truth of Overcoming *Dukkha* / 滅諦 *mettai*

The Truth of The Way / 道諦 *dotai*

The Noble Eightfold Path

八正道 hasshodo

Right Vision / 正見 *shoken*

Right Thought / 正思惟 *shoshii*

Right Speech / 正語 *shogo*

Right Conduct / 正業 *shogoh*

Right Livelihood / 正命 *shomyo*

Right Effort / 正精進 *shoshojin*

Right Mindfulness / 正念 *shonen*

Right Meditation / 正定 *shojo*

Appendix 3: Technique Families of Shorinji Kempo

Kenkei 拳形

Goho

Name	*Kanji*	Translation	Common features	*Waza*
Nio Ken	仁王拳	Two Deva Kings	single hand attack to *jodan*	23 *waza* e.g. *uchi uke zuki, kusshin geri*
Tenno Ken	天王拳	Heavenly King	combination attacks beginning with *jodan zuki*	9 *waza* e.g. *tsuki ten ichi, keri ten san*
Sango Ken	三合拳	Three Harmonies (Triad)	single hand or foot attack to *chudan, chudan geri gaeshi*	9 *waza* e.g. *shita uke geri, yoko tenshin geri*
Byakuren Ken	白蓮拳	White Lotus	*dan kobo*, flowing movement	9 *waza* e.g. *tsubame gaeshi, mikazuki gaeshi*
Chio Ken	地王拳	Earth King	combination attacks beginning with *chudan geri*	6 *waza* e.g. *jun geri chi san, fukko chi ni*
Kakuritsu Ken	鶴立拳	Standing Crane	gedan / kinteki geri attacks, hiza uke	5 waza e.g. kinteki geri hiza uke nami gaeshi

Juho

Name	*Kanji*	Translation	Common features	*Waza*
Ryuo Ken	龍王拳	Dragon King	*nuki waza*	32 *waza* e.g. *kote nuki, johaku nuki*
Ryuka Ken	龍華拳	Dragon Flower	*gyaku* and *nage waza*	59 *waza* e.g. *gyaku gote, kiri gote* 6 sub-families: *gyaku, okuri, oshi, juji, kiri, konoha*
Goka Ken	五花拳	Five Flowers	advanced *shikake* and *go ju nage waza*	26 *waza* e.g. *uwa uke nage, kannuki nage* 6 sub-families: *uwa uke, shita uke, katate, kannuki, bukkotsu, tembin*
Rakan Ken	羅漢拳	Arhat / Arahant	*dori, taoshi waza*	48 *waza* e.g. *sode dori, okuri tsuki taoshi* Also 35 *Rakan Appo waza*
Kongo Ken	金剛拳	Diamond / Vajra	*katame waza, bakuho*	27 *waza* e.g. *ude juji, ura gassho gatame*

Tan en Hokei

Name	*Kanji*	Translation	Features	Sequences
Tenchi Ken	天地拳	Heaven and Earth	*ren zuki* or *ren geri* attack	1 to 6
Giwa Ken	義和拳	Righteous Harmony	*jo chu niren kogeki* or *kobo*	1 to 2
Byakuren Ken	白蓮拳	White Lotus	*dan kobo*	1 only
Komanji Ken	紅卍拳	Red Manji	4 directions	1 only
Ryuo Ken	龍王拳	Dragon King	*kote nuki*	1 only
Ryuka Ken	龍華拳	Dragon Flower	*gyaku gote*	1 only

Shakujo Kata

Name	*Kanji*	Translation	Features	Sequences
Tenchi Ken	天地拳	Heaven and Earth	*sonoba zuki*	1 to 6
Giwa Ken	義和拳	Righteous Harmony	*sonoba zuki*	1 to 2
Byakuren Ken	白蓮拳	White Lotus	*dan kobo*	1 to 2
Komanji Ken	紅卍拳	Red Manji	4 directions	1 only
Ido Enren	移動演練	Moving training	*ikaku waza; shigoki zuki*	1 to 10

Other Hoki Kata

Name	*Kanji*	Translation	Sequences
Nyoi Ido Enren	移動演練	Short stick moving training	1 to 5
Dokko ken	独鈷拳	Vajra / *Dokko*	1 only

Appendix 4: *Bukai, Hokai* & *Sokai* Rankings

Bukai & Hokai – Technical & Philosophical Ranking

Bukai – kyu grades

rokkyu / 6th kyu (六級)
gokyu / 5th kyu (五級)

yonkyu / 4th kyu (四級)

sankyu / 3rd kyu (三級)

nikyu / 2nd kyu (二級)

ikkyu / 1st kyu (一級)

Bukai – dan grades

shodan / 1st dan (初段)

nidan / 2nd dan (二段)

sandan / 3rd dan (三段)

yondan / 4th dan (四段)

godan / 5th dan (五段)

rokudan / 6th dan (六段)

nanadan / 7th dan (七段)

hachidan / 8th dan (八段)

kyudan / 9th dan (九段)

Hokai – philosophical grades

The following are awarded with each bukai, from shodan

junkenshi 'provisional kenshi' (准拳士)

shokenshi 'small kenshi' (少拳士)

chukenshi 'middle kenshi' (中拳士)

seikenshi 'proper kenshi'(正拳士)

The following are awarded independently of each bukai, from godan:

daikenshi 'great kenshi' (大拳士)

junhanshi 'provisional master' (准範士)

seihanshi 'proper master' (正範士)

daihanshi 'great master' (大範士)

Sokai – Religious Ranking

shodoshi (少導師)
gonchudoshi (権中導師)
chudoshi (中導師)
gondaidoshi (権大導師)
daidoshi (大導師)
gonshohoshi (権少法師)
shohoshi (少法師)
gonchuhoshi (権中法師)
chuhoshi (中法師)
gondaihoshi (権大法師)
daihoshi (大法師)

Appendix 5: BSKF Gakka Topics by Grade

5th Kyu (verbal examination)	**Chapter**
Dokun: recite *Seiku, Seigan*	
Vocab list 1 (see below)	
How to Behave at the Dojo	I.3
How to Sit and Breathe During Zazen Meditation	I.6

4th Kyu (verbal examination)	
Dokun: recite *Seiku, Seigan, Shinjo*	
Vocab list 2 (see below)	
Basic Elements for Beginners	I.4
The Unique Nature of Shorinji Kempo	I.2

3rd Kyu (to be completed before grading)	
Doshin So and the Founding of Shorinji Kempo	I.1
On *Chinkon*	I.5
The *Dokun*	I.6
What is *Budo* and Why Do We Practise It?	I.7
Gyo – The Discipline of Shorinji Kempo	II.1
Half For Your Own Happiness, Half For Others'	II.2

2nd Kyu (to be completed before grading)	
Establish Yourself, Live in Harmony with Others	II.3
Ken Zen Ichinyo	II.5
Riki Ai Funi	II.6
Guidelines for Effective Training	III.1
The Growth Mindset	III.2
Ars Longa, Vita Brevis	III.3
Ichigo Ichie	III.6

1st Kyu (to be completed before grading)	
Shushu Koju	II.7
Fusatsu Katsujin	II.8
Go Ju Ittai	II.9
Kumite Shutai	II.10
Fuhai Shoju	II.11
The Three Levels of Mastering an Art	III.4
The Three Stages of Learning a Skill	III.5

1st Dan (to be completed before grading)	
What is True Strength?	
Your motives in starting Shorinji Kempo and your present state of mind	
(three subjects to be examined at grading)	
The Key Teachings of Shorinji Kempo	II.4-11
Guidelines for Effective Training	III.1
The Three Levels of Mastering an Art	III.4
The Three Stages of Learning a Skill	III.5
Types of Training	IV.1-7
The Five Elements of *Atemi*	IV.8
Sen	IV.9
Ma'ai	IV.10
Technical Principles	IV.11

2nd Dan (to be completed before grading)	
Half For Your Own Happiness, Half For Others'	II.2
On Self Defence	IV.12-13
(three subjects to be examined at grading)	
Establish Yourself, Live in Harmony with Others	II.3
The Power of *Ki*	V.1-5
Bodhidharma, Zen and the Shaolin Temple	VI.1
3 Vessels, 3 Systems, 25 Groups	VI.2
Gradings and Ranking in Shorinji Kempo	VI.3
History of the BSKF	VI.4
The *Manji* and the Meaning of the BSKF logo	VI.5
Keimyaku – all up to Shodan	

3rd Dan (to be completed before grading)	
Doshin So and the Founding of Shorinji Kempo	I.1
Gyo – The Discipline of Shorinji Kempo	II.1
(three subjects to be examined at grading)	
The *Dokun*	I.6
On *Kongo Zen*	VII.1
The Key Elements of Buddha's Teaching	VII.2
Dharma	VII.3
Fate and Free Will	VII.4
Karma and Destiny	VII.5
The Middle Way	VII.6
Keimyaku – all	

4th Dan (to be completed before grading)	
On Leadership in Shorinji Kempo	
The Four Noble Truths	VII.7
The Noble Eightfold Path	VII.8
Emptiness and Non-Self	VII.9
Buddhism and Morality	VII.10
Buddhism and Science	VII.11

Vocabulary List 1 (5th kyu)

migi	right
hidari	left
jun	front side
gyaku	back side / reverse
jo- / chu- / ge-dan	high / middle / low
kesshu	adopt *kesshu gamae*
rei	perform *gassho rei*
naore	return to *kesshu*
kamae	get into stance
hajime	begin
yame	stop
kiai	shout

ichi	1
ni	2
san	3
shi / yon	4
go	5
roku	6
shichi / nana	7
hachi	8
kyu	9
ju	10

Vocabulary List 2 (4th kyu)

tsuki (-zuki)	punch
keri (-geri)	kick
uke	block
ukemi	breakfall
nuki	release
kote (-gote)	wrist (reverse)
dori	take down
kiritsu	stand up
chakuza	sit down
seiza	kneeling
anza	cross-legged
o-negai shimasu	please
arigato gozaimashita	thank you

Figure 47 Demonstration at Polytechnic of Central London, 1974

Figure 48 BSKA public demonstration (top) and televised (bottom), both 1975

Figure 49 2nd British Shorinji Kempo Convention 1976 (top), BSKA tournament c1980 (bottom)

Figure 50 Tameo Mizuno presenting funds raised for Save the Children at Martial Aid, 1988 (top), and receiving a commendation from the Japanese Ambassador to the UK, 2000 (bottom)

BSKF Branch Directory

Branch	Contact details
Bristol	🌐 bristolshorinjikempo.org ✉ bristolkempo@gmail.com
Cambridge	✉ ukshorinjikempo@gmail.com
Edinburgh	🌐 www.edinburghkempo.com ✉ edinburghkempo@gmail.com
Glasgow University	🌐 www.gla.ac.uk/myglasgow/sport/whatson/club/shorinji/ ✉ captain-shorinji@gusa.gla.ac.uk
Leeds	🌐 shorinjikempoleeds.wordpress.com ✉ shorinjileeds@gmail.com
London:	
Camden	🌐 camdenkempo.com ✉ camden@bskf.org
Chiswick	🌐 chiswickkempodojo.blogspot.com ✉ skchiswick@gmail.com
City University	🌐 www.citykempo.com ✉ city.shorinjikempo@gmail.com
East London	🌐 www.eastlondonkempo.co.uk ✉ hello@eastlondonkempo.co.uk
Imperial College	🌐 www.union.ic.ac.uk/acc/shorinji/ ✉ shorinji@imperial.ac.uk
Marylebone	🌐 www.bskfmayfairbranch.com ✉ marylebonedojo@gmail.com
SOAS	🌐 soasunion.org/activities/society/SOASshorinjikempo/ ✉ soas.shorinji@gmail.com
South Wimbledon	🌐 www.wimbledonkempo.com ✉ info@wimbledonkempo.com

For latest branch information and training times visit: *www.bskf.org*

IKA Members

Country	Federation details
Czech Republic	Česká Federace Shorinji Kempo *www.shorinjikempo.cz*
Hong Kong	Hong Kong Shorinji Kempo Federation *www.hongkongkempo.com*
Indonesia	Persatuan Olahraga Kempo Indonesia *porkemi.com*
Ireland	Irish Shorinji Kempo Federation *adhgallery.com/shorinji-kempo*
Italy	Accademia Seido Kenpo Ryu *www.dojomessina.it*
Japan	IKA Japan *jskfgogokempo2015.jimdo.com*
Spain	Goierri Urola Shorinji Kempo Eskola *www.guske.es*
Switzerland	Swiss Kempo Union FR: *www.kempo-freestyle.org* DE: *www.swisskempo.ch*
UK	British Shorinji Kempo Federation *www.bskf.org*

Study online

If there is no BSKF branch or IKA federation near you, but you would still like to study or teach Shorinji Kempo, BSKF also offers a blended learning programme combining self-study and online tutorials with occasional in-person training visits.

For more details visit: *online.bskf.org*

Printed in the USA
CPSIA information can be obtained
at www.ICGtesting.com
LVHW081032030124
PP18016900003BA/20